R. Alec MacKenzie

Teamwork
Through
Time
Management

New time management methods for everyone in your organization

 **DARTNELL** CHICAGO / BOSTON / LONDON / SYDNEY

DARTNELL is a publisher serving the world of business with books, manuals, newsletters, bulletins, and training materials for executives, managers, supervisors, salespeople, financial officials, human resources professionals, and office employees. In addition, Dartnell produces management and sales training films and audiocassettes, publishes many useful business forms, and offers many of its materials in languages other than English. Established in 1917, Dartnell serves the world's complete business community. For catalogs and product information write: THE DARTNELL CORPORATION, 4660 Ravenswood Avenue, Chicago, Illinois 60640-4595 USA. Phone: 800-621-5463.

This publication is designed to provide accurate and authoritative information in regard to the subject matter covered. It is sold with the understanding that the publisher is not engaged in rendering legal, accounting, or other professional service. If legal advice or other expert assistance is required, the services of a competent professional person should be sought.

From a Declaration of Principles jointly adopted by a Committee of the American Bar Association and a Committee of Publishers.

Published by The Dartnell Corporation
4660 Ravenswood Avenue
Chicago, Illinois 60640
Chicago/Boston/London/Sydney

© 1990 The Dartnell Corporation
Printed in the U.S.A. by The Dartnell Press
ISBN 85013-182-0

Contents

List of Exhibits

Preface

This is a "how to" manual. Its principal purpose is not to explain *why*, but *how* to be more effective — not that reasons underlying recommended action will be ignored. To the contrary, probably the most complete summary of time management principles ever assembled is presented in Section 5. There are 68 of them in all. The purposes in assembling these principles are entirely practical. The first is to help the reader understand why certain proven management practices are effective and, therefore, to gain conviction regarding their value. The second is to clarify certain fundamentals of management which underlie these practices. The third is to provide a basis for managers to develop new tools and techniques of their own to enhance accomplishment of their objectives.

Practical managers will appreciate the hard-hitting approach. Issues are confronted directly. Blunt questions are asked, unequivocal answers demanded. A no-nonsense attack is made on a hallowed domain: executive effectiveness.

If the concern is with effectiveness at every level, what sense does it make to exempt the executive suite? Why should time and motion study be limited to production workers? Has anyone demonstrated or even suggested that productivity factors such as boredom, indifference, and resentment are any less evident in the manager's office than on the production line?

All managers should benefit from this manual. Home managers, team managers, specialists ranging from researchers to teachers and from attorneys to salespeople: anyone who manages tasks or people must manage time. Yet time is difficult to manage. While predictable in amount, it eludes control. While irretrievable, we think we can make it up. While it moves at a predetermined rate, it often *seems* to fly, sometimes *seems* to drag. And the greatest paradox of all: while no one has enough, everyone has all there is.

This manual will unravel the paradox. It will identify *more than 100* reasons why with all the time there is, there is not enough. Called "time concerns," these reasons will be identified as obstacles to effectiveness. They will be analyzed and solutions will be developed in a way that will allow their control or complete elimination.

A major breakthrough is claimed for this manual. It lies in the measuring of managerial effectiveness. You will identify *the two most current techniques* — appraising managers against objectives and appraising managers as managers. You will learn the shortcomings of these two techniques and how a third technique, appraising managers as time utilizers, permits measuring a manager's effectiveness and auditing his improvement over a fixed time period.

Other emphases will include:

- Managing the Time of Your Team.

- The Manager Secretary Team.

Finally, the technique and the art of time management will be advanced in a number of ways:

1. Identification of *more than 100* time concerns and time-savers classified by management function.

2. The examination of principles, concepts, tools, and techniques of effective management uniquely related to sound time management.

3. The presentation of a new method of attacking time concerns through systematic classification of causes and prioritization of individual solutions.

4. The measurement of the manager's effectiveness in controlling his principal time concerns and the auditing of progress in improving this control on a percentage of effectiveness basis.

5. The introduction of new diagnostic tools including the team time concerns profile; the managerial effectiveness audit; and quotients for interruption control, crisis management, achievement of objectives, delegation effectiveness, and meeting effectiveness.

One of the great timesavers is the ability to scan a book in advance to ferret out its real gems. Selectively reading those portions of greatest interest then ensures the reader maximum benefit with minimum effort. For the time-harried manager some of the most important and more interesting conclusions are presented here.

If this is all the time you have, you should make it worthwhile. If your curiosity is piqued to read on, if you'd like to save at least an hour or more a day from now on for yourself and your team as well, if you'd like to improve your effectiveness and that of your team from 20 percent to 100 percent—read on. An interesting adventure lies ahead.

Major Conclusions

1. There is the same universality among time concerns that has already been accepted for management principles. Current studies show a marked similarity of time concerns for managers at all levels, in all types of organizations, in all countries.

2. No one has enough time, yet paradoxically, everyone has all there is. Thus, the problem is not time, but how we use it.

3. While time is the most predictable resource of the manager (fixed amount, fixed rate of expenditure, irretrievability), it is also the most neglected, misused, and misunderstood.

4. In analyzing their time concerns, managers tend to blame outside influences first, such as telephone interruptions, drop-in visitors, and meetings. Upon analysis, they tend to see many personal or human characteristics such as indecision, procrastination, lack of self-discipline, and personal disorganization. Further analysis reveals yet a third major category of time concerns — that of neglected managerial skills such as lack of or ineffective communication.

5. Many of the most effective timesavers are also the most obvious — a "quiet hour" without interruption (by having a secretary take messages and intercept visitors); closing the "open door"; a written daily plan; stand-up meetings; disposing of in-basket items on first handling; doing nothing that can be delegated.

6. Time management is very personal. A time concern for one (daydreaming) may be a timesaver for another (creative thinking). A relaxed coffee break may refresh one manager, while making another, who is facing a deadline, extremely nervous.

7. Studies done on productivity strangely ignore executive productivity. Yet boredom, frustration, indifference, and resentment are as real and as destructive to effectiveness in the executive suite as on the shop floor. Based upon relative wages, the net result of managerial ineffectiveness must be far more damaging to overall productivity.

8. Managerial and professional effectiveness can be measured. Perhaps an answer to the great need for effective appraisal of executive performance is a combination of three techniques; appraising managers as time utilizers; appraising managers against objectives; and appraising managers as managers.

9. The best time generator is sound management. Effective time utilization and sound management are indivisible.

10. Our natural instincts frequently move in the opposite direction to sound time management. For example, although every hour spent in effective planning saves three to four in execution, and at the same time achieves better results, few managers are willing to spend the time required for effective planning. Consequently, they fail to gain the rewards of saving much more time than the planning took and the enhanced results as well.

11. There are a surprising number of myths concerning time—that it flies, that it can be saved, that no one has enough. On second thought, we see that these are myths. However, few of us give it that second thought.

12. Three of the world's most common time concerns—the telephone, drop-in visitors, and meetings—appear to most managers to be those most easily resolved. Far more difficult are lack of self-discipline, indecision, and procrastination. The former deal with environmental factors, the latter with basic, human characteristics.

13. Among the most amusing paradoxes of time concerns for particular groups of managers was the number one time concern for a group of 100 senior executives of a major telephone company. It was telephone interruptions. They had not learned, it seems, to master their own product. Another, for educators, was "enhancing the democratic process."

14. In time management seminars invariably there will be some managers who find it difficult, if not impossible, to choose their number one time concern for which they will develop solutions. Yet when it is suggested that their major time concern probably is indecision, they will deny it with good-humored vigor.

15. Time management principles apply equally in the home, at school, and in the office. Many homemakers discover not only that they are managing a tough little business, but that the problems they encounter on a day-to-day basis at home frequently include managerial tasks more difficult than many of those encountered at the office.

16. While many working women are unable to find time for all they want to do, many others find time to manage the home, manage a family, and hold down a responsible professional position. These examples raise a question for those of us who have only one major task to ponder: Is time the problem or are we our own worst problem?

17. The power of an individual to influence so-called "external" or environmental time concerns often exceeds his highest expectations. For example, a manager in Bell Laboratories complained about the time wasted in meetings waiting for late comers. Since he was not the chairman he assumed he could do nothing about it. I asked him what would have happened if he had suggested, "Why don't we start?" He answered that the rest of those waiting would have vocalized their agreement. I asked, "Then what would the chairman have done?" He responded, "Most likely he'd have started the meeting."

About the Author

For more than two decades business executives and their support staffs in more than 40 countries have attended Alec Mackenzie's seminars on time management, leadership, and the management process.

Indeed his landmark work, *The Management Process in 3-D* (published by the *Harvard Business Review* in five languages) has been widely acclaimed as the world's most accepted model of management and is regarded as one of the major catalysts of the business world's ongoing concern with time management. His book *The Time Trap* (AMACOM, 1972) has sold over 800,000 copies in 12 languages.

As president of Alec Mackenzie & Associates, Inc., in Greenwich, New York, Dr. Mackenzie actively promotes the management education and professional development of business people at all levels through publications, tape cassettes, films, seminars, and lectures throughout North and South America, Europe, and the Far East.

Dr. Mackenzie's other publications include: *Managing Your Time* (Zondervan); *The Credibility Gap in Management* (Van Nostrand Reinhold); *The Time Trap* (American Management Association [AMA] & McGraw-Hill Book Company-Paperback Division); *New Time Management Methods for You and Your Staff* (Dartnell); *About Time! A Woman's Guide to Time Management*, co-authored with Kay Cronkite Waldo (McGraw-Hill Book Company-Paperback Division); *Time For Success* (McGraw-Hill Book Company-Paperback Division); *Time Trap II* (AMACOM) and *Time Tactics*, his planner/organizer available through Alec Mackenzie & Associates, Inc. His writings have also appeared in *International Management* (England), *Les Informations* (France), *Expansion* (Mexico), *Canadian Defense Quarterly* and *Business Quarterly* (Canada), as well as the *ASTD Journal, Management Review, Personnel and Supervisory Management*, and *Association Management*. Dr. Mackenzie is listed in the 10th Edition of the *International Authors and Writers Who's Who*.

Dr. Mackenzie has been vice president of the Presidents' Association (AMA); vice president of the Erickson Foundation in Chicago; vice president of the Kartridge Pak Division of Oscar Mayer and Company; staff attorney for the Health Insurance Association of America; legislative assistant to U.S. Senator Alexander Wiley; and executive assistant to the director of Young Life Champaign, Inc.

His B.S. degree is from the U.S. Military Academy and his Juris Doctor degree is from the University of Iowa Law School. He pursued graduate studies in management and education at the University of Chicago and Columbia University.

"For what is Time? Who is able easily and briefly to explain it? Who is able so much as in thought to comprehend it so as to express himself concerning it? And yet what in our usual discourse do we more familiarly and knowingly make more mention of than Time? And surely we understand it well enough when we speak of it; we understand it also when in speaking with another we hear it named. What then is Time? If nobody asks me I know; but if I were desirous to explain it to someone that should ask me, plainly I know not."

—St. Augustine

SECTION 1

The Importance of Time

The Importance of Time

Many Meanings of Time

From the earliest periods of history, human beings have memorialized time. In the figure of Father Time we personalize time and ascribe to it a unique timelessness. On the other hand, by saying "time heals all" we attribute to time the quality of a force as powerful as an immutable law of nature. When we talk about the power of an idea "whose time has come" we suggest there may be a time and place for all things. And for certain critical events, it seems that timing or timeliness is the crucial element. In observing that "time marches on" we acknowledge the relentless, inexorable movement of time, its timelessness. Yet a moment in time of surpassing import may be caught by the phrase "when time stood still." Thus we see that time has many faces. It has come to mean many things.

Down through the ages man has recorded the passage of time. First, the shadow on the sundial, then the sand in the hourglass; now the hands of the clock have spoken their silent measure of time. Invisible, irretrievable, time was called the image of eternity by Plato. Immanuel Kant felt it had no real existence outside the human mind. Einstein designated it as the fourth dimension while the novelist Arnold Bennett called it the inexplicable raw material of everything. Napoleon said, "Ask me for anything but time." Faith Baldwin called time a seamstress specializing in alterations.

But rocks erode and stars grow dim, men age and empires decay, not because time works on them but because of the ebb and flow of energy systems operating within the physical laws of the universe established by God. If *space* is the dimension within which things exist, why not accept *time* as the dimension within which things *change*? Time is not a tyrant, a ravaging force of evil, an inscrutable judge, nor an omniscient healer. It is, as Webster put it simply, "the period during which action or process continues." Like sands in the hourglass are the days of our lives.

Misconceptions About Time

There are many misconceptions about time. One of them is that of "making up time." The pilot on the aircraft announced on the intercom that the 30-minute delay in departure from Frankfurt would be "made up" by arrival time in New York. Technically, we know that once spent, time is irretrievable. The 30 minutes lost will not be retrieved—they are gone forever. However, by increasing the speed of the aircraft, the fixed distance from Frankfurt to New York may be covered in 30 minutes less than normally scheduled time. This will require more effort by the pilot and navigator and greater expenditure of fuel. It may be accomplished, but at a determinable cost in other resources.

Another misconception is that "time will heal everything." "Time will take care of it," we say, instead of asserting more accurately that the condition will rectify itself, given the passage of adequate time. Still another misconception is that of not having enough time. "I don't have time," we protest, instead of admitting that the proposal is not sufficiently important in our priorities to warrant *taking* time for it. We always make time for the things that are important enough. A business friend of mine uses this technique candidly with friends. Instead of saying "I haven't had time" as his excuse for not getting something done, he simply says it hasn't had the priority necessary or he's had other more important things to do. He told me at a meeting that this candid approach to the matter has shocked a few people but generally it has been accepted and appreciated.

Paradox of Time

In seminars I ask how many managers have enough time. One manager in a hundred says he has enough. Generally one in 10 says he needs 10 percent more time. Four in 10 say they need 25 percent more time. Five out of 10, or one-half, say they need 50 percent more time. Then I ask them if they don't have *all there is*? They slowly begin to nod their heads as they ponder the great *paradox of time* — no one has enough, yet everyone has all there is! No, the problem isn't time, but rather how we utilize it.

The president of the American Management Association put it this way: "A person can be taught to use the tools of management more efficiently so that he will be more effective in the same amount of time. Time is the one element that eludes managers. We are forced to ask, however, is it time that is the culprit or is it our use of time?"

Myths of Time Management

Research into various concepts of time and their managerial implications has led to a collection of myths related to time and managerial effectiveness.

1. Myth of Activity

Managers who are the most active get the most done. In viewing the work of their subordinates, managers tend to confuse activity with results. Insecure workers often work at energy levels inversely proportional to their certainty of direction and confidence of results. A French manager at a seminar in Paris reminded the group of the motto of the French cavalry: "When in doubt, gallop." We also recall the story of the popular countryside pastor whose sermon notes were found by the custodian. In the margin, he read: "Weak point...shout!"

Even when the original objective is clear, managers frequently get enmeshed in the activity of getting there and forget where it is they are going! Activity, initially

4   © 1990 The Dartnell Corporation

designed to achieve predetermined ends, ultimately becomes the end itself. The politician, we are told, is one who, after losing sight of his objectives, redoubles his effort. The ultimate irony in this situation occurs when the manager, upon deciding to delegate another important task, looks about his apparently overworked staff and selects his best organized assistant because he's been going home on time. He thus rewards the most incompetent and penalizes his most effective team member.

2. Myth of Decision Level

The higher the level at which a decision is made, the better. There is a notion that people who are paid more money must make smarter decisions. Therefore the more decisions made at the top, the better off the whole organization will be. However, the management principle of decision level holds that decisions should be made at the lowest possible level consistent with good judgment and availablility of relevant facts. Among the justifications for this principle is the obvious fact that higher decisions cost more to make while lower decisions are based on greater familiarity with the circumstances involved.

One of the most common failings of managers is the tendency to keep on making the same kinds of decisions which they made in a previous position before being promoted. Outstanding salespeople are promoted to sales managers. If they continue to try to make sales instead of managing others in a way that will help them make sales, they will fail. Decisions inherent in the selling functions should be made by salespeople, not their superiors.

3. Myth of Delayed Decisions

Delay improves the quality of decisions. Arriving at the point of decision, many managers instinctively delay or procrastinate to avoid the commitment which follows the final decision. This syndrome has been termed "paralysis of analysis" by seasoned observers. Often, the longer a difficult decision is delayed, the more difficult it becomes to make. Also each delay lessens the time available for taking corrective action if it is wrong. The excuse is often given that the manager "needs more facts." But if 20 percent of the total facts involved in a given decision are critical to 80 percent of the outcome (Pareto Principle), the absurdity of "waiting till all the facts are in" becomes evident.

Norman Vincent Peale described the agony of saying "no" to requests to speak. He kept putting off the decision until he suffered real embarrassment due to the inconvenience his delay was costing others. It took him twice as long to explain why he had delayed. Learning the art of quick decisions saved him time and those who were requesting speeches a great deal of inconvenience. Many of them assumed from the start that he'd be too busy anyway. Some were angered by the delay because it was too late to arrange for an alternative speaker.

4. Myth of Delegation

Delegation saves time, worry, and responsibility. In the end, effective delegation saves time, but initially it takes time for planning what should be delegated, selecting and training competent staff to accept responsibility, communicating expectations, coaching and counseling for improved performance, involving the team in decisions affecting their work, and measuring and rewarding results accomplished. Therefore, delegation first requires time and in the end saves time only if done effectively. Nor is it a shortcut to avoid worry and responsibility. This would be "abdication." Ultimate accountability rests permanently and unavoidably with the top manager, regardless of who performs the work.

5. Myth of Efficiency

The most efficient manager is the most effective. Efficiency is often confused with effectiveness. Yet we know that to be efficient on the wrong tasks, or on the right task but at the wrong time, may be highly ineffective. What's the point, asks Peter Drucker, in trying to do more cheaply what should not be done at all? Effectiveness, as defined in Section 4, may be viewed as doing the *right* things right. Effectiveness is optimizing results—or achieving best results with the least expenditure of resources, including time.

6. Myth of Hard Work

The harder one works, the more he gets done. Our end results are seldom proportional to the buckets of sweat generated. As in the "myth of activity," managers tend to confuse perspiration with accomplishment. The time management principle of planning indicates that every hour spent in effective planning saves three to four in execution and ensures better results. Activity-oriented managers prefer action to thought and generally avoid planning at all costs. They would do much better to start nothing until they have thought the project through. For while planning takes time initially, only by investing that time can the savings of much more time be realized along with improved results. By confusing sweat with results, the "hard worker" winds up in the end having done things the hardest and least effective way. The key to the hard-work syndrome: work smarter, not harder.

7. Myth of Omnipotence

By doing it yourself tasks are achieved faster and better. By doing it themselves, many managers are convinced that they get things done faster and better. They think they not only save the time it would take to tell others how they want it done and to check up only to discover it's been done wrong—but also it will be done right in the first place and exactly the way they want it done. The fallacy in this reasoning is that by refusing to delegate the task to someone else, and taking the time to see that he knows how to do it right, the manager is ensuring that the *next* time he will have no choice but to do it again since no one else has learned how.

6

The illusion of omnipotence often arises, for example, from the successes most entrepreneurs enjoy initially. They seem quite willing to decide that they are successful *because* of their actions, not in spite of them. Concluding that no one else can do the job as well, they insist on doing many things they should have delegated so they would have time to manage. When he was president of Bell & Howell, former U.S. Senator Charles Percy observed that he was so busy doing things he should have delegated that he didn't have time to manage. He later came to emphasize not only delegation but also sound time management practices to ensure effective utilization of his time.

8. Myth of the Overworked Executive

Most executives are overworked. Many executives get illusions of indispensability along with omnipotence. Concluding that the enterprise couldn't survive without their continuous attention, they pass up vacations, work long days and weekends, and wonder why they aren't appreciated more. Their refusal to let others decide brings mountains of paperwork to their desk; their preoccupation with detail further clutters their stacked desks; their perfectionism places unrealistic demands upon themselves as well as their staffs; and their failure to delegate effectively forces everyone to come to them for answers to questions on the smallest details. We should pity the overworked, disorganized martyrs but recognize them for the liability they are. In keeping with this work-addiction syndrome, surveys of executive habits consistently show that the higher a manager moves in the enterprise, the longer hours he works. "Do a good job as a first-line supervisor working eight hours a day," observed one pundit, "and some day you may be fortunate enough to be a top manager and work 10 to 12 hours a day."

9. Myth of the "Open Door"

The "Open Door" policy improves a manager's effectiveness in dealing with his team. When "participative management" was first encouraged, its proponents logically suggested that availability of bosses to subordinates in time of need was an important element. To ensure this, they proposed that the manager's door be considered "open" to those subordinates who needed help. They did not mean physically open at all times. They meant open to those who needed help, when they needed it. Unfortunately the "open door" has come to mean open at all times. But being always available is no guarantee of success as a manager. On the contrary, the always-available manager finds it impossible to get his own work done, to think through to his own objectives and priorities, to concentrate on getting his own tasks accomplished. He falls prey to the corridor wanderer who, having caught up on his work, wonders with whom he can visit for a few minutes or more.

The open door is an invitation, except for highly placed executives in major corporations, for anyone who passes by to say "hello" or drop in for any other reason.

Experiments have shown how difficult it is for a person to walk by a friend's or associate's open door without a greeting. Given the average manager's instinct for socializing, his curiosity for the latest word, his desire for information, and his fear of offending—the open door can be viewed only as an insidious threat to effective management. Effective managers are virtually unanimous in their condemnation of the "open door." They agree on the imperative need for planned unavailability whether achieved by a "quiet hour," a skillful secretary taking call-backs, a hideaway, or simply staying at home for a few hours of concentration without interruption.

10. Myth of Problem Identification

Identifying problems is the easy part of problem solving. Much effort and time is wasted solving the wrong problems. Hence the axiom: a problem well-stated (thus identified) is half solved. A husband went down into the basement and discovered the floor covered with six inches of water. He called his wife to bring the mops. She called back telling him to turn off the tap first. A simple case of mistaken problem identification—the water was a symptom of the problem, not the cause. Some managers, like politicians, are known for their highly articulate answers to questions that haven't been asked.

11. Myth of Timesaving

Many managerial shortcuts are timesavers. If we have no choice but to spend time at a predetermined fixed rate, how can time be saved? Technically, it cannot. No one can elect *not* to spend time nor to spend it at a different rate. Nonetheless, managers talk constantly of saving time—often in ways which are unwise managerially and ultimately cost more time. Cutting an important conversation short in the interests of meeting another deadline may leave a festering problem unresolved only to erupt in a later crisis.

Hastening a decision without the critical facts has often returned to plague the hasty decision maker. Initiating action prematurely on a project without thorough analysis of alternative courses may later be revealed as the cause for taking the least desirable path—thus wasting much time, effort, and money in the end. "If you don't have time to do it right," asked one sage, "when will you have time to do it over?"

12. Myth of Time Shortage

No one has enough time. As mentioned in the Preface, no one has enough time, yet everyone has all there is. This seeming paradox forces managers to recognize that they do have all the time there is—there isn't any more. Therefore, time is not the problem, but rather how we utilize the limited supply we and everyone else have. Time shortage, therefore, is an illusion resulting generally from such forms of mismanagement as attempting too much in too little time, inability to say "No" to outside distractions, setting or accepting unrealistic time estimates, and confusing priorities by working on second things first.

13. Myth That Time Flies

Time marches on, we say. We've also been told, at a poignant moment, that time stood still. For most however, time flies. The most evanescent of all resources, it is present one moment, gone the next. And few know where or why. As fleeting as our fancy. . .illusory and invisible. . .inelastic and inexorable. . .we talk about it more than any subject except the weather, and we understand it less. We accuse it of running out, of flying, of being an enemy, of confronting us with deadlines every time we check our watch. Yet well-organized people count it as a friend. We never have enough. Others always do.

We say time passes. Yet in another sense it doesn't go anywhere. It is *we* who go. Time stays. It is ever present. Timeless. One of the few constants in the universe, time moves at a fixed rate. For each of us, it passes at the same speed. To say that time flies is to say that we are managing things in such a way that it *seems* to fly. Through inadequate planning and other comparable managerial mistakes, we are leaving ourselves with too much to do in too little time.

14. Myth That Time Is Against Us

The time-harried manager who is never caught up, who is busy fighting fires and missing deadlines, will always view time as an enemy. As in most things, however, we are our own worst enemy. Pogo puts it well: "We has met the enemy, and they is *us*." Time is on our side the moment we organize it.

Time—the Critical Resource

As executives attend seminars designed to enhance their skills in managing the resources at their disposal, they seldom ask what precisely *are* the managerial resources. The so-called 4 Ms of Management formerly described the commonly-referred-to men, money, machines, and materials. Occasionally methods were included. Never was time (minutes) included. Today we hear time referred to not merely as a resource of the manager but as the most critical resource. Peter Drucker put it this way: "Time is the scarcest resource and unless it is managed, nothing else can be managed." Therefore, management should view time as an asset and not as an enemy to be watched or feared.

The editors of *Business Week* in a March 14, 1970, editorial, observed that "executive time is the scarce resource—and it's going to become even more precious. Some companies soon may be making capital decisions on the basis of return on the investment of an executive's time." Management analysts increasingly agree with this prediction. Diagnosis of corporate-merger failures points to lack of appreciation of increased demands on the time of executives in the acquiring companies. An analysis of U.S. corporations related to decision-making models revealed scarcity of executive time as the critical element. One observer of the management scene proposes that minimization of demands upon executive time now deserves almost as much attention as maximizing profit. In some cases, return on time has been evaluated as a more important criterion than return on investment.

Effective executives are in agreement about the importance of time. When I asked the president of a major airline company how he viewed the importance of time, he replied without hesitation: "It's the most precious thing I have other than good health and a good metabolism." Frank Nunlist, former assistant United States Postmaster General, says of time: "It is like the real estate of the world, the most limited thing in existence. There is no more of it." A third executive, the president of a Fortune 500 company, expressed it this way: "Time is the most valuable thing we deal with. It can't be bought. It can't be recaptured. It must be utilized with the highest degree of effectiveness possible."

Gerry Achenbach, former chief executive of the supermarket chain Piggly Wiggly Southern for more than 20 years, concludes: "If one chooses to live a full life, he must appreciate the importance of time and of self-discipline. Appropriate utilization of time enables the manager to enjoy both his work and his leisure. Self-discipline means willpower to do those things you know should be done before doing the things you want to do because they are more enjoyable. By attacking rather than procrastinating, you will often find time enough to do both. Since it's your time you're spending, you should master your time, not let it master you. And you can't master your time until you're first willing to master yourself."

For Further Reading

Anderson, Richard C. and Dobyns, L. R. *Time: The Irretrievable Asset.* Watsonville, CA: Correlan, no date.

Christie, Les. *Getting a Grip on Time Management.* Wheaton, IL: Victor Books, 1984.

King, Pat. *Time, Making It Work for You.* Lynnwood, WA: Aglow, 1986.

Timpe, A. Dale. *Management of Time.* New York: Facts on File, 1986.

SECTION 2

Allocating Your Time

How Performance Skills Vary with Management Level

Not Letting Go of Your Job

Developing Skills in Relating to People

Managerial-Operational Model

Management Wheel

Time Profile of a President's Team

Managerial Time Cone

What Do These Managerial Models Have to Do with Time?

SECTION 2

Allocating Your Time

There are two fundamental questions to be asked about the allocation of the executive's time. The first is where *should* the manager's time go? The second is where *does* the manager's time go? In this section, we shall examine the first question—the ideal allocation of a manager's time. In Section 3 we shall be concerned with the actual allocation—where the manager's time really does go.

How Performance Skills Vary with Management Level

Exhibit 2.1 (see page 14) conceptualizes a view first articulated by Robert Katz of the University of Michigan concerning managerial skills of major importance at each management level. Athough Katz developed this model over 30 years ago, it is still regarded as a standard for depicting the relationships involved. As one moves up in an organization, one's attention ought to be focused increasingly on conceptual skills and less on technical skills. As the diagram indicates, the emphasis on human skills should remain fairly constant. Definitions of these performance skills are shown below the diagram.

Not Letting Go of Your Job

This model has important implications for the manager. Perhaps the most significant is the difference between the managerial (conceptual and human) and the operational (technical) activities of the manager. The tendency of managers to "hang on to" their old jobs as they are promoted up through managerial ranks has been well documented. There is a seeming reluctance to let go of a previous responsibility.

Observations of teachers with outstanding records failing as principals of public schools prompted the enunciation of the famous Peter Principle. Briefly stated, this principle holds that every managerial slot in hierarchical organizations is eventually filled with an incompetent because managers are promoted to their level of incompetence.

For a review of the fallacious part of the Peter Principle see "Principles of Time Management," page 71. Understandably, successful teachers would have an inclination to keep on doing those things which had earned them their success. If they were not given training in the new role of principal (a managerial role as opposed to the teaching or operational role), then the result could be readily predicted. As principals, they would continue to teach and would fail to accomplish the fundamental responsibilities of principals. In the light of the model, they would tend to continue to em-

Exhibit 2.1: Major Performance Skills Required At Various Management Levels*

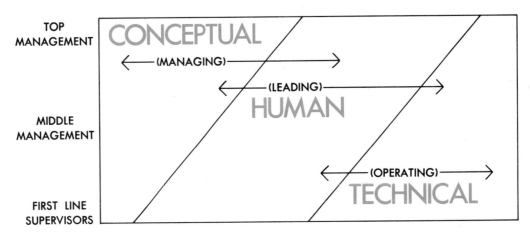

TECHNICAL—The ability to work with methods, processes, procedures, and techniques.
HUMAN—The ability to work effectively with people.
CONCEPTUAL—The ability to develop ideas, to deal with abstractions, to view the organization as a whole, to recognize how decisions in one area affect other areas.

phasize the technical aspects of their jobs almost to the same degree as before, rather than shift the emphasis to the conceptual skills as shown in the model.

Precisely the same phenomenon has been observed in industry. Many sales organizations have rewarded their top salespeople with positions in management but have neglected to instruct them in the different requirements of the new position. In some cases, the demonstrated skills for selling have not been accompanied by the development of corresponding skills in managing. Consequently, while the requirements of the job had changed significantly, the use of old skills and the emphasis given these skills by the salepeople continue as before. The failure to recognize this situation, of course, preordained unsatisfactory performance.

Developing Skills in Relating to People

Another fundamental illustrated by this model is the continuing importance for the manager to develop his skills in relating to people. If we define "managing" as achieving objectives through others, we could define "leading" as influencing others to achieve objectives. The most commonly accepted definitions of leadership include the concept of influence. We therefore can see the relationship between leadership and the center element of the model—the skill of relating to people. We see the model as one of the most basic to the entire field of management. It demonstrates relation-

*Graphic portrayal of concept described in article by Robert L. Katz, ''Skills of the Effective Administrator,'' *Harvard Business Review.*

ships between the fundamental concepts of management under the broad definitions of conceptual, human, and technical skills.

The parallel is considered to be important because of the common failure to distinguish between management and leadership. When asked to distinguish between the two, most managers say that in their opinion they are the same thing. Skilled observers, however, have long since made this important distinction. In its essence, the fundamental emphasis in management is accomplishment of objectives, while the fundamental emphasis in leadership is influence on people.

Managerial-Operational Model

Now that we see a relationship between conceptual and technical (managing and operating) skills, it will be useful to note a Managerial-Operation Model, Exhibit 2.2,

Exhibit 2.2: A Managerial-Operational Model for Managers

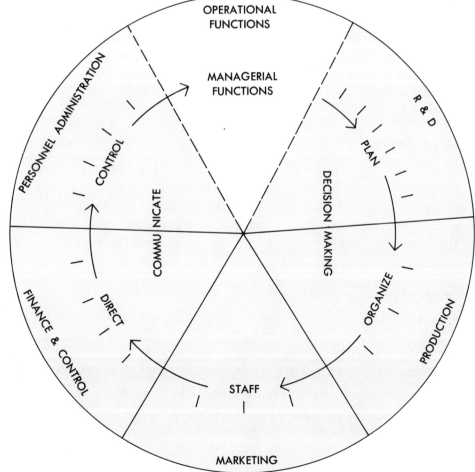

which demonstrates how the relationships between these two concepts can be made understandable. The middle band represents the sequential managerial functions such as planning and organizing. The term "sequential" is used to describe these functions because they generally occur in the order indicated beginning with planning and ending with controlling. The two "continual" functions of decision making and communicating are shown in the inner part of the circle to indicate that their occurence is more continual than sequential. All managers, with the exception of staff specialists, engage in all these managerial functions from time to time. The staff specialist engages in all with the exception of staffing and directing when he has no team reporting to him.

The outer band represents the most common operational functions beginning with research and development and concluding with personnel administration.

Whereas every manager engages from time to time in all the managerial functions, unless he is a chief executive over a division, a company, or an enterprise, the manager will be responsible for perhaps only one of the operational functions. The vice-president of production, for example, will have no line authority over the vice-president of marketing. Each will exercise responsibility and control over his or her own particular operational function. Thus we might view the middle band as rotating to demonstrate that any one of the separate operating functions in the outside band will be influenced by each and all of the internal managerial functions from time to time. That is to say the manager in charge of each one of the operating functions will be responsible for performing all the managerial functions with respect to his area of responsibility.

Management Wheel

The Management Wheel, in Exhibit 2.3 (see page 17), of the "Managerial and Operational Functions and Activities" brings together all the commonly accepted activities of both operational and managerial functions. One of the greatest values of this complete chart is to provide senior executives and division heads with a quick reference to the most commonly accepted activities in each of the functional areas under their control.

Time Profile of a President's Team

The usefulness of the model in Exhibit 2.3 respecting the allocation of time becomes even more apparent in Exhibit 2.4, Time Profile of a President's Team (see page 18). Here the concept of satellites is used to show the principal positions reporting to a president and the proposed allocation of time spent on managing functions and on operating functions for each position represented. The inner circle represents the allocation of time spent planning, organizing, etc. The outer circle represents the time devoted either to the operating functions (in the case of a senior executive) or the operating activities within each operational function (in the case of the operating executives).

Exhibit 2.3: The Management Wheel

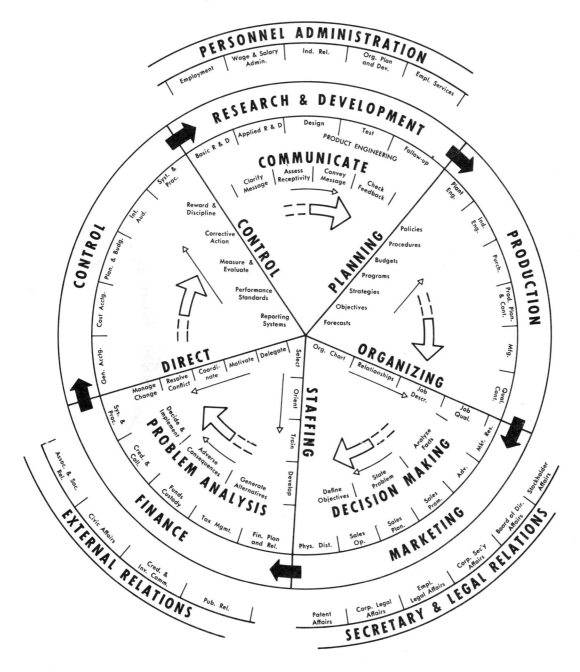

Exhibit 2.4: Time Profile of a President's Team

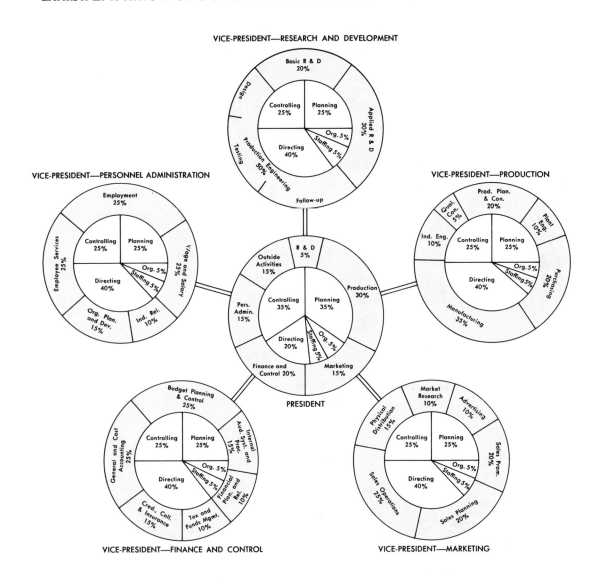

It has always been understood that the time which an executive ought to devote to planning increased with his level in the organization. In the beginning a supervisor is wearing two hats, that of supervisor for part of his time, and that of operator or doer for the rest of his time. That part of the time spent supervising or managing will be divided into some or all of the managerial functions mentioned previously. Of that time, however, perhaps relatively little will be spent in planning. As the supervisor becomes a middle manager, more time will be devoted to planning and less time to operations due to delegation.

It has been suggested that Exhibit 2.5 indicates the ideal relationships between the five most commonly accepted managerial functions. The importance of the two most critical managerial functions—planning and controlling—is shown to increase dramatically with organizational level. When all is said and done, it's a question of knowing where you want to go, planning the best way to get there, and controlling events to conform to that plan. A chief executive at the top level will spend much more time planning and controlling than organizing, staffing, and directing.

A chief executive like Ralph Cordiner, former president of General Electric Company, was known to observe that he would make as few as a half-dozen decisions a year. And of course, these decisions would be involved solely in long-range policy matters, never with purely operating problems. Saxon Tate, when he was managing director of the Canada and Dominion Sugar Company in Montreal, observed that increasingly in management his decisions had a longer and longer time span. By this he meant that the impact of his decisions would be felt further and further into the future. During an interview he presumed that at that time he made few decisions which had an impact on the company of less than five years.

Exhibit 2.5: Emphasis on Management Skills by Organization Level

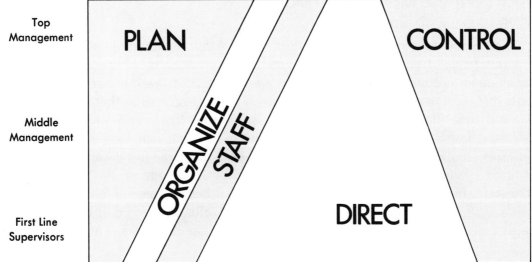

It should be observed that this model, like other models in this section, suggests certain relationships that have not been proven through empirical study. They represent the best thinking of those who have considered the matters involved. It is obvious that these models point to significant areas in time utilization and managerial effectiveness that are relatively untapped and in which future research might be exceedingly well rewarded. Questions to be asked could include: "How *should* managers spend their time at different levels of management?" and "How *do* managers spend their time at these levels?"

Managerial Time Cone

The Managerial Time Cone, Exhibit 2.6 (see page 21), presents commonly suggested proportions of time allocation for managing and operating at different levels in the organization. The Time Cone combines the basic aspects of several of the preceding models. Among the elements shown are the following:

1. The relationship between managing and operating time at various levels.

2. The fact that changes occur in relation to time allocated to managerial skills—e.g., planning—at various levels.

3. The fact that the managerial skills themselves remain the same despite the level and despite the operational assignment of the manager.

4. The idea that relative time spent in each of the operating activities can be demonstrated as segments of a circle.

This Time Cone is a useful tool for the senior executive who wishes to allocate a proportional emphasis to the various skills and activities that are demonstrated in the Management Wheel in Exhibit 2.3.

What Do These Managerial Models Have to Do with Time?

The reader may well ask at this point: Are we talking about management or are we talking about time? This question highlights a common misconception—that the management of time is something separate and distinct from the manager's job. We know that most managers have *tasks* that need managing, a *team* that needs managing, and *time* that needs managing. We assume that like manpower, money, and materials, time is a variable risk resource subject to the same managerial requirements, restraints, and limitations. Yet we saw in Section 1 that time is a completely unique resource—that it is unlike any of the other managerial resources. Furthermore, it is a constant, finite resource. Since the clock can neither be speeded nor slowed, in a very real sense time cannot be managed. It is the only resource that must be spent the instant it is received. As observed, the manager has no choice *whether* to spend

Exhibit 2.6: Managerial Time Cone
Relating Managerial and Operational Functions with Management Level

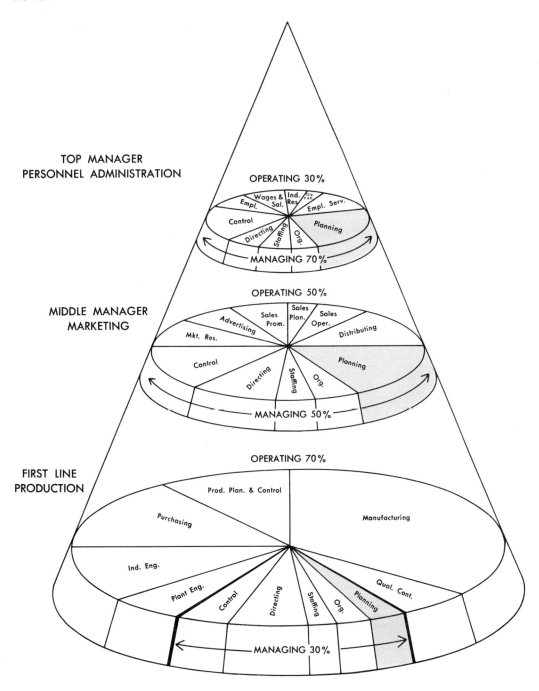

it; his only election is *how* it will be spent. Therefore we see time management as a misnomer. What is really involved is self-management. The real issues involved in the study of executive time are the issues of what executives do, and how effectively. Hence the emphasis is placed on the managerial and operational functions as well as the proposed allocations of time for each. The best time generator is sound management.

For Further Reading

Allen, Jane E. *Beyond Time Management: Organizing the Organization.* Reading, MA: Addison-Wesley, 1986.

Engstrom, Ted W. and Mackenzie, R. Alec. *Managing Your Time: Practical Guidelines on the Effective Use of Time.* Grand Rapids, MI: Zondervan, 1988.

Lieberman, Harvey and Rausch, Erwin. *Managing & Allocating Time: Industrial.* Cranford, NJ: Didactic Systems, 1976.

Management Update, Ltd. (ed.). *Making Effective Use of Executive Time.* New York: State Mutual Bk., 1986.

SECTION 3

Discovering Where Time Goes

SECTION 3

Discovering Where Time Goes

Introduction

Our perception of time varies greatly. We all know that the clock hand moves at a steady pace; yet we often say time flies. On other occasions time seems to stand still. There are great differences in psychological and clock times. If you are waiting for someone while it is raining and cold, five minutes can seem like an eternity. On the other hand, if you are completely absorbed in something you enjoy, minutes and hours disappear as if by magic! Thus, our perception of time depends a great deal upon the circumstances.

We often feel we use our time poorly: We know something is wrong but we cannot specify exactly what it is; there are symptoms that we recognize. Do you sense that you are working under constant, unrelenting pressure? That there are not enough hours in the day? Do you often feel overloaded and frustrated because you are not able to finish the jobs that are important? When critical matters arise, such as year-end reports and other urgent deadlines, do you spend evenings and weekends working to meet them? Do you then find yourself still working long hours when the deadlines have passed? Do you frequently feel assignments given you are too important to be entrusted to subordinates, and that to have them done right, you must do them yourself? If you recognize yourself in most of these symptoms, you need to gain control of your time.

In order to control time, it is necessary to understand what we presently do with our time. To discover this there is only one adequate tool—the time log. A time log is a complete diary of what we do during each day, recorded along with analytical observations. These observations enable us to evaluate the worth of our activities, how effectively our time is allocated to the most valuable activities, and what corrective measures can be taken. It is important to take a time log before attending a time management seminar. Three days should suffice if these are logged in detail. It is essential to provide a basic understanding of the allocation of our time and the nature and extent of the interruptions we experience.

Such a time inventory, or log, is necessary because the painful task of changing our habits requires far more conviction than we can build from learning about the experience of others. We need the amazing revelation of the great portions of time we are wasting to provide the incentive and the determination required to manage ourselves more effectively in this respect.

Taking a Time Log

Read the instructions for taking your log carefully. Be aware of these *pitfalls* in logging your time:

1. Recording at *fixed intervals* (e.g., every 15 minutes), resulting in most interruptions not being recorded.

2. *Terms too general* (lacking sufficient detail for analysis).

3. *Skipping less important actions* (socializing, day-dreaming, brief interruptions, etc.).

4. *Random, not continuous recording* (trying to remember after several hours).

5. Failure to assign priority.

6. Failure to analyze time use patterns.

7. Failure to think of and record corrective actions to take.

Record your log for at least three days with a plan to repeat after 30 days and thereafter quarterly. Following the blank log, you will find questions and information helpful in analyzing your logs. Special uses of the log are suggested on page 31.

Conclusions from a Sample Time Log

1. In the first 1½ hours, only one top priority was addressed.

2. Number 1 might have been completed in the first 20 minutes if needed information had been requested when it should have been.

3. Ten minutes was wasted on it and still no decision.

4. 10 percent (10 minutes) on #1
   20 percent (20 minutes) on #2
   35 percent (35 minutes) on #3
   35 percent (35 minutes) on #4

Exhibit 3.1: Instructions for Taking a Daily Time Log
1. Enter name, date, and goals.
2. Record each activity as the day progesses. Record all interruptions, their source and reason. Give as much detail as possible.
3. Set a priority on each action, so that you can check back at the end of the day to see how much time was spent on top priority work.
4. Comment on each action with a view to future improvements. Try to note suggestions for making these improvements.
5. Keep logs for minimum of three days; one week is preferable. Allow time to analyze your logs.
6. Use signs and abbreviations: Phone call out c→ Phone call in →c etc.

Sample Daily Time Log

Name: _____   **Date:** _____

Daily Goals: Deadline:

1. *Write up Contract* _____ 11:00   4. *Distrib. Mtg., Complete Agenda* _____ 3:30

2. *Report to S.K.* _____ 12:30   5. *Catch up on correspondence* _____ 4:30

3. *Staff Mtg. complete agenda* _____ 2:00   6. _____ _____

Priority: 1-Important & Urgent; 2-Important or Urgent; 3-Routine Detail; 4-Trivial

TIME	ACTIVITY	TIME USED	PRIOR	COMMENT/DISPOSITION
8:05	*Read newspaper*	20	4	*Could read at lunch — 1st 20 minutes wasted.*
8:25	*Read phone messages*	10	4	*Good time for update on calls before day gets going*
8:35	*Return c → B.R.*	5	2	*Good time to make calls, most in office at start of day*
	c → S.L.	5	4	*Good time to make calls, most in office at start of day*
8:45	*Got coffee, met Bill M.*	10	3	*Routine Problem*
8:55	*Opened, read mail*	25	3	*Sec. could open, sort, route and throw out junk mail*
9:20	*Dictate draft of contr. to secty.*	7	1	*Not really organized. Need decision from B.H. re: contract*
9:27	*c → B.H. — Problem re: contract*	3	1	*B.H. not available. Left cb.*
9:30	*Resume dictation to secty.*	15	2	*Dictating equipment would save time — mine and secretary's*
9:45	*c → S.K. Quests. re: report*		2	

Exhibit 3.2: Daily Time Log

Name: _____   **Date:** _____

Daily Goals: Deadline:
1. _____ _____   4. _____ _____
2. _____ _____   5. _____ _____
3. _____ _____   6. _____ _____

Priority: 1-Important & Urgent; 2-Important or Urgent; 3-Routine Detail; 4-Trivial

TIME	ACTIVITY	TIME USED	PRIOR	COMMENT/DISPOSITION

Daily Time Log—2

TIME	ACTIVITY	TIME USED	PRIOR	COMMENT/DISPOSITION

Analyzing Your Time Log

1. Pick one day from your logs and complete the form. See page 27 for the analysis of the Sample Log.

   How I Spent My Time

Priority	Minutes Spent	% of Time
1	_____	_____
2	_____	_____
3	_____	_____
4	_____	_____

2. In reviewing thousands of logs over the past two decades, we have found these typical conclusions:

   a. Many interruptions.
   b. Little time for top priorities.
   c. Too much time on low-value tasks.
   d. Doing many things that could be delegated.
   e. Easily distracted; short attention span.
   f. More productivity when logging.
   g. Takes longer to get results than previously thought.

3. Most time logs show the power of interruptions to fragment the day. Studies show that managers are interrupted on the average every eight minutes throughout their day. Secretaries and other support staff block interruptions for managers but fall victim to needless interruptions themselves.

   Typical interruptions that represent serious time concerns follow.

   _____ Telephone, drop-in visitors, socializing.
   _____ Unscheduled or rescheduling meetings.
   _____ Crises, shifting priorities.
   _____ Cluttered desk.
   _____ Inability to say NO.
   _____ Unfinished tasks.
   _____ Indecision.
   _____ Visual distractions, noise.
   _____ Mistakes, mechanical breakdown.
   _____ Wrong/lost information.
   _____ Self-interruptions.

   (Check your most significant ones.)

4. We allow interruptions because of:

_____ An illusion of courtesy.
_____ Image of availability.
_____ Presumption of legitimacy of interruption.
_____ Need to socialize.
_____ Desire to be informed.
_____ Low perception of value of own time.

(Check the reasons with which you can identify.)

Special Uses of Time Logs

We recommend:

1. *Periodic log* (quarterly for 3-day periods) to:
   a. Maintain awareness.
   b. Prevent regression into bad habits.

   Initially, we recommend that you log in detail as instructed and that you repeat quarterly for periods of at least three days.

2. *Occasional/specified log,* as needed to:
   a. Determine seriousness of particular time concerns.
   b. Measure progress in controlling certain time concerns.

   At intervals, you may wish to log only information regarding a specific time concerns, such as telephone interruptions, to determine seriousness and/or to measure progress.

3. *Continual/specified Log,* as needed to:
   a. Provide a continuing self-disciplining tool to:
      1) Monitor on-going effectiveness in utilizing time.
      2) Trigger immediate self-correction.

   A senior AT&T executive used the continual log every working day. He had discovered that it took very little time and alerted him immediately when time was being wasted. A self-correcting tendency always set in immediately to remedy the situation. This executive called the continual time log "the most powerful self-disciplining tool" he had ever encountered.

   A time log, used correctly, is the most important initial tool in time management.

Exhibit 3.3: A Typical Time Log for a Sales Manager

DAILY TIME LOG

Date: _____11-14-74_____
Name: _____Bill Grant_____

Goals:

1. *Finish Mgmt. Review*
2. *Sales Summary to Boss*
3. *Service Report to Boss*
4. *Staff Meeting*
5. *Catch up on Mail*
6. *Resolve Brown problem*

Priority: 1-Important & Urgent; 2-Important & NOT Urgent; 3-Urgent & NOT Important; 4-Routine; 0-Wasted

Comment/Dispostion/Results: Delegate to _____ .

Train _____ to handle.

Next time ask his recommendation.

Next time say "No."

Consolidate/Eliminate/Cut Time

Other

TIME	ACTION	PRIORITY	COMMENT/DISPOSITION/RESULTS
8:00			
	ARR 8:10 – Coffee	4	Could read over lunch
	Read W.S. Journal	4	(1st 20 min. wasted)
8:30	Review plan for day	1	Well spent. Anticipated two problems to
	Misc. notes to sec'y.	2	alert sec'y to.
	8:50 – wife called – plan for lunch	4	
9:00	9:05 – Secy's questions for day. BB called re budget	1 3	Switchbd. could have taken both messages.
	0	0	Must have been daydreaming – nothing done.
9:30	Dictation to sec'y	2	Not really organized for this dictation.
	Separated mail	4	Some sec'y. could have written herself. Let her decide; sec'y. will separate and prioritize.
10:00	Boss chatted re trip plans (pers.)	0	
10:30	0	0	
	Coffee	4	
11:00	Staff meeting		This staff meeting could have been completed in 30 min.
			Should not even have gotten into space allocation. 30 min. wasted.

Exhibit 3.3: A Typical Time Log for a Sales Manager (Continued)

DAILY TIME LOG

Priority: 1-Important & Urgent; 2-Important & NOT Urgent; 3-Urgent & NOT Important; 4-Routine; 0-Wasted

Comment/Dispostion/Results: Delegate to _____ .

Train _____ to handle.

Next time ask his recommendation.

Next time say "No."

Consolidate/Eliminate/Cut Time

Other

TIME	ACTION	PRIORITY	COMMENT/DISPOSITION/RESULTS
11:30	(Wrangle over new space allocation settled)	3-4	
12:00	Sign mail	4	Let sec'y sign routine mail
	Lunch	4	Could have met with boss for lunch and completed rules summary review — but wasn't ready when he suggested it.
12:30			
1:00	Lunch		
	Complete sales summary for meeting with boss	1	Urgent only because left until last min. Benefitted by experience.
1:30	CS drops in — social	4	Unnecessary interruptions. Could have waited
	Call BB on budget	4	
	Call JD — personnel replacement	4	
2:00	Mtg. with boss	2	If written report had been submitted earlier, boss could have reviewed. Then this meeting could have been cut to 15 min. or eliminated if he had returned the report
	Sales summary		
2:30	OK's delay on service report		with questions. 30 min. wasted.
	RM call info. systems in to ask boss when to	2	
3:00	expect decision re dept. revision and reorgan.		
	JJ call — personnel RM dropped in — Ques 'M' info. for sys.	4 4	Referred to HC. Referred to asst.

Exhibit 3.3: A Typical Time Log for a Sales Manager (Continued)

DAILY TIME LOG

Priority: 1-Important & Urgent; 2-Important & NOT Urgent; 3-Urgent & NOT Important; 4-Routine; 0-Wasted

Comment/Dispostion/Results: Delegate to _____ .

                      Train _____ to handle.

                      Next time ask his recommendation.

                      Next time say "No."

                      Consolidate/Eliminate/Cut Time

                      Other

TIME	ACTION	PRIORITY	COMMENT/DISPOSITION/RESULTS
3:30	Coffee		
	Distributor meeting		Attended only because of habit. Result some ques. directed to me instead of
4:00			my asst. Decision to leave these meetings to asst. unless he wants me to sit in.
4:30	Worked on mgmt. review (inter. by TM re staff mtg.)	1	This was #1 for day but left until end and then permitted interruption (needless).
5:00	Call pers. re Brown. Too late		Procrastination killed this one.
	Home		Where did the day go?
5:30			
Evening			

Making the Most of Your Time Log

Use for Both Scheduling Deadlines and Recording

The most effective executives see the time log as beneficial not only for recording where their time has gone, but for planning in advance how they wanted it to go. This can be done very simply by setting deadlines for each of the daily goals at the top of the time log. These self-imposed deadlines serve as an excellent planning device and establish targets to shoot for throughout the day. They provide an excellent excuse to resist interruptions. They also facilitate measurement and evaluation at the end of the day: (a) were the goals accomplished and (b) were they accomplished within the time span planned?

Detail in Recording

In how much detail should the time log be kept? Some managers instinctively and wisely take the time log as a challenge and record nearly every significant activity that occurs during the day. This kind of time log is immediately evidenced by some typical entries, such as the precise time that an activity started and the precise time it ended. This compares with the opposite tendency to record only the vaguest generalizations where half-hour segment after half-hour segment will show only one word or two such as "dictation." This type of entry raises the suspicion that the log was not taken seriously and may even have been filled in at the end of the day.

Two factors make this practice dangerous. First, such total dependence on memory is ill-advised, since no memory is that dependable. Second, the tendency to shape the log to make oneself look good may be irresistible. The majority of managers follow the middle path of a reasonably sincere effort to record detail, but with an obvious failure to catch the incidental interruptions of which most managers suffer a great number each day. Of what use is it to know that you received three calls in 10 minutes if you can't recall from whom they came or what was discussed? It is through sad experience that I have learned the importance of emphasizing the detail with which the time log must be kept. The rewards to the manager will vary in direct proportion to the attention given the details.

Almost invariably I find that the manager who was careless in this area—who used only broad generalizations—will come to the evaluative questions and have very few conclusions to draw. Dozens of times I have written the comment on these time logs, "If you had kept your log in greater detail, you would have had much more meaningful conclusions at this point." Takers of time logs would be wise to ensure that the instructions regarding detail are followed from the beginning of the project.

Analyzing Each Action at the Time

The columns titled PRIORITY and COMMENT/DISPOSITION/RESULTS should be completed while the action is fresh in mind. The best time is immediately. While it is possible to argue that delay provides time for reflection, it is my experience that little reflection is necessary. Furthermore, even that little reflection is not likely to be given *each action* if delayed. For all practical purposes the complete entry should be made at one time, steadily and regularly as actions take place throughout the day. With the use of simple code letters, which most managers utilize anyway, these entries need take very little time overall. As mentioned above, no memory is that dependable.

Allocating Time to Major Categories

Since the Management Wheel (Exhibit 2.3, page 17) lists all of the accepted managerial and operational functions and activities, 16 functions and 77 activities in all, the person who is selecting categories of concern should first look at the inner circle of this chart to determine which of the managerial functions to allocate, in what manner, assuming that all of them will be important at some level. On the outer circle are the operational functions. Then, on the chart on page 19 (Exhibit 2.5) the varying emphasis on the managerial functions, depending on one's organizational level, will be suggested. A glance at the Managerial Time Cone (Exhibit 2.6, page 21) shows at what levels certain activities may not be employed at all. For example, if she is a middle manager in marketing, she will not be responsible for all five or six of those marketing activities. She is apt to be involved with only one of them, perhaps market research, advertising, or sales promotion. By looking at these three exhibits, the manager will very quickly be able to determine the categories that are appropriate for any particular position.

Overall Analysis

One of the astonishing things about time logs is the frequency with which a manager will keep his log but fail to follow through with an overall analysis. At this point one must observe that perhaps this was his greatest waste of time during the period measured. What sense does it make to take the time to record activities for two days or for a week—only to neglect the analysis which would lead to conclusions, and make the invested time pay off? Suggestions for making an overall analysis will follow on page 40.

Planning

After the analysis has been completed, it is time for the manager to ask himself if this is the way he wishes his time to go. The third column in the time log requires an analysis of each of the major actions taken. A review of these conclusions will show the manager how he can improve his time utilization. Many activities simply should not have been undertaken at all. A number could have been done by other people, and therefore should not have been done by the manager himself. He should have delegated or referred them to others. In many cases they should have been screened by his secretary and rerouted without ever coming to his desk.

The time spent reading and deciding who should have handled a matter is a classic example of wasted time when a competent secretary could have handled it. One wit called this "reading your in-basket to see if you ought to be reading it!" Out of these conclusions should come a plan for systematic disposition of all actions which should not have been done at all or could have been done by others. A means of shielding the manager from needless interruptions should be developed and implemented.

Ways of consolidating or eliminating routine items which could be handled at the same time or dispensed with ought to be worked out. And most important, a method of setting daily objectives, priorities, and deadlines and of seeing that they are implemented must be devised. In most cases, the greatest help in this area is a competent secretary or assistant who can be assigned the task of monitoring progress in achieving the daily written plan.

Implementation

It is sad that a great many of the best-laid plans have gone astray for failure to ensure effective implementation. The causes of ineffective implemenation include lack of self-discipline and procrastination. A group of division presidents of a major midwestern corporation concluded after a one-day time management seminar that an excellent means of countering this problem would be a "buddy system." They would meet with others weekly for lunch to check up on how they were progressing against their weekly goals. The whole purpose of this would be to add a motivating monitoring influence which is needed as much at the top of the organization as at the bottom.

The president of a successful trucking firm in Oklahoma created a board of outside businesspeople to whom he wanted to be held responsible. He recognized that the president of a family-owned organization usually was missing this accountability element, and he determined that it was vital to his effectiveness as the chief executive. As a member of that board for a period of time, I can attest to the effectiveness of this system.

The Sales Manager's Analysis of the Time Log

Let us examine a sales manager's analysis of his time log. His answers to 10 questions follow:

Question	Answer
1. Did setting daily goals and deadlines improve your effectiveness?	Yes.
a. Why?	Helped me focus on essentials.
b. Were goals and deadlines demanding yet realistic?	Yes.
c. Which daily goals contributed directly to long-range objectives?	All.
d. Which could have been delegated?	None, really.

Question

Answer

2. What time did you start on your No. 1
goal?

   4:30

   a. Could you have started earlier?

   Yes.

   b. Did anything distract you from completing it?

   Yes, interrupted by TM, but late start
   real cause.

   c. Did you recover immediately (return at
   once to the task)?

   No. Too late.

3. To what extent did you achieve each
objective?

Goal	% Completed	Reason for Noncompletion
a. Finish management review	20	Late start. Interrupted. Too little time.
b. Sales summary to boss	100	Had to get it done (boss).
c. Service report to boss	0	Boss ok'd delay.
d. Staff meeting	100	Routine.
e. Catch up on mail	0	Only able to stay even. Too much to do.
f. Resolve Brown matter	0	Other things more important.

4. What was your longest period of totally
uninterrupted time excluding meetings and
lunch?

   About 30 min.

   a. Which period of the day was most
   productive?

   Early morning and late afternoon.

   b. Which was least productive?

   9:30 to 10:30 and 2:30 to 3:15.

   c. Is this likely a normal pattern?

   Yes. More or less.

   d. If yes, how could you program or pace
   your activities to take advantage of it?

   Question not clear.

   e. How could you make other periods of
   the day more productive?

   Don't know.

5. Who/what was your most frequent
interruptor?

   Boss and associates and team. But all
   necessary.

   a. What are the causes?

   Emergencies and other necessary
   communications.

   b. How can these be controlled,
   minimized, eliminated?

   They are my job, so why eliminate?

6. In order of importance list all types of interruptions with which you must contend, e.g., telephone, drop-in visitors, unscheduled meetings, unexpected crises, mail, self-interruptions, visual distractions, noise, etc. List two or three solutions for top three or four interruptions:

Interruptions

a. Unexpected crises

b. Unscheduled meetings
c. Telephone interruptions
d. Drop-in visitors

Steps to Control

No real solution. Hazard of the business.
When boss calls 'em, you go.
Have secretary screen.
We have an "open door" policy.

7. List the four most time-consuming activities which could have been handled by someone else or not done at all. How will you handle these next time?

Activity

a. Distributor meetings (3:30-4:15)
b. Staff meeting (10:45-11:45)

c. Unscheduled meeting (1:45-2:30)

d. Interrruptions throughout day, both drop-ins & phone.

How to Handle Next Time

Delegate to assistant.
Limit items on agenda and set time limit on meeting.
Give boss written summary. Let him review first and either return with questions or discuss more briefly.
Better screening by secretary; "quiet hour"; close door; visitors by apptmt; regular meeting times weekly with individual staff.

8. Did you tend to record "activities" or "results"?

Activities.

9. Did a self-correcting tendency appear as you recorded your actions?

Yes.

10. Of the solutions you have suggested on preceding page, which three will you implement immediately?
   a. Save meeting time by delegating attendance, limiting agenda, setting time limits, using memos instead.
   b. Control interruptions by coaching secretary in better screening of visitors and telephone interruptions.
   c. Implement "quiet hour" to concentrate on my own priority goals for the day.

Review of the Sales Manager's Analysis

QUESTION 1—*Did setting daily goals and deadlines improve your effectiveness?*

A review of the sales manager's analysis reveals a number of strengths and weaknesses in the area of time management. His response to Question 1 reveals his awareness of the importance of focusing on essentials. His conclusion that his goals were realistic as well as demanding does not seem to be borne out by his answers to Question 3. . .or he faces a sober conclusion that his record of accomplishment is pretty poor if in fact his goals were, as he says, realistic. It seems difficult to accept that all his goals contributed to long-range objectives, particularly goals 4 and 5, i.e., "staff meeting" and "catch up on mail." This response raises the question of credibility regarding his other answers.

It is difficult to disagree with his conclusion that none of his goals could have been delegated, yet at 9:30 he spent 15 minutes apparently separating mail. Indeed his secretary appears to have been underutilized and, fortunately, his recommended solutions clearly deal with this situation. Listing "staff meeting" as a goal appears too general. Given the total time that he felt was wasted in meetings, a better goal might have been to *avoid* holding a staff meeting or limiting it to 30 minutes as he indicates in column 3. Staff meetings (4) as well as catching up on mail (5) are routine items to be discouraged from appearing on serious lists of daily goals.

QUESTION 2—*What time did you start on your No. 1 goal?*

The sales manager's response to Question 2 indicates candor but little else. Assuming that he followed instructions and listed his daily goals *in order of priority*, there seems no excuse evident from the log for delaying the start of his number 1 goal until 4:30, the end of the working day. Even worse, to have allowed an interruption after getting only 20 percent of it finished, and finally, not to have returned to it at all, appears defenseless. Oddly, however, it is typical. The reader already must sense how valuable are the insights to be gained from the time log when seriously analyzed.

QUESTION 3—*To what extent did you achieve each objective?*

The responses to Question 3 betray an understandable defensiveness. His reasons for scoring only a 20 percent completion on his number 1 goal begin with the "late start" (candid). But then he states "interrupted" (an excuse). *Who* allowed the interruption? Next, disastrously, he laments, "too little time." Doesn't he have *all* there is? Since everyone has the same amount, is *time* the problem or is *he*? Whereas the boss appears to have provided the motivation for getting number 2 done, he uses him as the excuse for *not* even starting on number 3.

What does 100 percent completion of staff meeting mean? Since the term is so general, the total completion is without meaning. Hence the need for precise, measurable terms in goal-setting. His excuse for only "staying even" with the mail (can't most of this be delegated?) is "too much to do." Really? Or wasting too much time?

And the Brown matter failed to get resolved because he had other more important matters to attend to. Such as? Where do they appear on his time log? If they *were* more important, why did they not appear in the list of daily goals in the true order of their importance?

QUESTION 4—*What was your longest period of totally uninterrupted time excluding meetings and lunch?*

The response to Question 4, that early morning and late afternoon periods were most productive, is usual. Yet examination of the time log shows a curious use of these times. Note that the first two actions in the morning were acquiring coffee and reading the *Wall Street Journal*—neither of which would rank as a top priority for the day. It *is* true that at 8:30 the sales manager reviewed his plan for the day, appropriately ranked as a number 1 priority. He then made notes for his secretary in preparation for the 9:05 meeting to answer her questions for the day. Very few managers take these two vitally important actions—planning the day in advance and discussing these plans with the secretary.

In designating his least productive periods of the day, note that the sales manager identified a total of one and three-quarter hours *exclusive of meetings*. The effectiveness of his time in meetings was questioned above. The staff meeting apparently wasted one-half hour; the 45-minute meeting with the boss might have been handled another way; and the distributor meeting for another 45 minutes could have been handled by one of his team. Thus, two hours in meetings also were unwisely spent or almost totally wasted. Now the sales manager designates another one and three-quarter hours as least productive. So a total of three and three-quarter hours now appears to have been poorly spent. Is it any wonder that industrial psychologists and time management specialists agree that the average manager may be no more than 30 percent effective overall?

The question of pacing one's activities to take advantage of the most and the least productive times of day is a matter rarely, if ever, considered by managers. Yet virtually all management analysts propose, and most truly effective executives practice, this very principle. Managers who make it a habit to tackle the toughest or least pleasant task first have learned that several benefits result: 1) they are at their best and therefore will likely do a better job; 2) by getting it out of the way, the rest of the day is "downhill"; 3) if crises erupt, they can be more relaxed in handling them; and 4) if nothing else gets done, they can still leave at the end of the day without feeling guilty and with the assurance that the most important things got done.

Many managers find their energy depleted by midday and have a feeling of letdown after lunch. To offset this, some managers exercise, even if it is only to take a long walk. Others schedule the handling of mail and routine dictation during this period, thus matching the least demanding tasks with their least productive period.

QUESTION 5—*Who/What was your most frequent interruptor?*

To respond to Question 5 that all interruptions of his boss, associates, and subordinates are necessary is to blindly disregard his own conclusions recorded on his time log. At approximately 8:20 he read the *Wall Street Journal* while noting he could have read it over lunch. This was a self-interruption. Around 9:10 he took two calls but noted that the switchboard operator could have taken messages. At 9:30 he gets fouled up in dictation by not being prepared, thus dictating matters his secretary could have handled, which is another form of self-interruption.

Then he separated mail instead of delegating that routine matter to his secretary. Next his boss interrupted on a personal matter when the sales manager admits he should have been candid about being busy. And so on through the day. Thus, it is clear that a manager will typically record clear conclusions and still allow himself to completely negate these conclusions moments later when thinking in another vein. Perhaps it is the instinct of self-preservation that leads to the anomaly.

In responding that such interruptions are his job, the sales manager reaches a low of sorts in self-deprecation. Obviously, he thinks in terms of serious interruptions, not bothering perhaps to review his own conclusions in column 3 to see how unimportant and how avoidable many of them are. And to call these interruptions "emergencies" and "other necessary communications" begs the question. The most cursory review reveals that this conclusion is self-serving and is gross rationalization.

QUESTION 6—*List all types of interruptions with which you must contend.*

His responses to Question 6 may be the most discouraging since they seem to represent total capitulation to three out of the top four interruptions. Even a cursory second thought should reveal that crises *should be* expected. Murphy's famous Third Law holds, "If anything *can* go wrong, it will." So the experienced manager expects the unexpected and plans for it. How could emergency wards of hospitals be prepared for anything if the attitude "there is no real solution" prevailed?

And it makes sense, when the boss calls an unscheduled meeting, to suggest a better alternative, doesn't it? For example, you might ask, "Could we settle it now on the phone?" If it helps you accomplish more of the tasks you are trying to accomplish for him, why shouldn't you suggest it? Having your secretary screen telephone interruptions does make sense, especially since for managers worldwide, telephone interruptions are the number 1 time concern. However, the "open door" policy is a poor excuse for allowing drop-in visitors. Hundreds of thousands of managers leave their doors open but have established a climate of seriousness which prevents frivolous interruption.

Thousands of others have simply recognized that the so-called "open door" was not originally intended to be physically open at all times. It was meant to indicate the freedom of the manager with a problem to approach his superior whenever he had a problem which warranted the interruption. In other words, the door was "open" to that manager whenever necessary. One of the Fortune 500 international food companies has an "open door" policy. There is a concerted effort among middle and top managers in this company to modify this policy by closing the door whenever the manager chooses not to be interrupted and to make appointments whenever possible. Managers who have done this are virtually unanimous in their praise of this adaptation of a commonly misunderstood policy. "Open door" at all times for all purposes does not recognize the practical realities of the managing situation.

QUESTION 7—*List the five most time-consuming activities which could have been handled by someone else or not done at all.*

The sales manager's responses to Question 7 are very encouraging. However faulty or self-serving his analysis may have appeared in specific places, his proposed solutions for the most time-consuming activities which could have been handled by others are realistic and extremely promising.

QUESTION 8—*Did you tend to record "activities" or "results"?*

QUESTION 9—*Did a self-correcting tendency appear as you recorded your actions?*

QUESTION 10—*Of the solutions you have suggested above, which three will you implement immediately?*

His responses to questions 8 and 9 are normal. The three actions chosen for immediate implementation (Question 10) virtually guarantee that he will 1) save two or more hours a day and 2) increase his effectiveness several times.

How to Review a Typical Time Log Analysis

In reviewing your own or a subordinate's time log analysis, bear in mind that no two time logs will be identical, nor will their analyses. This means that while the above review of the sales manager's analysis will be instructive of items to question and points worth discussing, it will not be applicable uniformly to all situations. For example, few time logs will be as detailed as this sales manager's. The more general the time log, the more difficult the analysis. In extreme cases, the questions will not even be answered by the manager. In such situations I simply note that after spending the time required to take the log, it is a consummate waste of time not to have spent the extra few minutes necessary for the analysis and the greatest ultimate gain. I suggest that the manger either attempt (even though it may be difficult in retrospect) to analyze his log as recommended, or to repeat the entire process by taking a new time log and this time taking the assignment seriously. An advantage of this is that defects in the initial reporting on the first time log may be noted and suggestions made accordingly. Thus, the second attempt may be far more beneficial than the first might have been, even if it had been completed.

A typical complaint will accompany many time logs—the explanation that it wasn't a typical week. The best response to this is that few if any time periods are typical—that most managers never have what they would admit to be a typical week. So perhaps the atypical week should be accepted and analyzed for better or worse.

Watch for inconsistencies. Many were apparent in the sales manager's analysis. It takes a careful review to spot them, but in almost every time log there will be some. These may be extremely important in the case of the overconfident manager who acknowledges no timewasting. In such cases, reasons for this attitude should be sought in candid discussion.

Stay alert to evidences that the log was not kept while time passed but rather was filled in at intervals or even at the end of the day. One such indicator may be the same slant on all words and sentences in the entire log. Another clue is the brevity and generalization of entries combined with no indication that anything started or ended other than at the convenient 15-minute intervals. When all these evidences are present, the probability that this approach was used ought to be discussed. Be prepared for the quick response that the log was unreadable so it was copied over by the manager or his secretary. Such recopying would be a classic time concern in itself.

When a review of the Time Log Analysis reveals that one or more persons are repetitive interruptors, check into the possible reasons. Is it possible that the manager overcontrols, demands too much detail, doesn't allow independent initiative, or requires that his team check everything with him before proceeding?

Look for recognition of time concerns caused by himself, as opposed to those caused by others. If none appear, see the list of Time Concerns of 40 Senior Executives (Exhibit 4.2), on page 53. Discuss the reasons for the first set of time concerns being externally generated and the second list being internally or self-generated. Review with the manager those self-generated time concerns such as indecision, procrastination, stacked desk, lack of objectives, priorities, deadlines, etc. which he considers most important. Develop tentative solutions to the most serious ones to augment his own completed analysis.

Discuss with the manager what discoveries he made through the time log and its analysis. Then discuss what he might expect his team members to discover and how he might wish to introduce the subject with them.

Actual Time and Estimated Forecast—A Long-Range Comparison

Birger Wist, president of Bjarne Wist, in Trondheim, Norway, decided on a two-month period for his time log. He kept a detailed account with the help of his secretary and carefully analyzed the results which appear in the following summary. The column titled "Forecast" shows the percentage of total time that he thought he was giving to each function. The column headed "Actual" indicates the percentage of time actually spent in each activity.

Time Profile of a President

Activity	Forecast	Actual	Planned
1. Planning	50%	30%	40%
2. Reports and control	20	10	5
3. Staff meetings	15	21	10
4. Secretary	5	3	5
Dictation	—	—	5
5. Telephone	5	8	5
6. Civic activities	5	20	25
7. Plant visits	0	8	5
	100%	100%	100%

Wist's average working week totaled 35 hours plus time spent reading management literature. The greatest surprises to him, but not to his secretary, were the amounts of time spent on civic affairs and meetings and his overestimate of planning time by 20 percent.

As a result of Wist's survey of his use of time, he planned (see the third column of the summary) to spend 40 percent of his time planning and 5 percent on reports and control. The latter seemed to be taking longer than desired because of the number of reports he was reading unnecessarily and the number of questions he would ask that might have been answered in the reports if the information had been requested. He planned to reduce this time to 5 percent of his total by delegating to others the handling of many reports.

Staff meetings, Wist discovered, took much more time than desired. Better planning, careful preparation of agendas, stronger leadership, and better listening cut this time in half and resulted in faster decisions and more progress. Impromptu meetings, often held standing up to discourage socializing, were called frequently for short discussions and fast decisions.

His secretary handled all calls by responding that he was busy and would return the call later, unless of course it was a real emergency. Wist found this prevented the telephone from running him and allowed him to return calls at a time convenient for him. As a result, he was better prepared to respond since his secretary knew the purpose of the call and provided him with any necessary information.

Plant visits were better planned, and many questions were prepared in advance so that each visit had a definite purpose. Most interestingly, Wist decided that civic responsibilities ought to play an even more important part in his time allocation and he raised the apportionment to 25 percent.

"I lived with many timewasters for years," says Wist, "but I finally realized that I must do something about them if my business and I were to survive. Even then I found myself gradually slipping back into the old bad habits. So I decided that I would repeat the inventory at least briefly as a spot check twice a year."

For Further Reading

Drucker, Peter F. *The Effective Executive.* New York: Harper & Row, 1967.

Jungjohann, Kathy and Schenck, Becky R. *How to Understand and Manage Your Time.* Chicago: SRA, 1986.

Munzo, Tiszjji. *Time Mastery: The Beginner's Book.* Schenectady, NY: Illumination Society, 1987.

SECTION 4

Identifying Your Time Concerns

Definitions:

    Management
    Effectiveness
    Time
    Time Concern

Top 153 Time Concerns

Internal Versus External Time Concerns

Red Threads

Comparison of Time Concerns Abroad

Comparison by Occupation and Management Level

Identifying Your Top 10 Time Concerns

Team Time Concern Profiles

Confirming Your Time Concerns with Your Time Log

SECTION 4

Identifying Your Time Concerns

My experiences over the years have led me to conclude that time is inseparable from management and from life itself. Now, if time is so universal—if it is inseparable from life itself—it should not be surprising that the list of time concerns grows continually. Some time ago the list that I have been keeping reached 153, as Exhibit 4.1 shows. In identifying our time concerns, several definitions will be helpful.

Definitions

Management has been defined in many ways but perhaps the most commonly accepted definition is "getting things done through people." A more precise definition would be "achieving objectives through others."

Effectiveness is an elusive term which is often confused with efficiency. Peter Drucker has offered one insight into these two terms by suggesting that efficiency may be viewed as doing a job right, while effectiveness may be viewed as doing the *right* job right. Others have suggested that effectiveness should be viewed as achieving one's objectives with the most efficient utilization of resources available.

Time is perhaps the most elusive term in all of management. In the beginning section, we cited St. Augustine's difficulty in describing time. We also quoted Webster's definition: the period during which action or process continues.

A *timewaster*, or *time concern*, for our purposes, will be considered to be anything that prevents the manager from achieving objectives in the most effective way possible.

The importance of these definitions will be immediately apparent. The world's so-called number one time concern, telephone interruptions, may be challenged by some participants in any seminar. The challengers will be those who properly view the telephone as the most important instrument in their office and a great timesaver. How is it possible, they demand, to view the telephone as a time concern? Especially for the switchboard operator, this would be a ridiculous assumption. Switchboard operators achieve their objectives through the use of the telephone because their *job* is to handle incoming phone calls. However, an ineffective operator could waste a great deal of time in the handling of these calls.

The telephone operator will not have access to some of the solutions available to others in the organization—such as having telephone calls intercepted by a secretary or assistant. Nevertheless, there are many practical alternatives available. Examples include practicing brevity in handling phone calls, having instant access to a directory of numbers, and understanding the organization chart and the functional responsibilities of staff members, thus speeding the referral of inquiries on various subjects. Therefore, we see that a given tool or technique may be a great timesaver when used effectively, and yet it may become a time concern when used ineffectively.

Top 153 Time Concerns

We turn again to the composite list in Exhibit 4.1 (see page 51) of all the time concerns which have been suggested by a large number of managers with whom I have worked in 15 countries. Omitted are some on the light-hearted side ranging from the ridiculous "answering questions that should never have been asked" to the dubious "liquid lunches" and the sublime "daydreaming." I have been developing this list over the years and more recently have been categorizing the time concerns by management function. This categorization was extremely helpful, since it focused the search on the principal management functions. If time is indivisible from management—the best time-generator really is sound management—then it would seem reasonable that time concerns could be identified in each of the functional areas of management.

Internal Versus External Time Concerns

At this point, my quest for time concerns took a major turn. Until now, I had identified only the most obvious time concerns. These tended to be "externally" generated time concerns such as telephone interruptions, drop-in visitors, unscheduled meetings, and crises. Having identified that time is related to all managerial activities, I turned the search inward to what we might call "internally" generated time concerns. Here I began to identify a new class of obstacles to managerial effectiveness including failure to set objectives, priorities, and deadlines; cluttered desk and personal disorganization; ineffective delegation; unnecessary involvement in routine matters; attempting too much at once; unrealistic estimates; indecision and procrastination.

One of the most interesting time concern lists ever assembled, in my opinion, is found in Exhibit 4.2 (see page 53), an analysis by 40 chief executives of small electrical contracting firms. The list on the left was the first list compiled in the seminar as the presidents identified the time concerns which they thought most important. Then the group viewed the Peter Drucker film, "Managing Time." In this film the president, Ev Lansing, is shown wasting time in a number of ways ranging from not arriving at his own meetings on time to calling unscheduled meetings with everyone there. He consistently involves himself in small details and clearly attempts to get much more done than is realistically possible within the limits of time available.

After seeing the film, the 40 chief executives were asked if they could identify any new time concerns, and the list on page 53 was then developed. The striking characteristic of these two lists is that nearly all of those on the left, which were identified first, are externally generated—i.e., the presidents are blaming others for them. The list on the right is almost entirely made up of self-generated time concerns where

Exhibit 4.2: Time Concerns of 40 Executives (Electrical Contractors)

Before Viewing Film, "Managing Time"	After Viewing Film, "Managing Time"
1. Incomplete information for solution	1. Attempting too much at once
2. Employees with problems	2. Unrealistic time estimates
3. Telephone	3. Procrastinating
4. Routine tasks	4. Not listening
5. Meetings	5. Not saying "no"
6. Drop-in visitors	6. Doing it myself
7. Outside activities	7. Stacked desk, personal disorganization
8. Crisis management	8. Delegating responsibility without authority
9. Poor communication	9. Snap decisions

the presidents are blaming themselves. This deeper insight developed after they saw a film of another president wasting his time.

Thus, as the reader reviews this chart of time concerns, he should be alert to the different characteristics of the items which it contains. They could easily be divided into two groups—those that tend to be generated internally or self-generated, and those that tend to be externally generated or exist in the organization or situation in which the manager finds himself.

Red Threads

There is another interesting characteristic of these time concerns—many of them are interrelated. Consider how the inability to make realistic time estimates can lead a manager to attempt too much at once. Notice the relationship between attempting too much and doing it yourself. And note how doing it yourself, or refusing to delegate, could be a direct result of lack of confidence in staff.

There are some red threads, as German managers are wont to say, which run through a number of time concerns and link them together through a common element. For example, consider lack of self-discipline and how this could be viewed as a fundamental cause of a large number of time concerns. Certainly it would be viewed as a factor in failure to set objectives, priorities, and deadlines; in the cluttered desk and personal disorganization; and in indecision and procrastination. Undoubtedly there would be dozens of the time concerns which could be related to the red thread of self-discipline.

Another red thread might be the inability to say "No." This inability will accentuate the tendency of subordinates to delegate up, of visitors to drop in, of friends to telephone, of associates to ask more favors than they should. These consequences of the inability to say "No" could easily cause the manager to have to procrastinate and to allow his desk to become cluttered. The reader will very likely see other red threads—ineffective communication, just to name one, with its obvious impact on delegation, coordination, and motivation.

Comparison of Time Concerns Abroad

When traveling abroad I am often asked about similarities or differences in time concerns between managers in the United States and those in other countries. It has been my observation that while the opportunities for management development and continuing education are somewhat more limited in other countries, the apparent level of sophistication of their managers is not distinguishable from that in the United States. Their grasp of management fundamentals, their insight into the nuances of leadership situations, and the skill with which they articulate their opinions are for all practical purposes identical with senior managers' in America. Not surprisingly, the time concerns identified by managers abroad are virtually identical with those of managers in the United States. Since the principles of management are universal, and since time and management are indivisible, we would expect such similarity in time-related activities. (See Exhibit 4.3, page 55.)

Comparison by Occupation and Management Level

Almost all the principles which also apply to effective action of a manager in his office will also apply to family activities in his home. It is evident that a home without any planning or organizing or delegating or evaluating or communicating or decision making would be a shambles. In fact, it is my opinion that the homemaker runs a tough business and calls upon all the management skills that the office manager does. What interests me most about this, as observed earlier, is that many homemakers are succeeding in two professions by holding down a professional job in addition to managing the home.

As the administrative officer of the Bureau of Public Administration at the University of Maine said, "Homemakers who are also career women have to be better managers than most men for the simple reason they have two major jobs to manage." Flying back from Heidelberg, I found myself seated next to a woman from the midwestern United States who was the mother of three children, the wife of a professional engineer, a professional lecturer at educational conferences, and who had been a successful elementary school principal for 13 years. We will be talking a little more about her situation in Section 11, which is devoted to time management in the home.

If the principles of management are universal, it stands to reason that the time concerns from country to country, from enterprise to enterprise, and from management level to management level will be virtually identical. And this is precisely the case. With very few exceptions, you can list time concerns of managers from diverse backgrounds in different types of enterprises and from different countries and they will be virtually indistinguishable. Of course, there will be some exceptions. One

Exhibit 4.3: Professionals' Top 20 Time Concerns Worldwide

	USA	Canada	Latin America	Europe	Asia	Australia
1. Telephone Interruptions	2	1	1	1	2	3
2. Crisis Mgt., Shifting Prior.	1	2	7	4	6	2
3. Lack Obj., Prior., Plan.	3	4	3	6	5	1
4. Drop-in Visitors	5	5	2	5	4	6
5. Ineffective Delegation	6	6	4	2	1	7
6. Attempting Too Much	4	3	6	3	7	4
7. Meetings	11	8	5	7	3	12
8. Pers. Disorg., Cluttered Desk	7	7	9	8	10	5
9. Inability to say "No"	9	9	11	9	9	9
10. Lack Self-Discipline	8	10	17	11	19	10
11. Procrastination—Indecision	10	11	16	13	17	8
12. Untrained/Inadeq. Staff	13	16	10	10	12	14
13. Incomplete, Delayed Info.	20	—	8	14	8	20
14. Paperwork, Red Tape, Reading	12	12	15	17	—	13
15. Leaving Tasks Unfinished	13	14	—	12	13	11
16. Lack, Unclear Communication	18	19	12	16	11	—
17. Under-, Over-staffed	16	14	14	19	20	—
18. Confused Respons., Authority	17	17	18	15	13	16
19. Socializing	15	15	—	—	—	15
20. Lack Standards, Controls Progress Report	—	—	13	—	18	18

noteworthy exception is "enhancing the democratic process," which is a time concern that can be anticipated from groups of college presidents and occasionally from other educational administrators. It will rarely, if ever, appear as a time concern on the lists of other groups of managers.

For evidence of the universality of time concerns at different management levels, we need only to refer to the two lists of time concerns developed by the 40 senior executives of electrical contracting firms. If we had not known that these were suggested by presidents, it would be difficult to have guessed the level at which they were relevant or, indeed, to have excluded any levels at all. Perhaps the one time concern on this list which tends to give it away would be "outside activities." This can be a problem at middle levels of management, but is generally not a serious problem below the upper levels of management. At the senior executive level it can become a very serious problem indeed.

Identifying Your Top 10 Time Concerns

The chart in Exhibit 4.4 (see page 57) represents those time concerns which are most commonly cited. They are classified, as before, by management function. There is an extra benefit in this classification. When one's own most common time concerns are identified, it is possible to tell if they are concentrated in one or two of the functional areas of management. This provides a clue as to the broad management skills most in need of attention in one's own management development.

This chart has been widely used in management seminars in many countries to assist participants in the task of identifying their own top time concerns. They review this chart, checking all the time concerns they believe would be candidates for those on their list of the top 10. Once they have completed this tentative list, weighting their time concerns and completing the team profile is easy.

Exhibit 4.4: Sample Team Profile of Time Concerns—Professionals

Time Concern	A	B	C	D	E	F	G	W	R
PLANNING									
1. Lack Obj/Prior/Plan.	9	8	4					21	2
2. Crisis Mgt., Shifting Prior.		9	10					19	3
3. Attempt Too Much	10		3					13	6
4. Waiting for Planes/App'ts.									
5. Travel									
6. Haste/Impatience									
ORGANIZING									
7. Personal Disorg/Cluttered Desk	8	6						14	5
8. Confused Respons. & Authority									
9. Duplication of Effort									
10. Multiple Bosses									
11. Paperwork/Red Tape/Reading	1		1					2	
12. Poor Filing System									
13. Inadeq. Equip/Facilities									
STAFFING									
14. Untrained/Inadeq. Staff									
15. Under-/Over-staffed	7							7	10
16. Absentee/Tardiness/Turnover									
17. Personnel with Problems									
18. Overdependent Staff									
LEADING									
19. Ineffective Delegation	6	7	5					18	4
20. Lack Motivation, Indifference									
21. Lack Coordination/Teamwork									
CONTROLLING									
22. Telephone Interruptions	5	10	9					24	1
23. Drop-in Visitors		5						5	
24. Inability to Say "No"		3	2					5	
25. Incomplete/Delayed Info.	3							3	
26. Lack Self-Discipline		2	6					8	9
27. Leaving Tasks Unfinished									
28. Lack Standards/Controls/Rep.		1						1	
29. Visual Distractions/Noise									
30. Overcontrol									
31. Not Being Informed									
32. People Unavail. for Discuss.	2							2	

Your
Rank		Weight
1	=	10
2	=	9
3	=	8
4	=	7
5	=	6
6	=	5
7	=	4
8	=	3
9	=	2
10	=	1

Instructions:

1. Select your top 10 time concerns by assigning weights in descending order of importance. Give your top time concern a weight of "10", your next most important "9", etc. Record weights in column A above.

2. Record *weights* for the time concerns for each team member in Cols. B-G.

3. Total the weights for each time concern in Col. W.

4. Establish a *ranking* by weights in Col. R to obtain your team profile. The largest weight ranks No. 1, etc.

Exhibit 4.4: Sample Team Profile of Time Concerns—Professionals

(Continued)

Time Concern	A	B	C	D	E	F	G	W	R
COMMUNICATING									
33. Meetings	4		8					12	7
34. Lack/Unclear Communication									
35. Socializing									
36. "Memoitis"/Overcommunication									
37. Failure to Listen									

DECISION MAKING	A	B	C	D	E	F	G	W	R
38. Procrastination/Indecision		4	7					11	8
39. Wanting All the Facts									
40. Snap Decisions									

Your
Rank		Weight
1	=	10
2	=	9
3	=	8
4	=	7
5	=	6
6	=	5
7	=	4
8	=	3
9	=	2
10	=	1

Instructions:

1. Select your top 10 time concerns by assigning weights in descending order of importance. Give your top time concern a weight of "10", your next most important "9", etc. Record weights in column A above.

2. Record *weights* for the time concerns for each team member in Cols. B-G.

3. Total the weights for each time concern in Col. W.

4. Establish a *ranking* by weights in Col. R to obtain your team profile. The largest weight ranks No. 1, etc.

Exhibit 4.4: Team Profile of Time Concerns—Professionals

Time Concern	A	B	C	D	E	F	G	W	R

PLANNING
1. Lack Obj/Prior/Plan.
2. Crisis Mgt., Shifting Prior.
3. Attempt Too Much
4. Waiting for Planes/App'ts.
5. Travel
6. Haste/Impatience

ORGANIZING
7. Personal Disorg/Cluttered Desk
8. Confused Respons. & Authority
9. Duplication of Effort
10. Multiple Bosses
11. Paperwork/Red Tape/Reading
12. Poor Filing System
13. Inadeq. Equip/Facilities

STAFFING
14. Untrained/Inadeq. Staff
15. Under-/Over-staffed
16. Absentee/Tardiness/Turnover
17. Personnel with Problems
18. Overdependent Staff

LEADING
19. Ineffective Delegation
20. Lack Motivation, Indifference
21. Lack Coordination/Teamwork

CONTROLLING
22. Telephone Interruptions
23. Drop-in Visitors
24. Inability to Say "No"
25. Incomplete/Delayed Info.
26. Lack Self-Discipline
27. Leaving Tasks Unfinished
28. Lack Standards/Controls/Rep
29. Visual Distractions/Noise
30. Overcontrol
31. Not Being Informed
32. People Unavail. for Discuss.

Your Rank / Weight:
1 = 10
2 = 9
3 = 8
4 = 7
5 = 6
6 = 5
7 = 4
8 = 3
9 = 2
10 = 1

Instructions:

1. Select your top 10 time concerns by assigning weights in descending order of importance. Give your top time concern a weight of "10", your next most important "9", etc. Record weights in column A above.

2. Record *weights* for the time concerns for each team member in Cols. B-G.

3. Total the weights for each time concern in Col. W.

4. Establish a *ranking* by weights in Col. R to obtain your team profile. The largest weight ranks No. 1, etc.

Exhibit 4.4: Team Profile of Time Concerns—Professionals (Continued)

Time Concern	A	B	C	D	E	F	G	W	R

COMMUNICATING
33. Meetings
34. Lack/Unclear Communication
35. Socializing
36. "Memoitis"/Overcommunication
37. Failure to Listen

	A	B	C	D	E	F	G	W	R
33									
34									
35									
36									
37									

DECISION MAKING
38. Procrastination/Indecision
39. Wanting All the Facts
40. Snap Decisions

	A	B	C	D	E	F	G	W	R
38									
39									
40									

Your
Rank		Weight
1	=	10
2	=	9
3	=	8
4	=	7
5	=	6
6	=	5
7	=	4
8	=	3
9	=	2
10	=	1

Instructions:

1. Select your top 10 time concerns by assigning weights in descending order of importance. Give your top time concern a weight of "10", your next most important "9", etc. Record weights in column A above.

2. Record *weights* for the time concerns for each team member in Cols. B-G.

3. Total the weights for each time concern in Col. W.

4. Establish a *ranking* by weights in Col. R to obtain your team profile. The largest weight ranks No. 1, etc.

Team Time Concern Profiles

It is not uncommon for the top time concerns in a given group of managers to vary as we shall see in the following time concern profiles of various management teams. These appear in Exhibits 4.5–4.9 (see pages 61-64) as follows:

Exhibit 4.5   125 Managers of a Major Food Corporation
Exhibit 4.6   60 Managers of an Electronic Communications Corporation
Exhibit 4.7   75 School Administrators
Exhibit 4.8   50 Hospital Administrators
Exhibit 4.9   26 Women Managers

On each group profile exhibited, the number reporting indicates the total number of participants listing a particular time concern.

Exhibit 4.5: Time Concern Profile
125 Managers of a Major Food Corporation

		No.	Wt.
1.	Crisis Management/Shifting Priorities	66	196
2.	Meetings	43	125
3.	Lack Objectives, Priorities, and Daily Plan	55	113
4.	Telephone Interruptions	38	108
5.	Ineffective Delegation/Doing it Myself/Involved in Detail	36	94
6.	Drop-in Visitors/Open Door	43	90
7.	Confused Responsibility and Authority	38	88
8.	Inability to Say "No"	31	75
9.	Indecision/Procrastination	24	63
10.	Untrained, Inadequate Staff	13	45
11.	Unclear, Lack of Communication or Overcommunicating	15	44
12.	Socializing	14	40
13.	Stacked Desk/Personal Disorganization	16	35
14.	Inadequate Information, Waiting for Decisions	9	28
15.	Attempting Too Much at Once/Unrealistic Time Estimates	11	26
16.	Wanting All the Facts	11	25
17.	Lack Progress Reviews	6	14
18.	Multiple Bosses	4	13
19.	Failure to Deal with Poor Performance	6	12
20.	Overcontrol	2	10
21.	Personnel Changes	3	10

Exhibit 4.6: Time Concern Profile
60 Managers of an Electronic Communications Corporation

	No.	Wt.
1. Lack Objectives, Priorities, and Daily Plan	38	118
2. Crisis Management/Shifting Priorities	26	87
3. Drop-in Visitors	30	75
4. Unrealistic Time Estimates	27	72
5. Indecision/Procrastination	25	66
6. Ineffective Communication	22	65
7. Telephone Interruptions	23	63
8. Lack of Delegation	24	59
9. Stacked Desk/Personal Disorganzation	15	54
10. Confused Responsibility and Authority	17	45
11. Meetings	15	36
12. Socializing	10	26
13. Inadequate/Untrained Staff	10	25

Exhibit 4.7: Time Concern Profile
75 School Administrators

	No.	Wt.
1. Ineffective Delegation	31	69
2. Telephone Interruptions	30	57
3. Meetings	22	49
4. Drop-in Visitors/Open Door	19	42
5. Crisis Management/Firefighting/Shifting Priorities	18	33
6. Lack Objectives, Priorities, and Daily Plan	13	30
7. Confused Responsibilities	10	17
8. Paperwork	4	9
9. Indecision/Procrastination	5	8
10. Undercommunicating/Unclear Communication	3	8

Exhibit 4.8: Time Concern Profile
50 Hospital Administrators

	No.	Wt.
1. Telephone Interruptions	40	164
2. Drop-in Visitors (Open Door)	27	104
3. Ineffective Delegation (Involved in routine detail, refusing to let others do jobs)	34	89
4. Meetings	23	72
5. Inadequate/Understaffed (Secy.) (Occasionally—Absenteeism)	16	49
6. Lack Objectives, Priorities, and Daily Plan	18	44
7. Attempting Too Much at Once	19	43
8. Socializing	9	32
9. Stacked Desk/Personal Disorganization/Confusion	12	31
10. Crisis Management/Switching Priorities	13	29
11. Unable to Say "No"	11	28
12. Inadequate Info. for Decisions; Lack Info. from Other Depts., Getting Info. from Patients	8	27
13. Procrastination/Indecision	11	23
14. Lack Job Description, Duplication of Effort; Confused Responsibilities; Responsibility Without Authority	8	23
15. Lack Teamwork; Team Conflict	7	20
16. Fuzzy Communications	7	18
17. Lack Standards & Controls; Lack Feedback; Failure to Manage by Exception	9	17
18. Failure to Deal with Poor Performance	5	15
19. Lack Procedures and Policies	4	11
20. Personnel Problems	2	10

Exhibit 4.9: Time Concern Profile
26 Women Managers

	No.	Wt.
1. Telephone Interruptions	25	60
2. Drop-in Visitors	14	51
3. Crisis Management, Attempting Too Much, Switching Priorities	16	40
4. Responsibility Without Authority, Confused Responsibility, Two Bosses, Lack Job Description, Duplication of Effort	8	35
5. Involving Self in Detail, Doing Routine Tasks, Failure to Delegate	10	33
6. Understaffed, No Secretary	4	14
7. Incomplete Information, Lack of Communication, Lack of Feedback	5	13
8. Meetings	2	7
9. Lack Objectives, Priorities, and Daily Plan	2	7
10. Stacked Desk, Team Conflict, Unable to Say "No"	1	4
11. Socializing	2	4

The power of this time concern profile for a team is evident. It is an instant X-ray of the organization as it collectively views the principal obstacles to its effectiveness. This could become the basis of a major management development program. It should provide the basis for a highly effective attack on the principal problems visualized from a managerial perspective by the members of the management team itself.

We have thus laid the groundwork for attacking our time concerns, first those of the individual manager who now sees his top 10, and second, those of the team as represented by the profile. This profile provides the benefit of seeing those time concerns which the team believes are its most serious. We shall turn in the next section to the most effective means of solving these time concerns.

Confirming Your Time Concerns with Your Time Log

It is important to confirm your selection of time concerns with your time log. Most managers select their time concerns either in a seminar or upon reading a book on time management. Their judgment should be confirmed or revised through the time log explained in Section 3. This experience usually provides some surprises, since few managers know where their time is actually going. When the individual managers have confirmed their time concerns, the team profile can be readily confirmed.

For Further Reading

Bliss, Edwin C. *Getting Things Done: The ABC's of Time Management*. New York: Bantam, 1979.

Davidson, James. *Effective Time Management: A Practical Workbook*. New York: Human Sciences Press, 1978.

Fetner, Jack D. *Successful Time Management*. New York: Wiley, 1980.

Turla, Peter and Hawkins, Kathleen. *Time Management Made Easy*. New York: Dutton, no date.

SECTION 5

Solving Your Time Concerns

The Personal Element in Time

Approaching Time Haphazardly

The Ease of Saving an Hour a Day

Principles of Time Management

An Array of Principles

Time Management Tools and Techniques

Selecting the Time Concern to Solve

Time Concern Analysis

    1. Telephone Interruptions
    2. Drop-in Visitors
    3. Meetings
    4. Crisis Management
    5. Lack Objectives, Priorities, Daily Plan
    6. Cluttered Desk/Personal Disorganization
    7. Ineffective Delegation
    8. Attempting Too Much at Once
    9. Lack of or Unclear Communication
    10. Inadequate, Inaccurate, Delayed Information
    11. Indecision and Procrastination
    12. Confused Responsibility and Authority
    13. Inability to Say "No"
    14. Leaving Tasks Unfinished
    15. Lack of Self-Discipline

Solving Your Time Concerns

The Personal Element in Time

Nowhere is the personal element in time more evident than in the quandary of leisure time. The workweek is shortening. Time-saving devices proliferate. Yet for many people a strange dilemma results—what to do with the leisure time they have fought so hard to obtain. It may even be, ironically, that those who have the most are the least equipped to use it profitably.

A countervailing force to the drive for leisure is a seeming compulsion to work. Addiction to long hours and hard work is not an isolated occurrence. Yet who is to say what is work and what is leisure? Work to one person may be play to another. Some work primarily for pleasure, others solely for profit. For still others profit *is* their pleasure.

As people differ, so will their time—for time and life are indivisible. Most managers leave the management of their time to chance. Not many of them give it more than a fleeting thought. Fewer still have taken time to record where it goes, draw any conclusions from their observations, develop solutions, and implement improvements in their practices. For example, the manager who delights in opening his own mail to see who wrote to him today will nod assent to the suggestion that he should allow his secretary to open, screen, reroute, handle, and pass through to him appropriate portions of the mail. He might even agree that this would permit him to get more important things done. Yet having agreed to all that, he will likely persist in opening his own mail. Why? He likes to. Doing what we like instead of what we ought, putting second things first, allowing our pleasures to dictate our priorities: is this a familiar pattern?

Approaching Time Haphazardly

When we observe how few managers have taken the trouble to identify their time concerns, it is not surprising that fewer still have approached their solutions systematically. No doubt every manager from time to time comes across an idea in his reading or business contacts which seems worthwhile to him. He may take the trouble on occasion to jot down one of these ideas. If conditions are favorable, he may attempt to implement one of them. If the idea works exceedingly well, he may continue it. If it does not give evidence of performing up to his expectation, in all probability he will revert to his old habits.

I am convinced that one of the reasons for this disappointing situation is that in the process outlined above, few managers take the trouble to analyze the causes of their difficulties or to consider whether there are basic principles which could assist in their solution. Instead, the great majority of managers who have made the attempt to solve some of their problems will unfortunately jump to conclusions regarding quick and easy solutions without ever considering the causes or principles which may be involved. As one sage observed, knowing *what* to do will serve you well for a time. Knowing *why* will serve you well indefinitely.

In this section, we will be developing a list of principles, tools, and techniques, and a number of causes and solutions for each of the major time concerns. A technique for weaving these elements into a personalized time management strategy will be demonstrated.

The Ease of Saving an Hour a Day

There is no question that the piecemeal or haphazard approach of selecting one or two timesavers can benefit a manager who wishes to save time. The ease with which a manager can save time almost defies imagination. For example, there will be few, if any, managers who are reading this book for whom I would not readily guarantee the saving of an hour a day through a "quiet hour," better meeting control, improved planning, or speed reading. It can be swiftly demonstrated to the average manager that he can save considerable time with any or all of these simple techniques:

1. Statistics show that managers are interrupted on an average of once every eight minutes. Given a "quiet hour" without interruption of any kind, most who are well organized to take advantage of this opportunity will easily save one hour, and many will achieve as much as a half-day's work.

2. The average manager spends 10 hours a week in meetings, and 90 percent of them say half this time, or one hour a day, is wasted. For many administrators in the field of education the average hours per week in meetings are 20, not 10, and the amount of that time which is wasted would exceed 50 percent in their judgment. Applying the solutions presented later in the section, a saving of one hour per day should be practical and most likely conservative.

3. Improved planning is an accepted principle of time management. Every hour spent in effective planning saves three to four in execution, and obtains better results. The 20 minutes prior to leaving the office, if spent planning for the next day, could easily save an hour the following day.

4. The average manager spends one-third of his time reading, including all take-home reading, reports, correspondence, and the like. Those who have taken speed reading generally double their speed and retain or increase their rate of comprehension. Thus a savings of one-sixth of their time, or more than one hour a day, is possible.

However, the manager who limits his thinking to the saving of time, and not to the basic causes which underlie time concerns as well as to the fundamental principles involved in their solution, will save time with one technique and may lose all of the time he has saved through other time concerns which he has failed to analyze. Thus, it is clear that the manager who wishes to make a major difference in his own effectiveness must go beyond the short-range approach and move toward the development of a personalized time-management strategy.

Principles of Time Management

In my work with managers in different countries in time management seminars and consulting assignments, I have sought to collect, formulate, and catalog a list of fundamental principles of time management. Webster defines a principle as "a fundamental truth, a primary or basic law or doctrine, a settled rule of action, a governing law of conduct." My own preference for the meaning of principle is "a generalization of nearly universal application."

Many so-called "principles" are really a misuse of the term, or they are so weakly supported as not to merit serious consideration. On these grounds the well-known Peter Principle is excluded from this list. The assertion that managers tend to rise to their level of incompetence and therefore, ultimately, top levels in organizations will be filled by incompetent managers is partly obvious and partly absurd.

No one needs to be reminded that managers tend to rise in organizations and that every manager could be said at a given point in time to have a certain level of competence. The absurdity is the assumption that the level of competence of a given manager remains static and, therefore, all positions will ultimately be filled with incompetent managers. This conclusion ignores the factors which affect competence levels such as experience, reading, and training and development programs, as well as other factors such as attrition through retirement, leaving the company for better jobs, promotion to other departments, and the refusal of promotion. The real danger of such so-called principles is that the obvious aspect of the true portion misleads many people into uncritical acceptance of the absurd portion. The end result may be a serious disservice to the field of management.

The three Murphy's Laws are often cited: 1) nothing is as simple as it seems; 2) everything takes longer than you think; 3) if anything *can* go wrong, it *will*. Also cited, though less frequently, are two supposed corollaries of Murphy's Laws: 4) there is too much month left at the end of my money and 5) there is too much work left at the end of my time. The apochryphal sixth-century Irish king, Murphy, who is credited with these profundities, probably (a) was not named Murphy and (b) had not yet reduced his life's observations to such profound fundamentals.

Parkinson's Law, that work expands to fill the time available, certainly deserves careful consideration for inclusion in our list. Parkinson's observations came after a serious study of the British admiralty. He noted that while the number of persons employed in the admiralty understandably increased during wartime, the numbers inexplicably continued to increase in peacetime as well. This steady increase occurred despite cutbacks in both military requirements and military bases. Parkinson's Law alleges neither a fact so obvious that it needs no restatement nor a veiled absurdity.

There are many other so-called principles, some of which have been given the names of persons who allegedly invented them, or have been given other names deemed appropriate to their message. Perhaps the most interesting of these is the principle of "calculated neglect," which holds that despite their apparent urgency, some problems, if left alone, will go away. Such problems should be ignored in favor of more important priorities. While not proposed as a fundamental principle, this statement will be referred to in a later section, along with Pareto's Principle and Murphy's Laws, in a supporting or auxiliary role.

The manager who manages poorly is wasting his time and very likely that of the team. Time and management are indivisible. Hence practically every basic management principle in a sense could be said to be likewise a principle of time management. In the selections which follow, however, only those principles of obvious and direct relationship to time will be cited. Thus, the organizing principle of "commensurate authority" will not be cited whereas the principle of "planning" will be.

An Array of Principles*

Considering a principle to be "a generalization of nearly universal application," the principles listed in the following pages include most of those I have read, heard, or formulated which appear to warrant the designation "Principle of Time Mangement." (See Exhibit 5.1, pages 73-79.)

Making Time Productive (a seminar workbook), 12th Edition, R. Alec Mackenzie, 1987.

Exhibit 5.1: Principles of Time and Management

Planning Principles

1. Planning

   Effective long- and short-range planning produces better results in less time.

2. Objectives and Priorities

   Clear, measurable objectives which are prioritized according to long-range importance and short-range urgency are essential for effective planning, intelligent allocation of time and effort, and for optimum results.

3. Small Successes

   Small successes build confidence and increase long-term results, while large failures tend to destroy confidence and motivation. (Avoid setting excessively optimistic and unrealistic goals.)

4. Consolidation

   Grouping similar activities requires less time than doing each separately.

5. Flexibility

   Flexibility in planning promotes accomplishment by allowing adjustment for changing conditions.

6. Anticipation and Contingency Planning

   Effective contingency planning permits managers to identify the most serious and likely potential crises, and to initiate steps to anticipate and prevent their occurrence or to limit their consequences.

7. Punctuality

   Punctuality leads to predictability and improved human relations through meeting deadlines, avoiding inconvenience to others, averting crises, and even providing valuable time to think when others are late.

8. Limited Response

   Effective managers limit their response to the real needs of the situation, thus preventing overresponse, undue haste, mistakes, and wasted time and effort.

9. Optimum Scheduling

   Scheduling a little more work than is likely to be done provides fall-back tasks and prevents downtime when unforeseen problems stop progress on main tasks.

Organizing Principles

10. Organizing

    Resources are utilized and tasks accomplished more effectively when both are arranged and related optimally.

Exhibit 5.1: Principles of Time and Management (Continued)

11. Equal Distribution

    No one has enough time, yet everyone has all there is. It is the one resource which is distributed equally to all.

12. Awareness

    Recognition that one's time rarely is spent as one thinks encourages managers to log their time and to take corrective action to improve results.

13. Work Expansion

    Work tends to expand to fill the time available. (People tend to take as long as they have to finish a job, whether or not it could have been finished earlier. Give a person all day to do a job and the job will take all day.)

14. Commensurate Authority

    Responsibility must be proportional to authority for optimum results.

15. Single Reporting/Unity of Command

    To the extent that a person reports to more than one superior, he or she becomes less accountable to all.

Staffing Principles

16. Staffing

    Effective managers staff their organizations with competent, motivated people to ensure optimum results.

17. Complementarity

    Additions to staff should complement the capabilities and potential of present staff.

18. Potential Performance

    Personnel should be selected not only on the basis of capability to fill present needs but also on capacity for growth and potential performance in anticipation of future needs.

19. Orientation

    Achievement of goals is directly related to the degree of understanding of them, the means of achieving them, and of the background information relating to them.

20. Management Development

    Managers should be involved in training and development two levels below themselves to facilitate sound selection of replacements or additions to their own staff.

21. Reinforcement

    Training and development increase in effectiveness with the reinforcement of lessons learned through continued practice on the job and periodic review.

Exhibit 5.1: Principles of Time and Management (Continued)

Leading Principles

22. Leading

    Productivity tends to improve with the effective direction of well-planned and organized effort toward predetermined results.

23. Acceptance

    Effective managers accept things they cannot change, focus their time and effort on things they can change, and have the wisdom to know the difference.

24. Implementation

    Action implemented according to plan tends to achieve desired results. (The longest journey begins with the first step.)

25. Delegation

    Effective delegation improves overall results. (Managers should avoid detailed and low value tasks as well as decisions subordinates should make themselves.)

26. Completed Staff Work

    Delegating complete tasks aids achievement and prevents tasks from being returned undone.

27. Motivation

    Highly motivated persons tend to achieve more.

28. Initiative/Fast Start

    Results often vary directly with the timeliness of the start. Fast decisions and fast starts may yield either of two benefits: a competitive advantage if right, or more time to correct the course of action if wrong. Staying ahead is often easier than catching up. (Compare #65, Revocability.)

29. Meaningful Work

    Work that is meaningful and challenging motivates people to perform up to their highest potential.

30. Job Enrichment

    Overall results are enhanced when tasks are designed to be complete, to give the workers optimum control over how the work is done, and to provide direct feedback on how well the work is being done.

31. Coordination

    Coordination of related tasks tends to improve results through timeliness and unity of effort.

32. Timing

    To be effective, coordination must be achieved in the early stages of planning and policy making.

Exhibit 5.1: Principles of Time and Management (Continued)

33. Conflict Resolution

    When diversity of opinion is managed effectively, it strengthens the organization and improves results.

34. Change

    Results are improved when change is managed by anticipating it and planning to take maximum advantage of it while minimizing or preventing its negative consequences.

Controlling Principles

35. Control

    Effective control through periodic monitoring of progress against plans and corrective action to adjust for deviations will ensure better results. (Controls should be consistent with the situation with caution being exercised to avoid overcontrol.)

36. Effectiveness and Results Optimization

    When maximum results are achieved with minimum cost in resources, effectiveness or productivity is enhanced.

37. Energy Dissipation

    Energy not subjected to disciplined direction tends to dissipate itself ineffectively. (Managers who lose sight of their objectives need to be concerned with staying busy. They confuse activity with results, motion with accomplishment.)

38. Concentration of Effort

    Effective managers concentrate their efforts on the critical few events (around 20 percent) that will produce the major results (around 80 percent).

39. Visibility and Memory

    Visibility of those things one intends to do increases the certainty of achieving one's objectives.

40. Standards and Criteria

    Effective control requires measurable standards and criteria for determining whether planned objectives are being accomplished.

41. Optimal Overload

    Having more to do than can easily be accomplished tends to increase results through a sense of urgency and also provides alternate work options when unexpected delays occur. (However, carried to an extreme, overscheduling will tend to destroy morale, orderliness, accuracy, and quality of end results.)

Exhibit 5.1: Principles of Time and Management (Continued)

42. Deadlines and Realistic Time Estimates

   Effective managers impose realistic deadlines on tasks and decisions by building in reasonable cushions to allow for the unexpected. (By exercising self-discipline in adhering to realistic deadlines, effective managers counter the universal tendencies toward indecision, vacillation, and procrastination.)

43. Punctuality

   Punctuality leads to meeting deadlines, predictability in human relations, minimizing inconvenience, and saving the time of others.

44. Progress Reports

   Regular reports on progress toward goals at predetermined intervals permit identification and correction of problems, which enhance end results.

45. Exception Management

   Feedback on progress limited to only significant deviations from plan conserves time and energy.

46. Mistakes

   To the extent that mistakes are treated as lessons to be learned rather than errors to be criticized, the likelihood of their repetition will be lessened and overall results will be improved.

47. Interruption Control

   Reducing the number, duration, and impact of interruptions increases accomplishment. (Techniques for controlling interruptions include screening calls and visitors, completing tasks before permitting interruptions, planning for periods of limited unavailability such as the "quiet hour," hideaways, testing the legitimacy of interruptions by questions such as "Can it wait?" or "Could someone else help?")

48. Persistence and Task Completion

   Maintaining effort on tasks without interruption until completion tends to produce greater results.

49. Self-Discipline

   Managers who impose discipline on themselves enhance their results.

50. Habit

   Nearly all of a person's actions result from habit without thought. (To break the bad work habits of a lifetime requires thought, self-discipline, persistence, and reinforcement.)

Communicating Principles

51. Communication

   Joint effort and end results are improved with effective communication.

Exhibit 5.1: Principles of Time and Management (Continued)

52. Understanding of Objectives

    Communication is enhanced to the extent that the purpose or objective of the communication is understood.

53. Channel Selection

    Effectiveness of communication varies directly with the appropriateness of the channel selected. (Such channels include *verbal:* telephone, personal visit, meeting; *written:* letter, memo, notice, telex, cable; *nonverbal:* body language, facial expression, silence, closed door.)

54. Nonverbal Communication

    Effective communication is enhanced by an understanding of the physical signals emitted by speakers and listeners through actions, positions, expressions, and tone of voice.

55. Clarity and Ambiguity

    Understanding increases with clear, unambiguous language.

56. Brevity

    Brief communications tend to be better understood.

57. Attention and Listening

    A receptor's understanding is proportional to the level of attention.

58. Receptivity

    Communication increases in proportion to the receptivity of the receiver.

59. Line Loss

    Distortion of communiction is proportional to the line loss occasioned by the number of persons or stations through which the message must be transmitted.

60. Feedback

    Effectiveness of communication is enhanced to the extent that timely feedback ensures understanding.

Decision Making Principles

61. Decision Making

    Results tend to vary directly with the soundness of judgments and conclusions on which they are based.

62. Decisiveness

    Effective managers recognize that the ability to make up one's mind conclusively is vital as a counter to hesitation, vacillation, and procrastination, and therefore improves long-range results.

Exhibit 5.1: Principles of Time and Management (Continued)

63. Decision Tempo

When decisions are made hastily, impulsively, without adequate thought, or on the contrary, too slowly with unnecessary delay, effectiveness is diminished either through loss of quality or excessive time consumed.

64. Revocability

A decision which is revocable may be made faster and with fewer of the facts in hand. Thus, if the decision is incorrect, there is more time to take corrective action. The risk of making a wrong decision is much greater if the decision is irrevocable.

65. Problem Analysis

Indentification of real causes rather than symptoms increases the likelihood of developing effective solutions to problems.

66. Alternatives

Limited alternatives reduce the probability of selecting the best course of action.

67. Decision Level

Decisions made at the lowest level where appropriate information and judgment exist tend to be more effective.

Time Management Tools and Techniques

There are a number of tools and techniques which managers have found useful in managing their time more effectively. The chart in Exhibit 5.2 (see page 81) suggests a number of these tools and techniques classified by function.

Selecting the Time Concern to Solve

Selecting which time concern to solve first is worthy of some consideration. Some managers prefer to start on their number-one time concern as selected in Section 4. Others, sensing the danger of defeat and the desirability of early success, choose one they are quite likely to solve. This may be particularly wise where the number-one selection is unusually difficult, for example, the boss.

Time Concern Analysis

The form for analyzing a given time concern is shown in Exhibit 5.3 (see page 83). It calls simply for a column titled "Causes" and another titled "Solutions." The figure "80 percent" following "Causes" suggests that the greatest effort will be required to identify all possible causes contributing to this particular time concern. Most of the causes will suggest their own solutions. For example, the solution to meetings starting late is obviously to start them on time. Therefore, only 20 percent of the total effort ought to be required for developing solutions, once the causes have been identified. A priority for solutions is recommended to increase the likelihood that some actions will be taken. Having identified the two or three most important solutions, the manager is more likely to implement them than if he looks at 20 solutions with no indication of which are the most important.

A target of at least 10 causes would be realistic. For most time concerns it is not difficult to exceed 10 causes. It is helpful to categorize the causes *in sequence*, e.g., *before*, *during*, and *after* meetings; or *by source*, e.g., *internal* and *external* causes of wasting time on the telephone. On page 84 we see the telephone analyzed. In the left-hand column, internal causes are listed first followed by external causes. It is clear from reviewing these causes that "internal" means those generated from *within oneself*, while "external" means those generated by others or in the environment. Solutions are suggested for each cause. These solutions are all based on one or more of the 68 time-management principles. On the following pages sample time concern analyses are provided for the 15 most common time concerns:

1. Telephone Interruptions

2. Drop-in Visitors

3. Meetings

4. Crisis Management

5. Lack Objectives, Priorities, Daily Plan

6. Cluttered Desk/Personal Disorganization

7. Ineffective Delegation

8. Attempting Too Much at Once

9. Lack of or Unclear Communication

10. Inadequate, Inaccurate, Delayed Information

11. Indecision and Procrastination

12. Confused Responsibility and Authority

13. Inability to Say "No"

14. Leaving Tasks Unfinished

15. Lack of Self-Discipline

Exhibit 5.3: Time Concern Analysis

	Causes (80 Percent)	Solutions (20 Percent)	Priority
Internal			
1.			
2.			
3.			
4.			
5.			
6.			
7.			
8.			
9.			
External			
1.			
2.			
3.			
4.			
5.			
6.			
7.			
8.			
9.			

Time Concern Analysis No. 1: Telephone Interruptions

Causes	Solutions

Internal

1. Unaware of seriousness. — Take time log of phone calls. Evaluate origin, extent, and causes.

2. No plan for handling. — Develop plan to screen, delegate, consolidate.

3. Enjoy socializing. — Do it elsewhere. Stick to priorities.

4. Ego. Feeling of importance. — Recognize ego factor. Don't overestimate importance to others of your availability.

5. Desire to be available. — Distinguish between being available for business and for socializing.

6. No plans for unavailability. — Quiet hour; screening; set periods for taking calls.

7. Desire to keep informed. — Accomplish on planned, more certain basis. Recognize that your team members will naturally want to keep you informed of everything they are doing, rather than simply the essentials.

8. Desire to be involved. — Recognize danger of involvement in detail. Divorce yourself from routine matters and details.

9. Taking and placing own calls. — Delegate.

10. Lack of delegation. — Delegate more. Direct inquiries to persons responsible.

11. Not listing items to be discussed. — Organize yourself. Plan calls, and list points to be discussed.

12. Overdependent staff. — Refuse to make *their* decisions. Encourage initiative. Allow mistakes.

13. Facts not available. — Be prepared.

14. Fear of offending. — Don't be oversensitive. Professionals are not offended easily. Concentrate on priorities.

15. Lack self-discipline. — Develop plan, implement, monitor progress, assign responsibility to secretary or assistant.

16. Inability to terminate conversation. — Learn and practice techniques:
   • Preset time limit ("Yes, Tom, I can talk for a few minutes").
   • Foreshadow ending ("Bill, before we hang up").
   • Be candid ("Sorry, Joe, I've got to go now").

17. Unrealistic time estimates. — Secretary interrupts with reminder of urgent item demanding attention. Three-minute egg timer in front of telephone. Time yourself for one day. Recognize how much longer a call can take than is necessary.

Time Concern Analysis No. 1: Telephone Interruptions (Continued)

Causes	Solutions
Internal	
18. Lack ability to manage own secretary.	Study. Develop plan. Implement. Train or replace with experienced secretary requiring no training.
External	
19. Ineffective screening.	Analyze problem. Develop plan. Discuss with associates to avoid surprise and offense. Discuss with secretary to ensure understanding and confidence. Implement. Support secretary.
20. No secretary.	If you need one full or part time, do feasibility study to demonstrate need. If you have an assistant, use in place of secretary. If not, develop techniques to have messages taken at certain times. Use a hideaway. Cut-off switch.
21. Misdirected calls.	List of persons and numbers. Instruct personnel on directing of calls. Have "frequently called" numbers visible.
22. Confused responsibilities.	Clarify.
23. "Answer your own" policy.	Recognize waste of time and talent. Revise or eliminate policy.
24. Poor telephone system.	Study and update.

Time Concern Analysis No. 2: Drop-in Visitors

Causes	Solutions
Internal	
1. Unaware of seriousness.	Take time log of visits (business and personal; scheduled and unscheduled). Evaluate extent and causes.
2. No plan for handling.	Develop plan to screen. Arrange appointments.
3. Ego. Feeling of importance.	Recognize. Don't overestimate importance to others of your availability. Plan visits at coffee and lunch.
4. Enjoy socializing.	Do it elsewhere (coffee, lunch). Stick to priorities.
5. Desire to be available.	Distinguish between being available for business and for socializing.
6. No plans for unavailability.	Modified "open door," "quiet hour," screening, hideaway.
7. Desire to keep informed.	Accomplish on a planned and more certain basis.

Time Concern Analysis No. 2: Drop-In Visitors (Continued)

Causes	**Solutions**
Internal	
8. Desire to be involved.	Recognize danger of involvement in detail.
9. Fear of offending.	Don't be oversensitive.
10. Lack of delegation.	Delegate more. Direct inquiries to persons responsible.
11. Making decisions below your level.	Make only the decisions subordinates can't. Do nothing you can delegate.
12. Requiring or expecting subordinates to check with you excessively.	Manage by exception. Expect information concerning only deviations from plan.
13. Inability to terminate visits.	Go to *their* office. Meet *outside* your office. Stand up upon entry and keep standing. Preset time limit on visit. Foreshadow end. (Is there anything else before I leave?) Secretary interrupts to remind you of urgent matter. Be candid. (I'm sorry, I must get back to some other matters now.) Stand up and walk to door.
14. Unrealistic time estimates.	Take time log of all visits in one day. Recognize difficulty of estimating time requirements in socializing.
External	
15. Open door policy.	Recognize "open door" does not mean physically open, but open to those who need assistance. Modify your open door by closing it regularly for periods of concentration. "Quiet hour" is best.
16. Ineffective screening.	Train secretary to screen all visitors without offending. Locate secretary's desk in a strategic position to make screening easy.
17. No secretary.	If you need one full or part time, do feasibility study to demonstrate need. Use a time log for this. If you have an assistant, use in place of secretary. If not, concentrate on developing other techniques above.
18. Misdirected visitors.	Train receptionist. Advise others. Discuss problem.
19. Confused responsibilities.	Clarify responsibilities and publish.

Time Concern Analysis No. 3: Meetings

Causes	**Solutions**
Before	
1. Lack of purpose.	No meeting without a purpose; in writing if possible.
2. Lack of agenda.	No meeting without an agenda. Written agenda for scheduled meeting; verbal agenda if unscheduled to ensure that people come prepared and discussion is scheduled.
3. Wrong people/too many/ too few.	Only those needed present.
4. Wrong time.	Ensure opportune timing.
5. Wrong place.	Select location consistent with objectives of meeting, freedom from interruptions, physical equipment necessary, minimum of travel for majority of people.
6. No planning.	Allow for and schedule appropriate planning for most effective meeting.
7. Too many meetings.	Test need for "regular" meetings. Occasionally don't hold it—see what happens. Or cut time allowed in half for those tending to last a long time.
8. Too few meetings.	Assess need for participation, information, and coordination. Schedule accordingly.
9. Inadequate notice.	Provide written notice with all essentials including expected contribution and materials necessary for preparation.
10. Not starting on time.	Start on time. (By delaying for late arrivals, the leader penalizes those arriving on time and rewards those who come late!)
During	
11. Socializing.	Reserve socializing for better place. Get down to business.
12. Allowing interruptions.	Set policy and let everyone know. Wherever possible allow no interruptions except for clearcut emergency. Hold messages for delivery at coffee break and lunch times.
13. Wandering from agenda.	Expect and demand adherence to agenda. Resist "hidden agenda" ploys.
14. Failure to set ending time or time allotments for each subject.	Time-limit the meeting and each item on the agenda to place discussion time in accordance with importance of subject.
15. Keeping people after they are no longer needed.	Leave after expected contribution made.

Time Concern Analysis No. 3: Meetings (Continued)

Causes	**Solutions**
During	
16. Indecision.	Keep objective in mind and move toward it.
17. Deciding without adequate information.	Ensure requisite information will be available before convening meeting. Use it.
18. Failure to end on time.	End on time. Otherwise no one can plan for the time immediately following.
19. Failure to summarize conclusions.	Summarize conclusions to ensure agreement and remind participants of assignments.
After	
20. No minutes.	Record decisions, assignments, and deadlines in concise minutes. Distribute within one day of meeting.
21. Failure to follow up.	Ensure effective follow-up on all decisions. List uncompleted items under "Unfinished Business" at beginning of next agenda. Request status reports until completed.
22. Failure to abolish committees when business or objectives accomplished.	Take committee inventory. Abolish those whose mission has been accomplished.

Time Concern Analysis No. 4: Crisis Management

Causes	**Solutions**
Internal	
1. Unaware of importance.	Take time log of crises. Analyze source, causes, seriousness, controllable factors.
2. Lack of planning.	Categorize crises and causes. Assess probability of occurrence. Develop plan for contingencies to ensure most effective handling. Use project sheets for planning.
3. Failure to anticipate.	Expect the unexpected. (Murphy's 3rd Law—If anything *can* go wrong, it *will*.) Anticipatory action is generally far more effective than remedial.
4. Overplanning (attempting too much).	Plan less; leave 20 percent of day unplanned, thus allowing time to handle crises.
5. Overreacting (treating all problems as crises).	Limit your response by (a) ignoring problems which can be ignored; (b) delegating all the remaining ones which others can handle; (c) handling only those which you alone can.

Time Concern Analysis No. 4: Crisis Management (Continued)

Causes	**Solutions**
Internal	
6. Firefighting.	Recognize that it is more important to prevent new fires from developing than to spend all your time putting out old fires. Preventive action is preferable to remedial.
7. Procrastination.	Recognize danger inherent in putting off key actions leading to deadline pressures and often to impaired judgment under stress.
External	
8. Unrealistic time estimates (by manager or boss).	Recognize that everything takes longer than you think (Murphy's 2nd Law). Analyze characteristic underestimates, then add appropriate cushion to all critical estimates —e.g., 20 percent.
9. Switching priorities (by manager or boss).	Switching priorities means leaving tasks unfinished and damaging morale if done excessively. Calculate cost, discuss with boss, and make suggestions for reducing frequency of switches.
10. Mechanical breakdown/ human error.	Anticipate. Organize resources (human and otherwise) for rapid adjustment to compensate most effectively.
11. Reluctance of subordinates to break the bad news.	Develop a philosophy of treating mistakes as part of a learning process. Discuss with subordinates the idea that mistakes represent an opportunity to learn. Emphasize that last-minute reporting of bad news is most likely to lead to crises.
12. Inadequate, inaccurate, delayed information.	Determine information critical to planning, decisions, and feedback. Develop system to ensure its reliable delivery.
13. Overlooking possible negative consequences of a decision.	Analyze what could go wrong. Set up contingency plan.

Time Concern Analysis No. 5: Lack Objectives, Priorities, Daily Plan

Causes	**Solutions**
Internal	
1. Unaware of importance.	Recognize.
2. Lack system.	Use Time Tactics to develop Plan Sheet Daily Objectives, Priorities and Deadlines.
3. Lack time to plan.	Take it. Put first things first. Recognize that planning *takes* time initially, but saves three to four times as much in the end *and* gets better results.
4. Crisis-oriented (assumes crises are unavoidable).	Recognize fallacy. Except for acts of God, most crises are relatively predictable. Allow more time. Plan ahead for contingencies.
5. Successful without it.	Recognize success may be in *spite* of, not *because* of your actions. Planned results are predictably more successful than chance results.
6. Lack self-discipline.	Impose deadlines on yourself. Try objectives, priorities, and daily plan for one month. Enlist aid of secretary or assistant. Monitor progress. Evaluate results.
7. Action-oriented (would rather be moving than thinking).	Recognize most problems result from action without thought. Those who know *what* to do succeed once. Those who know *why* will succeed again and again. So take time to think it through. *Then* act.
8. Fear of commitment.	Recognize that while objectives mean commitment, they also mean knowing when you have succeeded.
9. Lack job description.	Recognize objectives are easier to develop when key result areas are clearly identified.
10. Difficulty of assigning priorities to tasks.	Not easy, but one of the most productive of all managerial pursuits. Determines where efforts should be concentrated.
11. Assumption that since few days are "typical" it is futile to plan, or that emergencies will spoil plan anyway.	Recognize that most managers tend to waste time in the same or similar ways every day. And while emergencies may disrupt a day, the damage can be minimized more easily if the day was planned and the most vital tasks completed before the emergency.

Time Concern Analysis No. 6: Cluttered Desk/Personal Disorganization

Causes   **Solutions**

Internal

1. Unaware of importance.

   Recognizes stacked desk as major interruptor and loser of documents (retrieval time). Take time log to assess retrieval time.

2. Lack of system.

   Plan Sheet for recording things you wish to remember so documents may be filed.

3. Ego (viewed by some as symbol of busyness, importance, indispensability).

   Recognize may also symbolize personal disorganization, indecision, procrastination, insecurity, confusion of priority, and inability to meet deadlines due to lost documents.

4. Fear loss of control.

   Use Time Tactics Project Sheet to provide better control than keeping all files on a cluttered desk.

5. Fear of forgetting.

   Proper calendaring and use of contact logs will be excellent memory substitute. No need to remember what can be retrieved.

6. Failure to delegate.

   Do nothing yourself you can delegate. You not only overload yourself with others' work but also deny them the experience.

7. Allowing interruptions.

   Screen. Set aside "time banks" for planned unavailability to complete your work.

8. Leaving tasks unfinished.

   Allowing diversions from tasks and not going back to finish them destroys effectiveness and cuts real results drastically. Practice task completion, require completed staff work, resist interruptions, finish the task before putting it down.

9. Procrastination/Indecision.

   Tackle toughest or highest priority tasks first. Self-impose deadlines and reward yourself. Eighty percent of tasks coming to your desk can be handled at once. *Do it now.* Keep the paper moving. Handle it once.

10. Slow reader.

    Screen and select with discrimination. Scan for essentials. Speed-reading course.

11. Lack objectives, priorities, and daily plan.

    Recognize that poor planning causes switching priorities, leaving tasks unfinished, and indecision. Plan your work. Work your plan.

12. Poor scheduling of tasks.

    Schedule by priority and realistic time estimates.

Time Concern Analysis No. 6: Cluttered Desk/Personal Disorganization
(Continued)

Causes	Solutions
External	
13. Ineffective secretary.	Train and authorize secretary to keep your desk clear. Information retrieval is secretary's responsibility, not yours. Label files not to be removed. Keep to minimum.
14. Failure to screen.	Secretary screens out junk mail, refers requests others can handle, types responses for your signature.
15. No secretary.	Minimize paperwork, respond on original. Simplify filing system. Keep only essentials.
16. Understaffed.	Indentify problem. Do feasibility study to show that cost of additional staff will pay off.
17. Paper blockade, memoitis, overcommunication.	Minimize overcommunication, emphasize brevity, verbal communication.

Time Concern Analysis No. 7: Ineffective Delegation

Causes	Solutions
Internal	
1. Insecurity—fear of failure.	Recognize. Accept risk as inherent. Allow mistakes. Learn from them.
2. Lack confidence in staff.	Train, develop, trust.
3. Involving yourself in detail and routine.	Do nothing you can delegate; divorce yourself from detail.
4. Delegating responsibility without authority.	Always delegate authority commensurate with responsibility.
5. Giving unclear, incomplete, or confused instructions.	Ensure clear, complete, unambiguous instructions. Ask subordinate to restate to ensure understanding.
6. Envy of subordinate's ability.	Laugh at yourself. Then give full credit where it is due. Develop your own replacement.
7. Can do job better and faster yourself.	Lower standards to what is "acceptable," not your own level of performance. Avoid perfectionism.
8. More comfortable "doing" than "managing."	Recognize that practice leads to success, which leads to comfort. Control.
9. Expect everyone to "know all the details."	Recognize that this should not be expected of someone who has delegated responsibility for handling.

Time Concern Analysis No. 7: Ineffective Delegation (Continued)

Causes	Solutions
Internal	
10. Failure to establish appropriate controls.	Establish plans, schedules with details, progress reports, monitoring of deadlines.
11. Overcontrol.	Relax. Emphasize goal-accomplishment methods and procedures. Measure results, not activity.
12. Failure to follow up.	Always check progress in time to take corrective action.
External	
13. Understaffed/overworked subordinates.	Limit expectations and reduce accepted responsibilities.
14. Inadequate, untrained staff.	Train, reassign, rehire, better selection.
15. Upward delegation.	Refuse to make decisions for subordinates. If they need help, ask the right question.
16. Problem not clear.	Be candid. Ask subordinate to figure out and keep you informed.

Time Concern Analysis No. 8: Attempting Too Much at Once

Causes	Solutions
Internal	
1. Lack of planning.	Set objectives, priorities, deadlines daily. Plan strategy to achieve them.
2. Unrealistic time estimates.	Recognize that everything takes longer than you think (Murphy's 2nd Law). Analyze characteristic underestimates, then add appropriate cushion to all critical estimates—e.g., 20 percent.
3. Starting late.	Plan ahead. Start early. Use Pert Chart or Time Tactics for even monitoring of projects.
4. Responding to the urgent.	Distinguish "urgent" from the truly "important." Be more discriminating in sorting priorities. Maintain perspective in balancing short-term demands against long-term objectives.
5. Overresponse.	Limit your response to the urgent *and* important demands. Learn to say "No" when necessary. Delegate.

Time Concern Analysis No. 8: Attempting Too Much at Once (Continued)

Causes	Solutions
Internal	
6. Sense of achievement.	Ask yourself what you are trying to prove. Be realistic. Keep perspective. Lower standards if too high.
7. Insecurity.	If over your head, check Peter Principle, cut back or switch to realistic assignment.
8. Desire to impress boss.	Take a second look at what boss really wants . . . to be impressed short run, or to succeed in the long run?
9. Difficulty in determining priorities.	Be discriminating. Check your priorities with boss periodically. Vitally important that you be on same wavelength regarding priorities.
10. Overambition.	Recognize. Trim back to realistic proportions.
11. Action-oriented.	Don't confuse motion with progress or activity with results. Work smarter, not harder. Slow down, think it through so you'll get there faster.
12. Ego. Overconfidence.	Beware. Control.
13. Desire to appear cooperative by never saying "No."	Say "No." There are many ways of doing this without offending. (Offer alternatives, apologize, etc.)
External	
14. Understaffed.	A common excuse for overwork. Why should boss hire an assistant if you get it all done without complaint? Do feasibility study. Show how more help is economically justified. Say "No" at appropriate time. If situation hopeless, look for another job.
15. Overdemanding job or boss.	Same as above.

Time Concern Analysis No. 9: Lack of or Unclear Communication

Causes	Solutions
Internal	
1. Unaware of importance.	Recognize.
2. Lack of time.	Take it. Priority warrants.
3. Not listening/Inattention.	Develop and practice listening skills. Concentrate.
4. Purpose not clear.	Clarify.
5. Use of wrong channel.	Select appropriate channel (phone, letter, memo, conference).
6. Poor timing.	Select appropriate time.
7. Poor articulation.	Check. Improve.
8. Overcommunicating.	Be brief. Don't repeat.
9. Insufficient communication.	Assess legitimate needs for information. Provide through staff meetings, house organ, memoranda.
External	
10. Lack policies and procedures to ensure effective communication.	Develop both to ensure organizational emphasis.
11. Lack of receptivity.	Test receptivity: "Would you like to talk about . . .?"
12. Meaning of words.	Recognize words mean different things to different people. Choose them well.
13. Differing value systems.	Recognize experience, training, and environment create different backgrounds for interpreting communication.
14. Distortion/Line loss.	Check interference, noise, activity. Assess potential impact. Take preventive steps. Minimize organization levels.
15. Language barrier.	Assess and adjust to accommodate.
16. Lack of feedback.	Get feedback. Take corrective action.

Time Concern Analysis No. 10: Inadequate, Inaccurate, Delayed Information

Causes	**Solutions**
Internal	
1. Unaware of importance.	Recognize and assign priority.
2. Lack system.	Determine what information is needed for planning, decisions, and feedback on results. Then ensure its availability, reliability, and timeliness.
3. Difficult to know what information is needed.	Discuss and decide.
4. Failure to test its reliability.	Make no assumptions. Too critical. Test periodically.
5. Providing information not needed or requested.	Avoid unnecessary communication. Stick to essentials. Avoid overkill.
6. Failure to assess priority or urgency of requested information.	Make assessment and allocate time accordingly. Standardize priority of information classifications.
7. Lack uniform method of screening priority and urgency of requested information.	Develop method.
8. Failure to anticipate probable delays in obtaining information.	Expect delays. Plan accordingly.
External	
9. Lack of authority to require information needed.	Clarify authority. Use "response deadlines."
10. Indecision or delay of others providing needed information.	"Unless I hear" memo.

Time Concern Analysis No. 11: Indecision and Procrastination

Causes	**Solutions**
<u>Internal</u>	
1. Unaware of importance.	Recognize.
2. Lack techniques for improving.	Set deadlines on all objectives and priorities, use reminders (egg-timer or wrist-alarm), have secretary check on progress, reward yourself (no coffee until you finish).
3. Lack self-imposed deadlines.	Set deadlines on everything.
4. Lack monitoring of progress.	Have secretray or associate check your progress against deadlines.
5. Uncertain of priorities.	Ascertain daily.
6. Shifting priorities. ("Why start? They'll just change it.")	Calculate cost; discuss; discourage.
7. Fear of mistakes.	Avoid fixing blame; ask what's been learned and how repetition can be avoided.
8. Attempting too much (ensures delaying some things!).	More realistic goals and expectations.
9. Unrealistic time estimates.	Recognize everything takes longer than you think. Allow more time—leave 20 percent of day unplanned.
10. Habit.	Break it! Develop better ones.
11. Doing what you like, postponing the unpleasant.	Do the unpleasant first, then the rest of the day is "downhill."
12. Doing the easy or trivial, postponing the difficult or important.	Do No. 1 first. Then you can relax. What doesn't get done will not be the most important.

Time Concern Analysis No 12: Confused Responsibility and Authority

Causes	**Solutions**

Internal

1. Failure to clarify precise responsibilities with boss.

Do so.

2. Lack of job description.

Write one. Discuss with boss. Get approved.

3. Job description overlaps others.

Identify areas of duplication. Eliminate.

External

4. Usurping of authority by others.

Identify. Discuss with boss. Clarify. Insist that if authority in doubt, then responsibility must be limited to match.

5. Responsibility without authority.

Insist on commensurate authority (equal to responsibility). It is mandatory that one have the power (authority) to carry out his duty (responsibility).

6. Ambiguous, confused communication or instruction.

Insist on clarity of communication or instruction. Request it in writing if verbal instructions are used inappropriately.

7. Nondescriptive titles.

Titles convey apparent authority to the world in which the manager works. They must be descriptive of real authority to avoid confusion.

8. Confused or no organization chart.

Organization charts provide the skeleton for authority relationships and are therefore essential to clarity of understanding of responsibility and authority within the organization. Clarify.

9. Lack of emphasis on assumption of responsibility and exercise of initiative.

Emphasize through accountability for results; through recognition and reward for exercise of initiative; through citation, consideration in performance and salary review, promotion, etc.

10. Subordinates unwilling to accept responsibility.

Select people with care. Train. Reward.

11. Weak promotion practices resulting in placement above level of competence.

Identify potential and improve selection for promotion; career development program.

Time Concern Analysis No. 13: Inability to Say "No"

Causes	**Solutions**
Internal	
1. Unaware of importance.	Recognize as seldom identified, but of major importance in wasting time.
2. Humanitarian desire to help others.	Don't overdo it. It will often be taken for granted.
3. Desire to win approval and acceptance ("Nice Guy" image).	Recognize possible trap—if desired results are *not* achieved, you may lose instead of gaining respect and feel resentful.
4. Fear of offending.	True friends are not offended by honest explanation. Develop techniques of saying "No" without offending. "Thanks for the compliment, but I'll have to decline." "I'm sorry I can't, but let me offer a suggestion...."
5. Possessing capabilities in demand.	Recognize this asset makes ability to say "No" even more imperative. Refuse to spread yourself too thin. *Concentrate your efforts!*
6. Belief that agreeableness enhances prospects for promotion.	Don't confuse continual assent with teamwork.
7. False sense of obligation.	Recognize prevalence of this cause. Examine reasons for this feeling. Discuss with family, friends, associates. Control.
8. Overdeveloped sense of sympathy, understanding, self-sacrifice, or impulsive generosity.	Be more realistic.
9. Insecurity or low self-esteem.	Recognize that always saying "Yes" may betray feelings of insecurity and low self-worth. Resist this urge. Say "No." Perhaps offer alternative proposal.
10. Guilt feelings or desire to convince yourself you are a good person.	Recognize. Assess whether failures are real or imagined.
11. Not assessing consequences.	Take time log recording all "Yes" responses that could have been "No." Assess time wasted.
12. Easier to say "Yes."	Assess consequences. (See No. 11 above)
13. Successful without saying "No."	Think it through. Develop several techniques as in No. 4 (above). Practice.
14. Not knowing how.	Recognize that mastering the art of saying "No" would likely enhance your success considerably. Develop techniques.

Time Concern Analysis No. 13: Inability to Say "No" (Continued)

Causes | **Solutions**

Internal

15. Timid approach—building up to saying "No" gradually by offering excuses first.

Recognize there are answers for all excuses. Say "No" *first* before too many hopes are raised. *Then* explain.

16. Lack excuses.

Don't be too sensitive. Sometimes no excuse is better than a poor one. Think of acceptable excuses ahead of time.

17. Fear that any excuses may not justify saying "No."

Don't feel every "No" has to be justified. Simply say "I'm sorry, but I'll have to say *no* this time."

18. No time to think of answer or excuse.

Count to 10 before saying "Yes." Give yourself time. Delay response.

19. Fear of retaliation.

If such fear is justified, recognize shaky foundation relationship is built on. Try to improve it.

20. To put others in your debt.

Practice the Golden Rule here.

21. Losing sight of own priorities.

Remember, the best excuse is prior commitment to your own priorities.

22. Lack of objectives and priorities.

Others will determine priorities for those who don't have their own.

23. Ambition or desire to be productive.

Better to do *less* well than *more* poorly.

External

24. Autocratic boss.

Balance the trade-offs—what you are learning versus what you are losing.

25. Tradition of organization.

Same as No. 24.

26. Refusal of others to assume responsibility.

Identify this and refuse to become its victim. (Note relation to false sense of obligation, No. 7.)

27. Thoughtless assumption by others that you will say "Yes."

Recognize that you have likely encouraged this assumption by never saying "No." Learn to say "No" especially to inappropriate or thoughtless requests or those that will make you feel bad if you assent.

Time Concern Analysis No. 14: Leaving Tasks Unfinished

Causes	Solutions
Internal	
1. Unaware of problem.	Take time log. Assess impact of leaving tasks unfinished. (Number, length of interruption, importance of tasks left unfinished.)
2. Lack objectives.	Set objectives to clarify those things which ought to be finished. Set deadlines on all important tasks to provide incentive to complete them.
3. Lack priorities.	Prioritize. (Arrange objectives in order of importance to clarify those things which ought to be finished *first*.)
4. Lack deadlines.	Set deadlines on all important tasks to provide incentive to complete them.
5. Failure to reward yourself.	Reward yourself with a list of items to be crossed off, by deferring pleasant diversions until certain tasks are completed, etc.
6. Responding to the urgent.	Recognize that urgent matters rarely are as important as they seem. Resist tendency to overreact, thus interrupting other tasks.
7. Overload, too much to do.	Assess capabilities to achieve tasks within limited time. Resist overload. When accepting new responsibilities, drop or defer old ones to make room.
8. Cluttered desk, personal disorganization.	Get organized to permit effective control of tasks. Be systematic in handling information. Recognize that sound organization saves time in retrieving information, processing decisions, and maintaining control over projects.
9. Lack determination to complete tasks (lack self-discipline, lazy).	Impose deadlines on yourself and announce to others. (Go public.) Employ assistance (e.g., have secretary remind you to ensure accomplishment). Monitor progress.
10. Inability to delegate.	Delegate task completion to someone else.
11. Accepting interruptions.	Train secretary to screen interruptions. Establish "quiet hour" for completing tasks.
12. Indecision.	Recognize that a willingness to decide is a primary characteristic of a successful manager.
13. Lack motivation.	Become aware of impact on your own effectiveness. Seek causes. Determine to correct.
14. Postponing the unpleasant.	Recognize danger that postponed tasks, if unpleasant but important, will become urgent, interrupting whatever else you choose to do.

Time Concern Analysis No. 14: Leaving Tasks Unfinished (Continued)

Causes	Solutions
External	
15. Shifting priorities.	Keep priorities current (reprioritize). Measure relative importance of new demands against current priorities. Resist unnecessary changes and resulting loss of time in leaving and later resuming tasks.
16. Incomplete or unreliable information.	Recognize need for adequate information and ensure its availability before starting tasks.

Time Concern Analysis No. 15: Lack of Self-Discipline

Causes	Solutions
Internal	
1. Lack of planning.	Recognize that planning encourages disciplined action. Lack of planning encourages undisciplined action. Plan your work; then work your plan.
2. Lack objectives or standards.	Set objectives in key result areas both personal and organizational. Develop standards (conditions that will exist when the job is well done) for routine tasks.
3. Lack of priorities.	Set priorities in order to focus effort on most productive areas. This ensures that what gets done will be most important...and what doesn't get done is least important.
4. Not setting deadlines.	Impose realistic but firm deadlines on yourself. Expect them of others.
5. Doing what we like (putting second things first).	Recognize this universal tendency. Question every action. (Is this trip necessary?)
6. Postponing the unpleasant or the difficult.	Schedule the unpleasant or difficult tasks first. Then the rest of the day is easy.
7. Responding to the urgent (postponing the important).	Resist the tyranny of the urgent by limiting your response: (1) ignore problems if they will go away by themselves, (2) delegate those which others can handle, (3) respond yourself to those only you can handle.
8. Not following up.	Recognize that people do what you *inspect*, not what you *expect*—and the same goes for *you*. So check your results against your plan. Are you progressing according to schedule? Have your secretary or assistant or associate monitor your progress.

102

Time Concern Analysis No. 15: Lack of Self-Discipline (Continued)

Causes	Solutions
Internal	
9. Not utilizing available tools and techniques.	Evaluate and utilize such aids as Time Tactics with integrated "To Do" lists (Must; Should; Can), daily written plans, deadlines, and project control charts.
10. Unrealistic time estimates.	Recognize that pursuit of unrealistic deadlines will lead to frustration and destroy self-discipline eventually. Be realistic in your own deadlines. Be candid in resisting unrealistic deadlines. Be fair in imposing them on others.
11. Lazy	Recognize. Determine to overcome. (See Bad Habits, No. 22.)
12. Unaware of this time concern (successful without self-discipline).	Recognize can be more successful with it.
13. Lack of interest.	Re-examine attitude toward job. Recognize that indifference makes self-discipline more difficult.
14. Inability to say "No."	Quit trying to be a "nice guy." Say "No" firmly and without offending.
15. Drifting into trivia.	Avoid nonessentials. Divorce yourself from detail! Concentrate on the critical priorities.
16. Cluttered desk.	Recognize as an impediment to an orderly mind. Use Time Tactics to record those things you do not want to forget. Clear your desk. Be systematic in procedures for routine matters.
17. Leaving tasks unfinished.	Recognize wasted effort in stopping and restarting tasks. Economy of effort dictates completing tasks before putting them down. Handle it once. Get it done the first time.
18. Carelessness.	Get it right the first time. If you don't have time to do it right, when will you have time to do it over?
19. Daydreaming.	Learn the art of concentration and practice it. Avoid distractions and self-interruptions.
20. Fatigue/Poor health.	Practice health fitness, exercise, recreation, time management.
21. Procrastination.	Identify tasks and decisions subject to procrastination. Set realistic deadlines. Go public by announcing them. Utilize secretary/assistant/associate to help you monitor results. Reward yourself when successful.

Time Concern Analysis No. 15: Lack of Self-Discipline (Continued)

Causes	Solutions
Internal	
22. Bad habits.	Make automatic and habitual as many useful actions as you can. This frees the mind for more productive work. To acquire a new habit, launch the practice as strongly as possible—announce it to discourage yourself from backsliding. Never let an exception occur until the habit is firmly rooted. Seize the first possible chance to act on your resolution.
External	
23. Undisciplined boss or organization.	Select boss or organization where self-discipline is respected and encouraged. Standards of behavior tend to gravitate to the lowest rather than the highest level in the group.
24. Switching priorities.	When a manager switches priorities on his team, he makes self-discipline difficult to practice. Take time log to record frequency, assess cost in morale and production; discuss with boss to seek ways of reducing problem.

For Further Reading

Drucker, Peter F. *The Effective Executive.* New York: Harper & Row, 1967.

Frank, Milos O. *How to Run a Successful Meeting in Half the Time.* New York: Simon & Schuster, 1989.

Parkinson, C. Northcote. *Parkinson: The Law, Complete.* New York: Ballantine Books, 1983.

Peter, Laurence J. *Why Things Go Wrong, or, The Peter Principle Revisited.* New York: William Morrow, 1985.

Peter Laurence J. and Hull, Raymond. *The Peter Principle.* New York: Bantam, 1969.

SECTION 6

Solving Your Team's Time Concerns

Developing Solutions with Your Team

Seminar, Education Program, or Both

Planning for Reinforcement

    Support from the Top
    A Time-Concern-a-Week Program
    Staff Meetings
    Measuring Results
    An Article a Month
    Buddy System
    Films and Cassettes

Team Sensitivity

Solving Your Team's Time Concerns

We discussed at the end of Section 4 the development of a team profile of time concerns. In that discussion, we observed that this team profile represents an instant "X-ray" of the obstacles to the team's effectiveness. This clearly becomes a powerful tool for the manager in implementing team improvement.

Some suggestions may be helpful in the preparation of this profile. With relatively large groups attending seminars, it is possible to get a good profile with each manager listing only his top five time concerns and assigning a weight of five points to his number one time concern; four points for his number two, etc. However, because most teams are relatively limited in size, and because it takes a certain number of entries to create a viable profile, it is recommended that the members of a team be asked to list their top 10 time concerns. The weights, as suggested in Section 4, would be 10 points for number one, 9 points for number two, etc.

It is important to take several other factors into consideration. One of these, of course, will be the average length of time that the manager has occupied his present position. A person who has just started in a new role may have some difficulty in identifying his time concerns with certainty. On the other hand, it is very possible that the same time concerns which afflicted him in his past position will also affect his performance in his present one. Nevertheless, one can expect that the new person will raise the objection that he is too new in his job to have identified any time concerns with certainty. A reasonable response would be that most time concerns relate to the person and are self-generated.

Another factor to be considered is whether time logs have been taken. The Principle of Awareness (Organizing Section) makes it clear that few managers have an accurate idea of how their time is actually being spent. Consequently, one may expect that the time concerns identified by someone who has not yet taken a time log may vary somewhat from those identified after taking a log. For this reason it is recommended in several places in this manual that the individual's list of time concerns and the team profile be validated with time logs.

These are but a sampling of the practical realities which the manager will wish to keep in mind as he approaches the problem of working with his team to cope with their time concerns. We turn now to various methods employed by different managers in approaching solutions with their teams.

Developing Solutions with Your Team

It is clear that the manager's style of leadership—autocratic, participative, or variable—will have a deep impact on his approach to solving time concerns with his team. At the very outset, one's approach to the use of time logs may vary widely. It is my recommendation that the time log be taken first by the senior executive for several reasons. It is helpful the person is familiar with the various problems which may hinder effective execution of the logs. Perhaps an even more important reason is the setting of an example by taking the time log. This demonstrates that the log is not to be feared, it may be of great benefit personally to the individual, and it is not intended to be used as a surveillance device or a monitoring mechanism.

By taking the time log, sharing findings with the group, then asking their assistance in solving some of his or her own time concerns, the senior executive takes an important step toward team involvement. It will be very difficult for the team to resist a later suggestion that they too may wish to gain the benefits from this device. A more autocratically disposed executive may well order time logs to be taken and run the risk that they will be feared, resented, and, of course, sabotaged.

Seminar, Education Program, or Both?

Since seminar work is the major part of my business, it is not surprising that the great majority of persons with whom I have had experience in developing team solutions have begun with the seminar approach. From an in-company time management seminar would normally come the selection by each of the participants of his/her top 10 time concerns and the development in the seminar itself of various team profiles as well as the overall company time concern profile.

This profile, of course, is the road map for attacking the time concerns of the team. It is always my suggestion that the individuals concentrate on implementing the solutions they have developed in the seminar itself. There is one problem with this, however; there are far too many recommended solutions for the manager to implement at once. Therefore, I strongly recommend that the participant prioritize his solutions on a very selective basis and record them on an "action item" list. Effective managers in my experience select carefully only two, three, or four items of primary importance for initial implementation. Thus, they are following the Principle of Concentration of Effort (Controlling Section) on the few items that will gain the greatest results.

In many situations an extensive team preparation program precedes the taking of a seminar. A five-star hotel in the South pursued a vigorous self-education program on time management for nearly half a year before sponsoring a time management seminar for its 50 managers and supervisors. In the course of this program, all managers and supervisors listened three times to an audiocassette program on time management* and read the assigned book on the subject.† When the time for the seminar came, all the managers were very well informed on the subject, had already identified a number of their own time concerns, had implemented solutions to some, had developed tentative solutions to others, and were prepared with questions on a number of relatively advanced aspects of time management.

The enthusiasm generated by such an approach provides a solid base for launching a successful effort with your team for managing their time. Of course, the subject itself is of commanding interest to almost every manager who recognizes that time is a person's most valuable asset. To be provided the tools for clearly identifying one's real problems in this area and developing viable solutions for them is a highly motivating activity.

Planning for Reinforcement

Of all the activities in a time management program, the follow-up or reinforcement step probably provides the greatest payoff in terms of time and energy expended. Although there are seven different types of reinforcement described in this section, it is not expected that a manager will use all of them. He should select according to the needs of his situation and make creative modifications as he sees fit.

Support from the Top

Active participation of the top management team provides strong motivation at all lower levels. In many in-company seminars, senior executives have been involved in the program. The most serious mistake that the senior executives can make is to suggest a program in management development for their teams but to abstain from participation themselves. This single oversight does more to kill the effectiveness of management development programs than perhaps any other factor. Support from the top is essential, and the very best way to show that support is direct and active participation by the entire top team. Tacit support for this principle is seen in the Presidents' Association of AMA where the members of a president's team are not allowed to attend the top management briefings until their president has attended the Management Course for Presidents.

This support can be continually demonstrated in a number of ways. Immediately following the seminars, I suggest a letter directly from the senior executive to all participants requesting their candid reactions to the seminar, a list of the ideas which the individual manager found to be the most helpful, and any suggestions from the seminar which are thought to be helpful for the organization as a whole. All the suggestions resulting from this survey, along with a summary of all of the actions thought to be of particular individual benefit, should be returned to each of the participants for reinforcement purposes.

---

*"Managing Time," R. Alex Mackenzie

†*The Time Trap—Managing Your Way Out,* R. Alex Mackenzie

In addition, the suggestions for the organization which receive the most support and are consistent with organizational objectives ought to be acted upon immediately and those actions made known to the participants. This has a very dramatic effect on the participants. It shows them that the organization is taking the time management program seriously and intends to implement it. A very strong though subtle implication is clear—the company is doing its part; how about you? A common suggestion often acted upon in this manner by top management is the "quiet hour." It is viewed enthusiastically by almost all managers as soon as it is explained. They usually suggest to top management that it be implemented company-wide.

A Time-Concern-a-Week Program

One of the most appealing and forceful recommendations for follow-up in the time management program is the concept of beginning to work immediately on the organization's time concern profile. (Refer back to Exhibits 4.5 and 4.6, pages 61 and 62, for sample corporate profiles.) Beginning with the number-one time concern, the management team can attack "a time concern a week." Thus, every manager will have before him the task of doing his part to help the organization solve this time concern in any way he can. Mutual reinforcement generated in this way enables the organization to capitalize on one of the most powerful forces in management development. It should be evident why this is such a powerful force. Many of the time concerns involve relationships with other people (telephone, visitors, meetings, etc.).

When an entire team is concentrating on eliminating its number-one time concern, members can help each other. Throughout a given day, whenever a manager may have momentarily forgotten about the number-one time concern, it is probable that he will be reminded of it by someone else. Hence, the team effort in the achievement of almost any goal multiplies many times the probability of its success. We know that the probability that an intended event will occur increases directly with the systematic application of effort toward its realization (Principle of Probability of Occurrence).

Staff Meetings

It is my recommendation that, beginning with the senior executive, every staff meeting in the organization list time management as a subject on the agenda to be discussed at least weekly for two or three months, and then at least monthly thereafter. This ensures that the subject will be brought up and discussed by the manager and his team on a regular, periodic basis. This periodic exercise should serve as an excellent reminder to everyone of the importance of time management. It should provide a measure of periodic progress and excellent reinforcement. Three questions should be asked at these meetings: 1) What *progress* are we making in time management? 2) What *problems* are we encountering? 3) What are the *plans* for next week?

Measuring Results

It is also strongly recommended that as time concerns are identified for solution, criteria be discussed and accepted on which the measurement of progress in this area will be made. A list of possible criteria for the top seven time concerns follows in Exhibit 6.1 (see page 112). These criteria can be measured by taking a one-week time log every month for four months and measuring the progress in controlling the time concerns directly from each time log. If changes were measured in percentages, it would then be possible to record monthly progress on such a basis. This could apply to the management of the individual's as well as the team's top concerns. Thus, since these time concerns are the manager's chief obstacles to effectiveness, we would have developed an entirely new measurement device for evaluating the effectiveness of managers. In Section 9 we shall examine further the details of such a program.

An Article a Month

Monthly or periodic readings in time management are highly recommended as an auxiliary reinforcing tool. Every training director is concerned about follow-up and reinforcement, but it is a very difficult objective to fulfill. In fact, some analysts have estimated that the billions of dollars spent each year in training and development are mostly wasted because the initial impact is lost due to ineffective or nonexistent follow-up. There are a large number of articles on the subject of time management, some of them outstanding. One response by the president of a large Venezuelan bank has been this kind of follow-up:

Once a month his key managers receive a copy of a selected article on time management with two or three suggested questions to be discussed with their staffs after all of them have read the article. The benefit of this plan should be obvious. Every four weeks a reminder of the importance of the subject arrives at the manager's desk in the form of an article written in an interesting and persuasive manner. New ideas are constantly brought to bear and old ideas reinforced. Furthermore, the managers discuss these articles with their teams, which is another way of ensuring the ongoing concern of the entire team for the effectiveness of their managerial performance.

Buddy System

One of the best devices for sustaining interest within a team for a time management program is the buddy system. Here two or more managers agree to meet regularly (probably weekly) for lunch to discuss their progress in managing their time. They check on each other's performance for the past week and make certain commitments about things they plan to achieve during the next week. This form of "going public" leads to a sense of commitment. They arrange that progress toward these commitments will be reported and assessed at the following meeting. Such a plan was discussed with the presidents of the divisions of one corporation as a solution to the problem of regression—the tendency to fall back into our old, bad habits. The training coordinator of a major food marketing corporation proposes to the field service

Exhibit 6.1: Criteria for Measuring Impact of Time Concerns On Managerial Effectiveness

1. Telephone interruptions

Number of calls taken unnecessarily.
Number of minutes spent beyond reasonable requirements.
Number of calls placed unnecessarily.
Extent to which objectives were achieved.

2. Drop-in visitors

Number of visitors who should not have been received.
Number of minutes spent beyond reasonable expectations.
Extent to which objectives were achieved.

3. Meetings

Ratio of optimum to actual time spent in meetings.
Extent to which predetermined objectives were achieved.
Participants' views on both of above criteria.

4. Crises

Existence of written strategy for crisis management by
    a. Categorizing types of crises anticipated.
    b. Written plan for handling each.
Percent of potential crises anticipated and prevented or
    effectively minimized.
Number of cases of "overreaction" (treating problems
    unnecessarily as crises).

5. Lack of objectives, priorities, and deadlines (daily plan)

Existence of written long-range and short-term objectives.
Percent of progress toward objectives in measured period.
Existence of priorities and deadlines for all objectives.
Percent of deadlines met in measured period.
Number of No. 1 priorities achieved daily.

6. Cluttered desk and personal disorganization

Responsibility assigned in secretary's job description for
    orderliness of manager's desk, papers, files, appoint-
    ments calendar, meetings, etc.
Effective daily plan in writing and monitoring process for
    checking progress against plan daily.
Amount of time lost due to searching for misplaced docu-
    ments, mistakes made or deadlines missed due to disor-
    ganized desk and/or person.

7. Ineffective delegation and involvement in routine and detail

Ratio of actual to potential delegations during logged period.
Amount of time spent on routine matters which could have
    been delegated, eliminated, consolidated.
Amount of time spent unnecessarily involved in detail.
Ratio of refusals of inappropriate requests for information,
    opinions, suggestions, or decisions, to the total number of
    such requests from subordinates (upward delegation) or
    from associates.

managers attending his seminars that they utilize this method of maintaining progress concerning the important areas they have decided to implement during the seminar.

Films and Cassettes

Films and audio tapes in the time management area can serve as periodic reinforcers of the basic concepts and techniques of time management. Audiocassettes have advantages, particularly for people who travel, since they can use earphones to play the tapes while riding on public transportation or use tapedecks while driving.

Team Sensitivity

It is important to remember that time management is essentially a team effort. This being the case, sensitivity to the time requirements of other people and, more consequentially, sensitivity to the impact of your own actions on the time requirements of other people are important, continuing responsibilities.

E. B. Osborn, a chief executive and leading exponent of time management, whose time management style is outlined in Section 8, makes a point of this important concept. Osborn bases the success of the relationship between the boss and secretary as well as between the boss and team on this fundamental concept. Osborn says the reason the quiet hour is so effective is its immediate benefit to every member of the team. Similarly, in planning meetings with another person, he recommends being sensitive to the other person's time requirements by asking well in advance when it would be convenient to meet.

Teamwork itself implies the coordination of activities, the assisting of one another, the mutual synchronizing of efforts to ensure optimum results. Sensitivity to the needs of others will significantly enhance the effectiveness of this effort, while the lack of sensitivity will destroy the effort.

Such sensitivity may also prevent a problem which otherwise may arise. This is the problem when one manager's solution to a time management problem in effect becomes the problem of another manager. Delegation is a classic area where this may occur. A superintendent of a public school system jokingly told me that following the time management seminar for the administrators of his system, a principal returned to his office, packed all of the piles of papers on his desk into a cardboard box, put it on his secretary's desk and said, "Here, this is your problem." While the twinkle in his eye revealed that the story was apocryphal, it was not without its point.

Overdelegation, delegation that in effect could be called "abdication," is visiting the problems of a manager onto the subordinate. Such delegation without regard to availability of time and competence to perform the task would certainly be imposing the solution of one problem onto another person in the form of a new problem. Sensitivity and teamwork are essential to see that this kind of abuse of time is not permitted.

For Further Reading

Kieffer, George David. *The Strategy of Meetings*. New York: Warner Books, 1988.

Kobert, Norman. *Managing Time*. New York: Boardroom Books, 1980.

Mackenzie, Alec. *The Time Trap*. New York: McGraw-Hill Publishing Co., 1975.

McCay, James T. *The Management of Time*. Englewood Cliffs, NJ: Prentice Hall, 1977.

SECTION 7

The Professional Secretary/Assistant—Key to Managerial Effectiveness

with Billie Sorensen, International Lecturer on the Office Professional

The Professional Secretary/Assistant— Key to Managerial Effectiveness

The key member of the manager's team should be the secretary. We have not included the secretary in earlier discussions of the boss's team, precisely because we believe that the secretary's role is unique, and needs special emphasis. The secretary is the key to effective utilization of executive time.

Answer for the Harried Executive

Executives who have turned over their calendars and the management of their time to their secretaries or assistants strongly defend this way of functioning. The general manager of a major airline says it this way:

> Were I to suggest to any other harried executive one single method of improving his work day, it would be to hire a competent, understanding and compassionate secretary, and then make her such an integral part of his working life that she becomes an extension of his right arm. Your secretary must know not only the operational details, your function in the operation and your responsibilities, but even your likes, dislikes, prejudices, biases and the way you think, if she is to function most effectively.

Still, in time management seminars, managers frequently respond with a chorus of dissent to the statement that the secretary is the key to effective utilization of their time. They protest that allowing a secretary to schedule their hours in the office, often making the decision of who sees the boss during his working day and freeing him or her of routine detail of operations as much as possible, actually means turning over to the secretary the running of the office. They fear the secretary will become overly protective, even dominant, and may offend associates or clients. While exceptions are always possible, we have yet to hear such a comment from managers who have actually tried it. Invariably they discover that the secretary/assistant handles many situations more easily and effectively than they.

What Is a Secretary/Assistant?

Defining the word "secretary" or "assistant" is not simple. The job runs the gamut from the young novice with little or no experience in handling telephones or computers to the executive confidential assistant who may well have a secretary or two. It encompasses the ambitious college graduate who wishes to climb the ladder of management and the middle-aged, competent homemaker-turned-secretary who wants to do a good job in an upgraded position but, having family and community interests, has no desire for the responsibilities of management.

With a bit of humor and a measure of truth, an anonymous writer listed these qualifications for a secretary/assistant:

> She must have a diplomat's tact, a mule's endurance, a chameleon's effacement, a salesman's enthusiasm, the sun's punctuality, the speed of light, a sister's loyalty, a rhino's hide, an Einsteinian brain, a mother's sympathy and the patience of Job.

To become a professional secretary, able to act as a real assistant to the boss, a period of training, usually on the job, is required. Secretarial schools used to do little more than teach their students how to take shorthand and type well. The graduate of such schools arrives on the job ill prepared to take command of managing the boss's day. The short period of orientation given by most companies for new employees adds little to the knowledge needed to handle the job competently. Today's office professional must have computer and management skills. If she is lucky, her boss has been working with a professional secretary/assistant and knows how to work with the new arrival to increase her effectiveness within a comparatively short period of time. Managers complain about the difficulty of obtaining a qualified secretary. They say that if she is topnotch, she will be available only to presidents or board chairmen and that it will be their lot to struggle along with something far less. Our experience has shown us the fallacy of this assumption.

This does not negate the tremendous need for improved secretarial training by both secretarial schools and businesses. Many business schools and universities are now offering management courses for the secretary.

On the other side of the coin is the professional secretary, well trained and with years of experience, who all too frequently remains at a fixed responsibility and salary level. The lack of opportunity for advancement, with limited possibilities for increased income, often contributes to lack of motivation even in the most highly qualified secretaries.

Mission of the Secretary/Assistant

The advent of word processing/administrative support teams and desktop terminals has raised questions concerning the future role of the secretary. This development is discussed in Section 13. We believe the role of the professional secretary is secure. The long-time practice of giving senior executive secretaries the title and responsibilities of administrative or executive assistants will become more widespread and will occur at lower levels.

If the manager's job is achieving objectives through others, the mission of the professional secretary/assistant should be helping the boss achieve his or her objectives most effectively.

A Boss/Secretary Team in Action

The changes that took place in the office of the department head of systems training in a major national electronics firm illustrate well the importance of an evolving boss/secretary relationship. Fred was the department manager with a staff of about 50. Virginia was his secretary and had the support of two clerical people. According to Fred, at first she did largely steno-clerical kinds of jobs—a reflection of what she had learned in high school courses.

Later, Fred and Virginia systematically examined together the boss/secretary functions of their office, then allocated each one either to boss or to secretary. The principle they followed was to give Virginia as many substantive functions as possible, making her job more interesting and challenging and freeing Fred to get to the most important part of his job. With this added responsibility, Virginia became overloaded with work, and routine duties were allocated to other office clerical personnel.

With training and encouragement from Fred, and considerable personal effort, Virginia has become a knowledgeable secretary. With minimal instruction she is able to carry out a variety of office projects, many of a managerial nature; with the sketchiest instructions, she can disseminate information to Fred's supervisory team. She works well with others, including being able to say "No" without offending; she has organized her own work to make the best use of her time.

Virginia made the following list of attitudes, procedures, and policies, many of which were instituted as a result of attending a boss/secretary seminar on time management:

1. Look at the job from boss's point of view. Be sensitive to time limits and priorities and the need to plan and organize accordingly.

2. Maintain a schedule of boss's time: calendar, meetings, projects. Keep a "to do" list for boss, being sure it is of workable size. Prioritize the items. Prepare folders for meetings boss will attend, giving him all pertinent materials needed.

3. Schedule regular meetings with boss to review office operations.

4. Keep interruptions to a minimum; screen visitors, making an effort to handle requests or problems, discern which ones must be handled by boss.

5. Answer boss's phone, handle as many calls as possible, refer calls where applicable.

6. Open mail, answer letters where possible, draft answers to others if possible.

7. Act as interface between boss and department, writing notes and memos for boss.

8. Attend boss's staff meetings as part of the management team.

9. Maintain and monitor a list of general reading projects.

10. Review articles on time management and office operations.

Fred and Virginia say memorandum writing has been cut appreciably. Virginia sends to each member of Fred's team a copy of his weekly schedule (see Exhibit 7.1, page 121). This informs the team of Fred's availability without having to check with Virginia to see where he has open time. They have a reminder of meetings they are to attend. She sits in on staff meetings and takes minutes of action items. Following the session, Virginia distributes a list of action items so that each member has a record of what he or she has agreed to do. She follows up to be sure action items are actually completed. She maintains a "to do" list to ensure that current projects are brought to Fred's attention. (See Exhibit 7.2, page 122.)

One of the most interesting developments has been the value Fred has obtained from keeping a daily log of his activities. He finds it a great help in disciplining his time as he goes through the day. When his log shows time is being wasted, an automatic connection takes place. Although initially it took a conscious effort, he now finds it almost automatic. He feels that the time it takes is inconsequential compared to the benefit. The log consists simply of an abbreviated notation of each activity with its starting and ending time. Rarely does the list exceed one page. An example of an actual log of Fred's is shown on Exhibit 7.3, page 123.

The Secretary/Assistant-as-Ally Concept

In Fred's view today's professional secretary functions as an "ally" to her boss's team. While a protector of her boss's time, she is sensitive to the needs and personalities of those who contact him, especially members of his team. She seeks to aid them in achieving their goals. When this is not possible, she explains tactfully without offending. Because her aim is to help her boss effectively achieve his objectives, she needs skills as a manger, including how to set objectives and reach them; how to organize resources including time; how to handle matters to be delegated by her boss to team members but left to her to implement; how to motivate other people to help her boss achieve his objectives; how to follow up on managerial details; how to communicate effectively yet diplomatically; how to make decisions in the boss's absence and what to bring to his attention when he is there.

She attends top management meetings, and her viewpoint is sought because she brings a unique perspective to the boss's problems. As an ally of the manager's team, she is able to present their point of view to the boss, and his to them.

One of Virginia's more useful managerial tasks is what Fred calls "dispensing friendly advice," especially to new or less experienced people. The abrasion of a boss's criticism can leave a pretty deep wound. A word from his secretary can come more as a friendly tip-off than an admonition. Corrective action can be taken in advance without a lot of stir. A professional secretary doesn't always have to be told when this is necessary and may often give a precautionary nudge in the right direction.

Exhibit 7.1: F. L. Stevenson Weekly Schedule

Iss. Date _____

From _____

To _____

	TIME	MEETING WITH	PURPOSE
4/8 MON.			
	9:30	RMS, DE, JJT	Curriculum Proposal
4/9 TUES.			
	All day	TAC Members	Training Advisory Council
4/10 WED.			
	10:00	JRW, HOH	Review work assignments
	1:30	AC, HOH, SP	Rehearsal of ILC/NSPI Presentation
4/11 THURS.			
	10:30	RC, BR	To discuss curriculum committee meeting
	lunch	SPP	To discuss IMS Curriculum Proposal
	1:30	Mr. Justice	Tour of ILC
4/12 FRI.			
	2:30	C. Martinetz	Debriefing: Administrator's Workshop

⬭ INDICATES CHANGE

Exhibit 7.2: "To Do" List

F. L. Stevenson

Date _____
       Month   Day   Year

THINGS TO DO

For JHV/VAV; value of training and PSD technology

Prepare for Montreal symposium*

Review RK's memo on dictation*

AMA Management Training Course*

Meet with J. J. Tannenbaum and R. D. Pederson on Kaplan studies*

Gard, Shaw, Green, Levin

Call Karlin re: 4-120 videotape course this fall (?)

JJR re: BISCOM subcontracting

Everett re: permanent position

VAV re: production system* (memo, if possible)

Review Sloan's proposal*

RO/EL/JJT re: "This is PSD" videotape

Note to HOH re: Swayzer's performance reviews*

Letter to Walther*

_____

Note from Mrs. Torgrimsen: This list is usually updated once a day, but it will depend on how many new items he may have. The asterisk (*) means that he must refer to written information included in the folder always attached to the list. This folder has three dividers: Priority 1, 2, and 3.

Exhibit 7.3: FLS Time Log

_____
(date)

Today:

1. Whalen re Smith transfer
2. H.F. Symposium paper
3. Set up project briefings
4. Check MJK audiotape
5. Sloan proposal

7:35	Review budget summary
8:15	Notes for RDP meeting
8:35	B. Bauer—shipmt in Mon. City
8:40	RDP & JJT re audiotaping MJK's presentation
8:45	JJT re Fauver contract
9:05	VLT—mail & planning for day
9:15	HOH—CAI project—line & terminal—continue 1 month—PSS Test project
9:25	RDP re holding up on disconnect of terminal
9:30	ULT—planning
10:00	To RDP's staff meeting
10:45	ILL—reviewed quarterly student load date with Fran
11:00	Changed dental appt. (?)
11:05	Geiger (Travel) not in X6868 Kirshner 4877 back after lunch
11:10	VLT—reviewing voucher problem
11:35	Lunch with Swayzer Green re Learning Center opus
1:10	Geiger—not in—will call
1:15	RDP re personnel assignments
1:30	Continued work on HF symposium paper
2:06	Dean Fiery—AT&T—inquiry about PSD help for syst. devel. project AT&T Corp. project comm.—Longlines will staff
2:20	Continued work on HF symposium paper
2:35	Jim George, WE Co.—Media Task Force—referred to Bishop
2:40	Continued work on HF symposium paper
2:50	Geiger—will get info from TWA & advise
3:15	Continued work on HF symposium paper
4:30	VLT—misc. items for tomorrow
5:00	

Related to this talent is the tact required of a secretary in turning back to the originator's attempts to delegate upward. Subordinates frequently bring to the boss a task that should be done on a lower level. An efficient secretary sees this quickly and turns it back to the team member for completion, without offending in the process. A simple suggestion will often suffice: "I'm sure the boss would be pleased if you went ahead and used your own judgment in the matter."

A secretary, given greater responsibility, will also assume a greater workload, willingly. As Meralon Hartwell, former executive secretary, expresses it: "There's a difference between an overworked, unchallenged secretary and an overworked, happy, involved secretary." After time management training was instituted, with its added responsibilitites for secretaries, often she would stay overtime and work through a problem because she felt she was doing something significant.

Meralon noted that the executives at Pacific Western, once they were trained in good time management practices, realized that by simply being informed on corporate problems and goals, the secretary can answer many questions of subordinates, saving hours of the boss's time and adding immeasurably to the company's effectiveness. In one company, of 16 secretaries who met for lunch to discuss their progress one month after attending a time management seminar, 14 reported they were doing considerably more work thanks to increased delegation by their bosses, and were enjoying their work much more.

Beginning the Team Relationship

Have you ever sat down with your secretary to find out how things are going? To learn from her what suggestions she has for managing your time? What could she do that you are now doing? Margaret Jacobs, former associate personnel manager for General Foods in White Plains, New York, says that by utilizing to the fullest her secretary, Heather Ferguson, she increased her own effectiveness by as much as 300 percent and Heather found her job much more interesting and challenging. Not only was there no additional clerical help, but Margaret shared Heather with her boss, John Bulger, the personnel manager.

As Margaret and Heather described their situation, the telephone was the source of almost constant interruptions. The two bosses learned that Heather could answer or refer about 80 percent of those calls, permitting them to handle priorities for which there previously had been no time. Initially Heather encountered a great deal of opposition. One manager refused to talk to Heather or leave a message. On the fifth try he finally got through to Margaret. His problem: to enroll one of his men for a training course. Margaret's answer: "Just a minute, I'll put you on hold — my secretary handles all the enrollments!" The effective manager supports his or her secretary as a full-fledged member of the management team.

Margaret and Heather instituted the "quiet hour." The first week was so discouraging they considered giving it up. Margaret was completing long-delayed projects, writing memos, piling work on Heather, who was now also handling John's telephone calls and calendar. The workload was so tremendous that Heather was getting further behind every day. Margaret's desk was slowly clearing, but Heather's was steadily looking worse. Another week went by, and they began to see that Heather's work was leveling off and to realize that because of the quiet hour Margaret had been able to clear the enormous backlog of work, long unfinished because of daily interruptions. With her quiet hour, she was able to keep current.

On occasion, Heather's desk did get stacked with work. At such times her bosses answered their own phones for an hour, so that she could get the typing done. By agreement, if the phone rang three times, one of the bosses would answer it. This allowed Heather to continue work on some essential task without interruption.

Because there are always exceptions to screening of phone calls and visitors, Margaret kept Heather well informed. The first 15 minutes of her day was reserved for Heather. This permitted planning for the day. When it was necessary that Margaret be located and interrupted wherever she was, there were no embarrassing surprises. Heather was able to use discretion in handling each situation as it arose.

A most interesting timesaver was discovered when Margaret decided not to spend so much time in meetings. Heather, while consulting Margaret's calendar, would ask the caller how long it would be necessary for her boss to be in a given meeting. On many occasions, she was able to manage for Margaret to attend briefly for relevant discussion, then leave. Margaret estimates her total meeting time was cut in half!

Developing Joint Profiles of Time Concerns

The first step toward effective time utilization for boss/secretary teams is making two joint profiles of time concerns, one for each member of the team. Each will develop two lists of time concerns—his/her own and the other person's. For example, the boss will list his own time concerns on Exhibit 7.4 (see page 126) and his secretary's on Exhibit 7.5 (see page 127). At the same time the secretary will be listing her own time concerns on *another* copy of Exhibit 7.5 and her boss's on *another* copy of Exhibit 7.4. When each has completed the two lists of the top 10 time concerns, they exchange so that each has his/her own. The boss has his own two lists, one developed by himself, the other by his secretary. The secretary has her own two, one she developed herself, the other listed by her boss.

At this point each is ready to complete his/her own joint profile shown in Exhibit 7.6 and Exhibit 7.7 (see pages 128 and 129). Each lists his/her own top 10 in descending order of priority (thus allocating weights of 10, 9, 8, etc., to time concerns 1, 2, 3, etc.). Then the appropriate weights from the second list are added in column B and any new time concerns not shown on the first list are added at the bottom with their given weights.

If the team consists of two bosses and one secretary, or one boss and two secretaries, then the one team member relating to two others must fill out three lists, one for himself and one for each of the two bosses (or secretaries). When the boss having

Exhibit 7.4: Boss's Time Concerns

Select 10, weighting as you go—10 for No. 1 time concern; 9 for No. 2, etc.

Telephone interruptions	_____
Drop-in visitors	_____
Meetings	_____
Crises	_____
Lack of objectives, priorities, and deadlines	_____
Cluttered desk and personal disorganization	_____
Ineffective delegation	_____
Attempting too much at once	_____
Lack of or unclear communication	_____
Inadequate, inaccurate, and delayed information	_____
Indecision and procrastination	_____
Confused responsibility and authority	_____
Inability to say "No"	_____
Leaving tasks unfinished	_____
Lack of self-discipline	_____
Others _____	_____
_____	_____
_____	_____
_____	_____

Exhibit 7.5: Secretary's Time Concerns

Select 10, weighting as you go—10 for No. 1 time concern; 9 for No. 2, etc.

Not being kept informed by boss: of his whereabouts, of company
policy, of department plans _____

Lack of objectives, priorities, daily plans _____

Attempting too much (unable to say ''No'' to boss) _____

Lack of organization on part of boss _____

Interruptions by boss while trying to complete his deadline work _____

Office procedures not established, confused responsibility and authority _____

Unclear instructions; incomplete, inadequate information _____

Procrastination, indecision _____

Socializing, drop-in visitors _____

Switching priorities, confused priorities _____

Poor, inadequate filing system _____

Multiple bosses _____

Equipment problems _____

Errands, trips to copying machine _____

Redoing letters because of incorrect dictation by boss _____

Leaving tasks unfinished _____

Rescheduling of meetings and other appointments _____

Not delegating enough to others _____

Lack of independence, overcontrol by boss _____

Telephone _____

Mistakes, ineffective performance _____

Failure to listen _____

Exhibit 7.6: Secretary's Profile of Time Concerns

1. List your time concerns in order of importance in Column A below.

2. In Column B record weights for your time concerns listed by your boss. Boss probably will list time concerns different from your own. Spaces to add those are provided below your list.

3. Add Columns A and B (and C if necessary) to get total weights for Column W.

4. Establish ranking by weight in Column R (largest weight ranks No. 1, etc.) to get your profile of time concerns.

A		B	C	W	R
My top time concerns	Weights	Boss's Weights	Boss #2's Weights	Total Weights	Rank
	10				
	9				
	8				
	7				
	6				
	5				
	4				
	3				
	2				
	1				

Exhibit 7.7: Boss's Profile of Time Concerns

1. List your time concerns in order of importance in Column A below.

2. In Column B record weights for your time concerns listed by your secretary. Secretary probably will list time concerns different from your own. Spaces to add those are provided below your list.

3. Add Columns A and B (and C if necessary) to get total weights for Column W.

4. Establish ranking by weight in Column R (largest weight ranks No. 1, etc.) to get your profile of time concerns.

A		B	C	W	R
My top time concerns	Weights	Secty's Weights	Secty #2's Weights	Total Weights	Rank
	10				
	9				
	8				
	7				
	6				
	5				
	4				
	3				
	2				
	1				

two secretaries, or the secretary having two bosses, receives lists from each, then both columns B and C will be utilized (in Exhibits 7.6 and 7.7).

One problem which occasionally arises is the fear that listing the other person's time concerns will imply criticism. The boss may have to be told that he attempts far too much, the secretary that she interrupts her boss unnecessarily at times. Honesty and candor in listing such areas where improvement is possible are absolutely essential. Otherwise team members will be deprived of valuable help in improving their own effectiveness.

It sometimes is difficult to list 10 items. However, upon reflection, it will be clear that a good profile requires 10 items from each member of the team. Even though it may seem difficult, when pressed to identify 10 areas where some improvement might be possible, success is almost always achieved rather quickly.

Where the team members have not worked together before, one of two options is open. Either find other members of the group who have worked with them and who will list time concerns for them to make a joint profile possible, or eliminate that step completely and simply wait until the others have completed their profiles. Then progress to the developing of solutions, utilizing each one's own list. It is important to keep in mind that this is a joint effort for improvement of both members of the team. It is essential that all areas where improvement is possible be identified.

Attacking the Time Concerns

To clarify the process of combining the two lists into one profile, the composite profiles of the "boss," Alec Mackenzie, and Billie Sorenson, the narrator of the section that follows, are shown in Exhibits 7.8 and 7.9 (see pages 131 and 132). While a fair degree of similarity is evidenced in the two views represented by both profiles, this sometimes is not the case. The key to remember in writing down the second list is to simply add new ones at the bottom of your own list of 10.

As you see from our profiles, a time management consultant, like everyone else, has problems with time. We found that Alec, because of his broad interests and creative thinking but lack of time to follow through, was generating far more projects than could possibly be completed in the limited time available. This could account for his leaving tasks unfinished—my opinion, not his. There simply were not enough hours in the week or sufficient staff. As he traveled around the country meeting new people with interesting ideas, we would find ourselves with a list of books and articles to be written, tape-recording sessions, meetings, and a mountain of frustration. We had the difficult task of selecting what projects might be completed within a three-month period, what could be delayed for six months, and what we would consider long-range possibilities.

The list was then prioritized and proved an efficient aid in keeping us on a realistic track. To keep work moving, I was forced to plan my own time. Necessarily, Alec's priorities and objectives were my own, since it is my job to see that his work is com-

Exhibit 7.8: Secretary's Profile of Time Concerns—Billie Sorensen

1. List your time concerns in order of importance in Column A below.

2. In Column B record weights for your time concerns listed by your boss. Boss probably will list time concerns different from your own. Spaces to add those are provided below your list.

3. Add Columns A and B (and C if necessary) to get total weights for Column W.

4. Establish ranking by weight in Column R (largest weight ranks No. 1, etc.) to get your profile of time concerns.

A		B	C	W	R
My top time concerns	Weights	Boss's Weights	Boss #2's Weights	Total Weights	Rank
No objectives, priorities, daily plan	10	10		20	1
Telephone	9			9	6
Leaving tasks unfinished, indecision, procrastination	8	3		11	4
Switching priorities	7			7	8
Unclear communication	6	2		8	7
Multiple bosses	5	8		13	2
Ineffective delegation, not delegating enough to others	4	6		10	5
Lack self-discipline (in keeping boss informed)	3	9		12	3
Socializing	2			2	12
Failure to listen	1	1		2	12
Personal disorg., stacked desk		7		7	8
Not "on top" of job		5		5	10
Not screening junk mail		4		4	11

Exhibit 7.9: Boss's Profile of Time Concerns—Alec Mackenzie

1. List your time concerns in order of importance in Column A below.

2. In Column B record weights for your time concerns listed by your secretary. Secretary probably will list time concerns different from your own. Spaces to add those are provided below your list.

3. Add Columns A and B (and C if necessary) to get total weights for Column W.

4. Establish ranking by weight in Column R (largest weight ranks No. 1, etc.) to get your profile of time concerns.

A		B	C	W	R
My top time concerns	Weights	Secty's Weights	Secty #2's Weights	Total Weights	Rank
Attempting too much, unrealistic time estimates	10	10		20	1
Lack of, ignores self-imposed deadlines	9	8		17	2
Shifting priorities	8	7		15	3
Inability to say "No"	7	2		9	5
Paperwork	6			6	8
Socializing (telephone)	5	3 & 6		14	4
Personal disorganization, stacked desk	4	5		9	5
Indecision, procrastination	3			3	10
Too critical of others	2			2	11
Expecting others to conform to my schedule	1			1	12
Leaving tasks unfinished		9		9	5
Involved in routine		4		4	9
Junk mail, trivia		1		1	12

pleted. Planning would not have been possible, however, had I not also handled his calendar and scheduled all appointments. With speaking engagements three days a week, travel requiring almost another full day, we are left with one working day a week for projects to be completed. If that day is not scheduled carefully, interruptions cause our goals to be completely lost.

When Alec and I both agreed that lack of objectives, priorities, and daily plan was my top time concern, we disagreed on others. I listed telephones, noting that getting a call through to Germany had just required one hour's time (one of many such occurrences). Alec's view is that it's part of the job and handled without wasting time. He doesn't note my switching priorities as I do, and I don't see my desk as stacked as he does.

With Alec's travel schedule, it is essential that the office function without him. My assistant and I make his appointments, handle details of his seminars, and keep up-to-date with a heavy load of typing, mail, taped interviews, etc. One of the greatest rewards we receive is to find other managers turning over responsibilities to their secretaries as a result of working with us. The initial contact with our office is almost always made by a company executive. When he discovers that we are capable of giving the right answers and handling matters efficiently, we find other secretaries being allowed to respond to our mail and telephone calls. On the other hand, it is distressing to speak with secretaries who are obviously intelligent and interested but unable to answer questions because their bosses have not kept them informed.

The Ideal Boss from a Secretary's Viewpoint

When we sought to obtain a description of an ideal boss, we found not one secretary who mentioned that he should bring his own coffee and never ask her to do personal errands. If a secretary is functioning as a member of the managerial team and knows that her work and time are important to her boss, such occasional favors are incidental. When we asked one of the most effective secretaries we have ever encountered to describe qualifications for an ideal boss, she said, "That's easy, I'll just describe my own boss." Here is her list:

1. He is respected by his business associates for his just and honest dealings and by his staff for his personal interest in them.

2. Having an even temperament, he can be relied on to give an analytical and objective response in any situation, however critical. A sense of humor is a necessity.

3. Keenly aware of time management principles, he saves his secretary's time by organizing his work and allowing time for his secretary early in the day, keeping appointments as scheduled or advising of any changes.

4. He is aware when his secretary's workload is at a peak and gives her uninterrupted time.

5. He does not hesitate to criticize his secretary's job performance, kindly of course, so that she continually evaluates, refines, and improves her work habits.

6. He keeps his secretary apprised of important happenings in the company regarding projects and policies so that she may more effectively assist him as a member of his team.

7. He helps his secretary work to the outer limits of her capabilities, giving her responsibilities that require initiative, making her job more challenging and interesting.

How to Utilize Your Secretary Effectively

In order to maximize the effectiveness of the boss/secretary team, it is essential that the boss take the initiative. He should develop a "team approach" to the job. A job description should be discussed, agreed upon, and written down.* A useful test for the advanced secretary developed by the National Secretary's Association is described in the same source.

To work at her best, a secretary must enjoy your confidence. Provide her with background information to enable her to understand your decisions, contribute to them, execute them, inform others of your intent, anticipate problems, answer questions of others, and use her judgment independently when necessary.

Allocate the first minutes of each day to her, so that she may get answers to her questions and directions for the day. Give her the time she needs—for most teams from 5 to 10 minutes are sufficient. Give her the freedom to inquire and have access to your desk during the day. This will often enable her to give a fast answer to an inquiry which otherwise might be delayed or even held for you to answer.

Encourage your secretary to take initiative; anticipate problems; screen trivia; prioritize mail, projects, requests; organize your desk and keep it organized; keep you informed; make appointments; handle routine correspondence and reports; suggest better ways of doing things; improve procedures; ask questions; remind you of what needs doing.

Ask your secretary how and when she would like to receive dictation; how she would like to handle your mail; what she would like to know about your projects, assignments, objectives, and priorities; how she would like to handle phone calls, visitors, and meetings; how she would like to handle calendars and keep up with changes; what she could do that you are now doing; what suggestions she has for better utilization of your time and hers.

Review progress at least once a week. At the morning planning session, some review of the previous day's progress will be natural. At a set time on Friday or Monday, a planned review of the entire week and a look ahead at the next week will be

---

*The Time Trap, American Management Association, 1972. McGraw-Hill Publishing Co., 1975; Time Trap II, American Management Association, In Press 1990.

useful. When this review session is scheduled on a regular basis, it is easy for both persons to note items for discussion as they occur during the week. Talk over how things are going. What got "off the track" and how can you prevent it from recurring? Each should ask the other how he or she can help the other be more effective.

Remember that most secretaries can and want to contribute much more to the success of the team. Few managers utilize their secretaries' skills and abilities to the maximum. And finally, what my boss believes about the future role of the secretary:

> The career path of a capable woman should lead through the professional secretary rank into the rank of the professional manager. Let's get something straight. The professional secretary must be considered part of the managerial team. Many top managers concede she is the most important team member because she is managing the organization's most valuable asset—executive time. It is inconceivable that she not be considered a member of the team. Of course, this has radical implications on the sometimes grossly unjust salary range of secretaries. Opportunities for promotion should be inherent, including the right to be considered for the boss's job. She may be the most qualified person to fill that job when it becomes vacant. Yet, who will deny that some managers retain their present position primarily because of the skill, knowledge, and expertise of their secretaries? To deny these obvious facts is simply to perpetuate the archaic injustices of our essentially autocratic hierarchies. We are talking simple justice, as well as the long-range effectiveness of the entire organization.

For Further Reading

Mackenzie, Alec. *The Time Trap*. New York: McGraw-Hill Publishing Co., 1975.

Reynolds, Helen and Tramel, Mary E. *Executive Time Management*. Englewood Cliffs, NJ: Prentice Hall, 1979.

Winston, Stephanie. *The Organized Executive*. New York: Warner Books, 1983.

SECTION 8

Characteristics and Strategies
Of Effective Time Managers

W. R. Harris

> "I am a Timewaster"
> Importance of Secretarial Relationship
> Measuring Effectiveness of Meeting Time

Victor Milke

> End of Overtime Work
> Time Concern Chart on Wall for Visibility

Gerry Achenbach

> Need for a Philosophy of Time
> No Need for Crisis

Mark Dundon

> The Key is Planning
> Importance of Controlling Interruptions
> Controlling Meeting Time

Bruce Peterson

Characteristics and Strategies Of Effective Time Managers

Over the years, my travels in 40 countries have resulted in encounters with outstanding time managers. I have selected the following 10 because of their novel and extremely effective adaptations of the basic tools and techniques of time management, for example Hummel's recognition of the tyranny of the urgent and de Marsano's "prima donna itch." Shown after the names of each of these selected individuals will be the title they held at the time of my interview with them.

1. Dr. Charles D. Flory

Dr. Flory, partner, Rohrer, Hibler and Replogle, summarizes the characteristics of the most effective managers in his experience. Rohrer, Hibler and Replogle, with over 700 clients including many of the largest companies in the world, *enjoys an unparalleled reputation among psychological firms* to industry. As a senior partner, Dr. Flory edited their well known *Managers for Tomorrow* and *Managing Through Insight*. He has spent a lifetime personally consulting with board chairmen and presidents of a number of these corporations. This experience, combined with his rare insight, has given Dr. Flory a unique perspective of what makes top managers effective.

Flory observes that since every executive has all the time there is, it is the degree to which he organizes and utilizes this time which determines his fitness to ask others to work under him. "Anyone who can't organize himself is unsuited for major managerial responsibility," says Flory.

Common Characteristics of Effective Top Managers

When I asked him what common characteristics he had observed in the most effective top managers, he listed the following:

1. *The ability to do it now.* At least 80 percent of the things coming over the desk of an executive can be handled immediately. The effective executive disposes of it if it is not useful, delegates it if appropriate, and does it himself if necessary.

2. *The ability to delegate to the most qualified person.* This is not easy for the average executive who wants to do what he *can* do well. Many managers are more comfortable *doing* than *managing*. The effective executive sees that he has qualified people; selects the appropriate ones for a given responsibility; delegates with clarity to ensure understanding of the assignment; and

follows up with regular progress reports to ensure that the intended results are achieved.

3. *Willingness to take time to support, encourage, and evidence concern for his subordinates.*

4. *The ability to sift out critical issues for decision.* The effective executive avoids being trapped in trivia. He recognizes that the perfectionist tendency will draw the unwary manager into unnecessary detail. He avoids detail by leaving routine tasks and operating decisions to others. The cluttered desk is a clue to the executive who allows himself to get drawn into unnecessary detail. The key to solving this is the ability to organize and to decide. Indecision is probably the biggest thief of time.

5. *Refusal to waste time on the "impossible."* Admits defeat and moves ahead; is forward-oriented; wastes no time regretting or rationalizing.

6. *Projects himself into the future. Gains quick closure.*

7. *Possesses a sense of timing — a feel for the situation.*

8. *Possesses a real sense of time passing.* Ability to estimate time requirements realistically.

2. E. B. Osborn and Philip T. Perkins

E. B. Osborn, chairman of the board, Economics Laboratory, St. Paul, Minnesota, is a recipient of the Honored Company Award from the Harvard Business School Club of Minnesota. This award is given for ability, efficiency in management, response to unusual challenges, achievement of long-range objectives, community responsibility, and meeting the appropriate needs of the consumer. As will quickly be apparent to the reader, time management practices in Economics Laboratory (EL) have penetrated every level of corporate management. For this reason, I elected to interview two different members of EL's executive team: the chairman of the board and one of the vice-presidents, Philip T. Perkins.

Unique Features of the Time Management Program In Economics Laboratory

There are a number of unique features of the time management program at Economics Laboratory. The first is that E. B. Osborn is the spearhead. He has written an executive development manual devoted to the enhancement of managerial effectiveness which is based almost exclusively on the principles of time management. A second distinguishing feature is that these principles have been accepted and actively implemented at every level of management in the company. At least every two months (usually monthly) an executive development meeting is conducted by the corporate staff to review progress, problems, and plans for enhancing the time management program in the company. A third highlight of the program is its foundation on a weekly Plan Sheet, one of the most powerful tools ever devised in any time management program. The Plan Sheet, if well executed, virtually ensures the manager's control of both time and tasks. This much can be said of no other single tool in the realm of time management.

My introduction to the Economics Laboratory plan came from Phil Perkins, then vice-president of marketing, consumer division. When I asked Phil to speak at a time management seminar on the time management practices at Economics Laboratory, he brought copies of his own Plan Sheet and explained how this relatively simple device enabled him to manage all of the details, maintain constant perspective on his objectives, and ensure that his priorities were accomplished. He described the impact of the system on the entire organization as profound. "When you find that something works as well as this," he concluded, "you're going to use it. No two managers in the system use it in exactly the same way. But I don't know of a single manager who does not employ the basic time management principles in one way or another. The concepts have penetrated our company so completely that it would be impossible to calculate its benefit."

I found E. B. Osborn in his spacious White Plains office in a relaxed and thoughtful mood. He was obviously delighted with the request to explain his preoccupation with time management. His *Executive Development Manual*, he admitted, has found its way into many countries of the world. News of an idea that works, he commented, travels with great speed. Friends ask for copies of the manual, they show it to friends of theirs, and requests for copies and reactions to the concepts have come from a surprising number of countries.

"There's a kind of paradox," said Osborn, "about the typical manager's concentration on long-range planning from one to five years and on short-range, tactical planning for fiscal and budgetary procedures as opposed to his lack of corporate interest in day-to-day planning. Yet, this is the stuff from which others spring. The things we tell ourselves we want to do and the things we have been requested to do—these really are the job. In the *Executive Development Manual* we seek a team effort as well as to encourage in each individual manager executive work and planning habits that will get him the fastest and easiest way to maximum accomplishment and in a manner that dovetails with the efforts of others."

Story of the Frustrated Executive

Then Osborn recounted the story of the frustrated executive described in the manual. In Economics Laboratory this executive had found the pace increasing, the workload burgeoning. He was getting more and more done, but found less and less satisfaction in doing so. Increasingly, he wondered if he was getting the right things done. There didn't seem to be enough thinking done. When he thought about delegating he realized that his assistant was buried, too. Therefore, the most obvious solution to his problem was not available—passing along part of the load. Clearly, an assistant already overloaded is not going to be of much help in relieving any manager of his burden. "We decided," said Osborn, "to examine this executive's workload, and this is what happened:

> "1) We studied his workload. 2) We studied the workload of his assistant to determine whether extra people were needed. Actually they weren't. 3) We greatly changed and improved delegation. 4) The executive made a concentrated effort with his secretary to put his day together from the time he reached his desk until nightfall when he went home—minus the briefcase. 5) Certain filing and paper handling reforms were made. 6) Finally, the Plan Sheet began to operate to pull him out of the maze he was in."

Osborn concluded from this experience that you cannot find the time to think and accomplish the big things until you are less busy. You cannot be less busy until the man who reports to you is less busy, so you can pass part of the load along.

Guidelines for Managing the Executive's Daily Operation

Guidelines for managing the executive's day-to-day operation, according to Osborn, include the following:

1. He organizes and delegates:
   a. Organizes his own day, with "first things first."
   b. Prearranges conferences with adequate notice to the persons involved.
   c. Knows the importance of doing one thing at a time, of "clustering" related subjects.
   d. Does not allow his desk or his memory to become cluttered.
   e. Uses his file system to store facts and to jog memory; flags important facts for quick recall.
   f. Assigns work to others.

2. He knows his own problems and weaknesses, and those of others.
   a. Plans for interruptions, phone calls, etc.
   b. Anticipates interruptions, wherever possible, at a time convenient to him, thus conserving more valuable time later.

3. He gets an airplane view of his job through use of a Plan Sheet, which:
   a. Unclutters his desk.
   b. Unclutters his mind.
   c. Facilitates review of things accomplished and remaining to be done.
   d. Ensures that the big things are cleaned up first and the little things not forgotten.

It is in the issue of delegation that the Osborn concepts approach the unique team element. Delegation implies there is someone to whom to delegate. But if the time-harried manager's subordinate is likewise working under tremendous pressure, is frequently distracted by emergencies, works around the clock, and achieves results through sheer stamina, that subordinate is obviously not a likely candidate for delegation without creating additional problems or pressures beyond endurance. As explained in the *Executive Development Manual*, the subordinate is restricted in his own growth if he is unable to assume greater responsibilities. This is something he cannot do if he is unable to organize and manage his own affairs. Thus, the necessity for time management implementation at every level in the organization becomes an absolute imperative for organizational effectiveness.

Shown in the following Exhibit 8.1 is an actual Plan Sheet of Phil Perkins to demonstrate the practical working out of this device two levels below the chief executive officer, E. B. Osborn.

The Plan Sheet

I visited Philip T. Perkins to discuss the detail of the Plan Sheet as he utilizes it. The interview ranged across other time management practices of extraordinary interest, so I am presenting his views below in question-and-answer form.

Q—"Phil, why is the Plan Sheet so highly regarded by executives who are using it?"

A—"Its purpose, Alec, is to furnish the executive with the tool for self-management and for maintaining control over all the facets of his job—including emergencies and the constant pressures beaming in on all managers. It's a means of organizing one's thinking and planning all in one place, in the least amount of time, with maximum effectiveness."

Q—"Is it of equal benefit to all managers, those who are already well organized and those who are not?"

A—"The Plan Sheet is designed to help the manager who is well organized and to bring a sense of calm and control to the executive who is not. Its principal asset is to provide a way out of the chaos when his job is at its worst. When his 'to do' list contains 30, 40, or 50 items, the Plan Sheet becomes a practical imperative and probably the only real way for bringing order to this chaotic, but common, situation."

Q—"In what ways does it help the manager?"

A—"In addition to its obvious memory value, the Plan Sheet provides for effective scheduling of individual or group conferences and the subjects to be discussed in order of importance. It is a practical means of establishing priorities and of assuring that the most urgent matters will be disposed of first. It provides a means of responding to unpredictable and often unavoidable interruptions with minimum distraction from primary purposes."

Q—"What is its broad format?"

A—"The general categories of phoning, writing, general meetings, and lunches, followed by a page of names of colleagues routinely worked with, provide the basis under which most of the things to be remembered can be conveniently grouped."

Q— "Speaking of remembering, wasn't E. B. Osborn one of the first executives to articulate what we now think of as the principle of visibility in time management?"

A— "Yes, I believe so, Alec. He says it this way: 'It is essential to keep visible those things you intend doing. You can't do what you can't remember.'"

Q— "Would you explain how the Plan Sheet works?"

A— "Perhaps I should first explain what it is *not*. It is not simply a list of things to do each day, with which most executives seem to operate. The Plan Sheet is not just a listing of things to do with priorities attached representing relative importance at some previous time when the effort was made to indicate relative priority. Nor is it simply a memory jogger, nor just a schedule of what has to be done. Instead, it is a systematic means for organizing all of your day, your week or even a two-week period. By a quick daily viewing of all the things the executive must do, wants to do, or has been asked to do, matters that had no priority yesterday often become real priorities today. Activities are categorized in such a way that the manager will be managing his own time instead of surrendering its control to outside forces."

Q— "Would you give us the details of your own Plan Sheet—the one we are now looking at?" (See Exhibit 8.1, pages 145-146.)

A— "Yes. Here on the first page are the general categories referred to above. At the top right are luncheon appointments for the next two weeks. This enables my secretary or myself to make tentative dates subject to my confirmation. It saves a great deal of my time and gives better control. If the secretary has put down a tentative date—notice your own initials, A.M., with a parenthesis on Friday—she will be able to suggest to another person inquiring about lunch that next week might be better. She thus avoids possible conflicts. At the left side of the page at the top we have a section called 'phoning,' which we fill in as we go through all of the phone calls we want to make. I generally keep this in pencil because this section of the Plan Sheet may fill up quickly with the number of phone calls that will normally take place, even in the course of a day or two. Notations in pencil can be erased, and this column will be useful for a longer period of time. Phone calls are interoffice as well as outside.

"Below that, space is provided for planned correspondence and general, then there is a list of executives, superiors, and those reporting to me, and you will note there are things to be discussed with each of them. Of course, your secretary should be listed on the Plan Sheet because she is part of your

Exhibit 8.1: Philip T. Perkins Plan Sheet

PHONE

1   ✔ *EBO lunch Fri.?*
4   ✔ *Greg – travel plans*
     KMM – Re Moving Policy
     Ross – Friday store visits O.K.
3   ✔ *JMH – 90 Day Travel Plans*
     RWP/TMO R&D Coordination
     ✔ *Lunch Mon. – JMH*

LUNCH

Fri.	7/12 Hideaway
Mon.	7/15 JMH
Tues.	7/16 JJK
Wed.	7/17
Thur.	7/18
Fri.	7/19 EBO
Mon.	7/22 St. Paul – GKC
Tues.	7/23 St. Paul – JAL
Wed.	7/24 St. Paul – KMM
Thur.	7/25 St. Paul – MM Meeting
Fri.	7/26 AM (Tentative)

CORRESPONDENCE

5   ✔ *Send EB info on December meeting – cc:FTL*
     JMH – competition raising quantity discounts?
     Send FTL copy of Acquisition Screen

GENERAL

Finalize acquisition screen
Sales meeting agenda
Do linear charts for Division by title

SECRETARY

2   ✔ *Digest for St. Paul*
     Need acquisition screen file

EBO

Acquisition Plans
Division strategy document (D)
Linear charts by title
New Finish package design (D)
Marketing Plans Review dates

FTL

Division strategy document (D)
City Desk consolidation
Progress Report schedule (D)
Attendance at National Sales Meeting
New Finish creative strategy
Marketing Plans Review dates

JMH

Review past/future six month plans
Need to revise coverage control cards
Regional Managers sales coverage on Star
6a   *90 day travel plans (D)*
     Consumer field – regional expense control
     Regional Managers Meeting – analyze all reports
     Regional Office Executive Development Meetings

Exhibit 8.1: Philip T. Perkins Plan Sheet (Continued)

JJK

1	*Status new advertising copy*
	Job standards (D)
2	*Military marketing plan*
6b4	*90 day travel plans*
	Status Trendex Report
	Cost SAMI – 3 Test Markets
3	*Products on Bonus Program (D)*
6	*Nielsen coupon handling charges*
5	*Organization charts – Review (D)*

---

team. There will be many things you would like to review with her, or ask her to do for you. In this manner you have one place to list all of these items so you will not forget them. When the opportunity comes for discussion, all of your ideas are in one place and you are much less likely to forget something."

Q—"When will you normally be setting up or making additions to this Plan Sheet?"

A—"Well, in my case, as with most of the executives in Economics Laboratory, there are two times during the day which are set aside by joint agreement. The period from 4 to 5 o'clock is generally used for reviewing the day's results and getting organized for tomorrow. For example, you will note that under "correspondence" are listed things I want to write about. If it's a matter relating to incoming correspondence, it would be set aside and a small "w" in a circle would be placed to remind me that I want to respond to that letter which is under the dictation flap on my desk. The actual dictation might likely occur in the morning during the period from 9 to 10 o'clock. That time is set aside for all executives to be getting their own things organized, placing calls, and handling other matters that do not require meetings. No meetings are held before 10 o'clock. The "general" category is for all matters of a general nature, any projects, deadlines, etc., not covered by other categories.

"You will note in the left margin a priority marking which I always keep in pencil so that erasure is possible and new items of high relative importance can be added and given a high priority."

Q—"In your experience, do most managers have difficulty in setting priorities?"

A—"Yes, I think it's a major problem. Two fundamental concepts of prioritizing become clear as soon as you operate with a Plan Sheet. Relative importance of the item, of course, should be the primary criterion. We give great emphasis in Economics Laboratory to getting the most important thing done first, rather than postponing it until smaller details have been cared for. Getting number one done first is one of the fundamental keys to success of the effective executive. When the most important thing is done, the rest of the day is downhill—almost coasting.

"The second critical element in prioritizing is the timing or the timeliness of a given action. Some people prefer to call it 'relative urgency.' It is not always true that the most important thing needs to be done first, because of deadlines often imposed by external factors. If a colleague has to have a bit of information immediately in order to accomplish one of his requirements, this may very well have to be placed first on the executive's list of things to be done. Even though it in no way could be ranked as the single most important thing he has to get done for the day, it may still be the *first* thing he'll do.

"Another great benefit of the Plan Sheet, of course, is the overview it presents of all of the items to be accomplished and the prospect for intelligent delegation thus provided. The scanning of all things to be done permits not only relative prioritizing, but sound decisions as to what matters can best be handled by other members of the team."

Q—"I note a number of symbols or telegraphic notes on your Plan Sheet. Do you find yourself resorting to this time-saving practice almost automatically?"

A—"Yes, of course. Many managers seem to resist taking time to write things down and to prioritize them. Shorthand notes have a very logical place in offsetting the desire not to spend any more time than is necessary in this exercise."

Q—"Are you sure you can justify the time that such a Plan Sheet takes?"

A—"Without doubt. Don't forget, Alec, that time spent in effective planning repays itself many times over, and also gets better results. I have no doubt that the Plan Sheet itself saves me on the average of from one to two hours a day."

Q—"If it is that beneficial, why isn't it mandatory for all executives?"

A—"I really don't know the answer to that question. It ought to be. On the other hand, all managers are different. An interesting point here is that probably no two executives in Economics Laboratory utilize the Plan Sheet in exactly the same way. Each one seems to tailor the concept to his own desires. I'm convinced, however, that the manager who refuses to utilize some comparable system for organizing himself and the things he needs to get done is refusing to manage. Basically, the program is repeatedly *sold* not *told* to all levels of management. Monthly meetings help."

Q—"By the end of the day, then, you have not only reviewed the things accomplished during the day, but you have also gotten yourself organized for the next day?"

A—"By five o'clock, I have a good idea what's going to happen the next day and the order in which I want to get my major tasks accomplished. Also, my secretary knows the same things, and she finds this a great benefit in arranging and controlling her day."

Q—"Is numbering of priorities one of the real keys to the Plan Sheet?"

A—"Yes, it is. In numbering you have to first designate priorities. It may be that the first thing you want to do is sit down with your secretary and arrange for a trip itinerary and next, to cover some correspondence with her, and then complete phone calls. You may also want to sit down with two of your executives on some matters that are under their names on the Plan Sheet. And it may even be that you have 10 items to discuss with the executives but the time pressures of that day may permit only two of them to be discussed. Because they are critical and must be handled at that time, you would, of course, place your priorities accordingly on the Plan Sheet. Any papers that will be needed to support this discussion will be in a desk file or a desk flap, and you will mark this on your Plan Sheet with a 'D' for discussion with that executive."

Q—"Does an executive sense a feeling of ease when his day is planned ahead in this manner?"

A—"Of course. Most managers leave work late after a hard day's work carrying a briefcase and a large feeling of guilt. The Plan Sheet goes a long way toward removing the excuse for all of that."

Leaving the Briefcase

Q—"How often do you carry your briefcase home?"

A—"Rarely. I will frequently take my Plan Sheet home so that I can jot down any new ideas in an appropriate way so as not to forget them. Once I have written it down, it's off my mind and I can rest easy. I much prefer to finish my work at the office even if it might mean staying a few minutes later. In my opinion, the managers who take work home as a rule are not managing their time well. They usually are victims of others wanting to talk to them during the day. Time gets away from them and they wind up being squeezed at the end of the day, working late and taking work home. That way they have no chance to recharge their batteries.

"Working at home is generally not for effective executives. Unless you are organized with an office there, you will be working in an inconvenient place without adequate equipment, files, and secretary. Getting organized with a Plan Sheet in the way we have been discussing saves you enough time to get it all done in the normal hours. Before coming to Economics Laboratory, I worked for several other companies where I tried to make out with listing everything in a column on a sheet of paper and without any organized way to categorize or prioritize. It makes a great difference to know at the end of the day that you have gotten a good day's work done and that none of it is going home with you. You feel well organized and ready for the next day's activities—in effect, you are master of your own time.

Teamwork—the Key

Q—"What difference does it make that time management is practiced at every level in Economics Laboratory?"

A—"All the difference in the world. Everyone else knows what you are trying to accomplish. You respect their time and they respect yours. Effective time management is much easier and much more effective when it is embraced throughout an entire organization. If I can save one or two hours a day simply by using a Plan Sheet, you can imagine what the total gain in my effectiveness must be from utilizing all of the concepts together. When you consider that every manager in an organization is operating at the same cruising speed, the total impact of time management on an organization is simply incalculable."

The Hideaway

Q—"You are the first one who ever described the 'hideaway' concept. Would you tell us about it?"

A—"This came about as a result of the need for executives who are traveling to have a period of uninterrupted concentration after their return. With so many things piled up on their desks, decisions pending, and matters awaiting discussion with many of their peers, the demands on the returning executive's time can sometimes be unbearable. Instead of being able to catch up, he seems to be getting farther behind. We first found that it was simple to agree that any desk temporarily vacated by a traveling executive or someone sick could be available for the person wishing to be uninterrupted. We agreed that when a manager was at another person's desk, it was for the purpose of not being disturbed, and his desire was honored.

"Now we have formalized the policy and have two company suites, one here in White Plains and another in New York City, which are used exclusively for this purpose. We call them our 'hideaways' and any executive may sign up in advance for the period of time he feels necessary for undisturbed concentration. In this environment you are more at ease, you are more in control of the work in front of you, and you are not at the mercy of others trying to phone you. The executive gets on top of his 'pile-up,' sorts out the subjects or disposes of informative material, gets 'action' items on his Plan Sheet where he now has an overview, and can assign his own time for the ensuing day or days.

"There is a great temptation, you know, to respond to the knock on the door—especially when it's just for a moment of your time. The concept is really so simple that it's amazing to me it hasn't been more widely adopted years ago. All you are doing, in effect, is extending your absence from the office one more day. However, this extra day is for the sole purpose of getting caught up with your work."

Q—"Can you give me an example of the kind of project which is very difficult to accomplish without such a period of uninterrupted time?"

A—"A performance appraisal would be an excellent example. This requires a good deal of time, thought, and effort, and it is not a project that one welcomes because of the difficulty of the task. During the average day, you would normally put it off because you would want to get all of the little things done first. What invariably happens is that the little things comsume your whole day, and you end the day with a feeling of frustration that the big job wasn't started."

Energy Conservation in Meetings

Q—"I've heard you refer to conserving energy in meetings. That's a rather intriguing concept. Would you explain?"

A—"We often talk about frittering away our energies on little things, while we put off the more important things until we are too tired to handle them. Well, the same concept can operate in a slightly different fashion in meetings. How many times does a meeting move into a position of two opposing points of view—each being expressed more vigorously and with increasing conviction? We have found that a great deal of time and energy can be wasted (with fatigue beginning to set in) by pressing on in such meetings and attempting to force the group to one conclusion or the other.

"We have found that adjourning the meeting at the point this trend is identified and resuming at 10 the next morning can bring about some remarkable gains in group effectiveness. Oftentimes, reflection overnight, getting back to the desk at 4:00 p.m. for handling other affairs, and the change of pace that results bring a new perspective to the group. Oftentimes dishar-

150

mony is transformed into harmony, and a great deal of time and energy has been conserved. We have seen meetings, which might well have lasted for three more hours into the evening, resolved in 30 minutes the following morning—and to the satisfaction of all participants.

"Another thing we have found in setting meetings is to try to look ahead at least a day and to place a phone call to ask the other person when would be a convenient time for him to get together to discuss the items you have listed. This gives him a chance to fit this discussion into *his* schedule and to be prepared for a better contribution. We also find that by listing the items for discussion on the second page of the Plan Sheet under the name of the appropriate person, a great deal of time is saved in what would otherwise have been an interruption every time you thought of something you wanted to discuss. By the time you have three, four, or five items on your list for a person (and quite possibly he may have an equal number) it is clear that five, six, eight, or 10 items may conceivably be disposed of in one meeting. This is cutting time lost through interruptions a great deal.

"Still another idea when calling a person for an appointment is to ask, 'Are you in a meeting?' This eliminates the necessity of the other person explaining that he has three or four people in his office and could he return the call? This is extending a courtesy to the person being called and also a courtesy to those people with whom he is meeting. The executive who will accept calls in the middle of a conference with one or more other persons is, of course, extending the ultimate discourtesy to his visitors. On the other hand, if he knows the other person is in a meeting, but the call is an extremely urgent one, he is now alerted to the fact and will manage to cover the subject in a very few brief sentences. This is still extending respect to the other person. I never ask, 'Are you busy?'"

Q—"I have heard both you and E. B. Osborn talk about 'consideration of the other fellow.' This seems to be fundamental to your concept of teamwork and time management?"

A—"Yes, it is. If everyone is respecting the rights and interests of the other persons, the benefits in terms of time saved and harmonious efforts are immeasurably enhanced."

Plan Sheet for Trips

Q—"Do you recommend a special Plan Sheet for trips?"

A—"Yes. If I'm going to our home office [in St. Paul], my secretary prepares a special Plan Sheet. She prepares this up to two weeks in advance. Since I will be seeing a number of executives, this permits me to begin organizing my thoughts for discussion with each of them and to be filing matters for discussion. All of this goes into a folder marked 'home office' [St. Paul]. This provides me the information necessary for determining how much time to request with each executive. When I arrive, I give a copy to the receptionist on the 18th floor. She will then know my whereabouts at all times during my stay. This saves a tremendous amount of time in searching for me when calls come in from the White Plains office or from outside parties. The final Plan Sheet, of course, will show all items to be discussed in the form of an agenda for each of the meetings, and they will be prioritized. This is a tremendous help in keeping me organized and able to manage my time while in the St. Paul office."

Digesting Mail

Q—"What happens in your office while you are gone?"

A—"The most important thing my secretary does is what we call 'digesting.' We divide our mail into three different classifications: Action (correspondence written directly to me); Mail (copies of correspondence written to someone else on matters of interest to me), and Reading and Routine Correspondence (periodicals, etc.). My secretary will read the action mail and summarize it in two or three sentences. It is interesting that all these memoranda that have to be so vitally sweated over can be digested by a secretary in three or four sentences.

"If I am going to be out of town for a week, on Monday my secretary will mail the digest page to me for receiving on Wednesday wherever I am. If there is anything of a critical nature, I can contact the individual concerned. I can dictate answers or items for discussion or follow-up on a portable recorder and send it back to my secretary, if I am going to be away for a sufficiently long period. When I return to my office, instead of having a great stack of mail to go through, I am fairly well in control. At least 90 percent of it already has been handled, one way or another. Either I have talked to her on the phone, or mailed her a tape or a crossed-out digest page with notes advising things she is to throw away, file, or answer. This way I don't have the problem so many executives face of wondering what is piled up on the desk and when I'm going to get to it. I don't have a crisis. The system is of tremendous benefit in keeping the work flowing during travel time away from the office."

3. Dr. Charles E. Hummel

Tyranny of the Urgent

Dr. Charles Hummel, President, Barrington College, Barrington, Rhode Island, is one of two educators I have known whose emphasis on time management practices marks them as unique in the field. For over 20 years, I have been acquainted with Hummel and his unrelenting efforts toward maximizing his effectiveness in a minimum amount of time. One of the many highlights in his time management style is his recognition of the "tyranny of the urgent." As he puts it:

> When we stop to evaluate, we realize that our dilemma goes deeper than shortage of time; it basically the problem of priorities. Hard work does not hurt us. We all know it is to go full speed for long hours, totally involved in an important task. The resulting weariness is matched by a sense of achievement and joy. Not hard work, but doubt and misgiving produce anxiety as we review a month or a year and become oppressed by the pile of unfinished tasks. We sense uneasily that we may have failed to do the important. The winds of other people's demands have driven us onto a reef of frustration.
>
> We live in constant tension between the urgent and the important. The problem is that the important task rarely must be done today, or even this week. But the urgent task calls for instant action—endless demands, pressure, every hour and day.
>
> The momentary appeal of these tasks seems irresistible and important, and they devour our energy. But in the light of time's perspective, their deceptive prominence fades; with a sense of loss we recall the important tasks pushed aside. We realize we've become slaves to the tyranny of the urgent.

Another of the highlights from this unusual educator's life style is his complete commitment to the practical necessity of setting aside time for planning. Although admitting that it is not always physically possible to take the time set aside, emergencies being what they are, Hummel nevertheless usually sets aside a few minutes daily to plan the next day; a significant time at the end of the week to plan the following week; as much as one day a month to plan the following month; and a long weekend with his administrative team to plan the following year. With his board, of course, he is responsible for maintaining a 5-year plan and, in the case of Barrington, he extends this from time to time to a 10-year look ahead.

Planning Discussions with Team Members

Another element of Hummel's effective time management deals with planning for and following up discussions with his team members. On the Plan Sheet following, Exhibit 8.2 (see page 154), he lists items for discussion with each of his team. This list is, of course, comparable to the similar section of the Economics Laboratory Plan Sheet described in the preceding interview. Hummel's adaptation of the weekly Plan Sheet for categorizing and prioritizing his action items follows in Exhibit 8.3 (see page 155). His analysis of managing versus operating and action versus reaction characteristics enables him to periodically assess these aspects of his management style.

Exhibit 8.2: Barrington College Plan Sheet

Items for Discussion   **Week:** _May 13_

Dean of Faculty:

Priority	Subject
1	Report to board — 5/25
3	New Faculty Appointment
2	Summer Institute
4	Plans for Library

Business Manager:

Priority	Subject
2	Board Financial Statement — 5/25
5	April Computer Printout
8	Sale of Kenyon
1	Cash Flow — 6/30
3	New Secretary — Development
4	Mortgage Negotiation — Early Childhood Center
6	Annual Budget
7	Summer Vacation Schedule

Dean of Students:

1	Exit Interview for Seniors
3	Personnel — Summer Plans
2	Financial Aid Policy Review

Director of Development:

3	Alumni Fund Drive
1	New Secretary
4	Trustee Fund Drive
5	Annual Budget for (Dept)
2	Income Projections for Year

Director of Admissions:

1	Status of Admissions, Applications and Funds
3	New Brochure
4	Advertising Expenditures
2	Letters to New Students

Director of Communications:

1	Final Newsletter — 6/24
3	Budget for Year
4	New Logo for College
5	Mailing List
2	75th Anniversary Plans

Exhibit 8.3: Barrington College Plan Sheet

Week: _May 13_

Morning

    8:30 — Evaluation
    9:00 — Dictation
    9:30 — Phoning
    10:00 — Meetings

Afternoon

    1:30 — Phoning
    2:00 — Meetings
    4:00 — Miscellaneous

Lunches

Mon.	_Faculty Committee_
Tues.	_Rotary_
Wed.	_Student Assn. Officers_
Thurs.	
Fri.	_Trustee Richardson_

Phoning

Mon.	_J. Brown_
	H. Williams
	Dr. Jones
	M. Wilson
	Univ. R.I.
Tues.	_L. Buck_
	T. Mallion
	R. Helms
Wed.	_R. Vicks_
	T. Freiburg
Thurs.	_Univ. Club_
	H. Shaw
Fri.	_New York Visits_
	for May 20-21

Writing

A	_Board Newsletter_
A	_Gift Receipts_
	(key donors)
A	_Foundation Proposal_
	Review
A	_Bulletin Editorial_

Meetings

M	_Administration Council_
M	_Budget Review Comm._
O	_75th Annv. Comm._
O	_Faculty Mtg._
R	_Dean of Students_

General

O	_Mortgage Negotiation_
M	_Annual Budget_
O	_Donor Calls_
O	_Foundation Call_
M	_Five Year Projection_

M - Managing   A - Action
O - Operating   R - Reaction

How the Control Matrix Works

Hummel's method of ensuring follow-up is the "control matrix." He uses it as a device for keeping current with projects being worked on by his staff. His explanation will have a familiar ring for most readers:

> In my administration at the college during the first few years, I found my greatest weakness was the element of supervision. In a conference with one of my department heads I always had an agenda on which I took notes as we made progress indicating items for further action. Usually, I would observe him writing on his own page, but I had no way of knowing what he was recording. When the conference was over, there was often a disparity between his thinking and mine regarding the nature and timing of subsequent action.
>
> Also, I would send out a memorandum requesting information. Days and weeks would go by and unless I thought to ask for it, the information would rarely return. Department heads, like their supervisors, usually apply grease to the wheel which squeaks, so when I squeaked loud enough I would get action on a particular request. However, if for some reason it moved out of my action orbit, nothing would happen until it caught my attention again or a special need arose.
>
> I discussed the matter one day with the chairman of our board. He told me that he solved the problem by using a "control matrix" and sent me a copy. I revised his form to suit my needs, and I've used it regularly ever since. It is so simple that I wondered why I had not thought of it myself and so effective that it amazed me that I had not seen something like it before in my reading, or heard about it in conversation with other managers. Since then I have found that most other managers have the same problem, and I've been happy to share this solution with them. The department head and I both have copies of this matrix. Simultaneously, we write down in the appropriate box the title of the project and date initiated. The upper half of the next box has the action plan with projected date for completion. Let us assume that it is one week from now. When we convene a week later, on that date, he reports the action taken. It may be necessary to have an extension, in which event we make note of this fact and set a new projected date. Or, if that phase is completed and more work remains to be done, a further date is set until such time as the project is completed or terminated.

A partially completed form of the control matrix, Exhibit 8.4 (see page 157) illustrates how it is used.

Exhibit 8.4: Barrington College Control Matrix

Department <u>Development</u>

Project/Date	Action	Action	Action	Action
1. On-Campus Executive Luncheon 1/20	Plan: Finalize program 1/27 Action: Program settled 1/27	P: Invite guests 1/31 A: Roster complete 1/31	P: Luncheon 2/6 A:	P: A:
2. Estate Planning Project 1/27	P: Attend seminar and report 2/9 A: Seminar evaluated	P: Prepare direct mail program 2/23 A: Approved	P: Initiate mailing 2/27 A: Delay in mail room	P: Reschedule mailing 3/3 A:
3. Alumni Telethon 1/27	P: Prepare timetable 2/3 A: Approved	P: Recruitment of volunteers by 2/17 A: Completed 2/17	P: Training seminar 2/24 A:	P: Telethon 3/3-7 A:
4. Parents Fund Appeal Letter 1/27	P: Draft approved 1/29 A: OK	P: Mail 2/3 A:	P: A:	P: A:
5.	P: A:	P: A:	P: A:	P: A:

4. H. Saxon Tate

Time—the Third Resource

H. Saxon Tate was managing director (chief executive officer) of the Canada and Dominion Sugar Company in Montreal when I interviewed him. Later he became chief executive of the parent organization, Tate and Lyle in London, the largest sugar company in the world with some 35,000 employees. Saxon calls time the "third resource." "Yet, unlike the other two recognized resources, capital and labor, time is irreplaceable. If you've wasted it, that's it. Its importance is so fundamental that it must be obvious to any executive who is fighting the battle of the bottom line," he explains.

"Yet isn't it strange," continued Tate, "we're taught about managing all other resources except time? That certainly is the first obstacle. Another is our tendency to do things we like, rather than things we ought to do. Another problem with time is the failure of others to recognize the impact of their actions on your time—insensitivity, I guess you would call it. A fourth obstacle I've encountered in the management of time is the general failure of managers to utilize travel time. For the majority of managers this is dead time. Very few seem to utilize it for essential reading, thinking, or writing. A final obstacle to time management would seem to be the burgeoning reams of meaningless paperwork that are engulfing executive ranks. It requires a real discipline to sort it out and to insist on reducing the flow to the minimum of essentials."

Like most effective executives, Saxon Tate is committed to the concepts of professional management. "The key question in determining a manager's effectiveness," he explained, "is whether he is conducting himself as a manager or an operator. If he is managing, he will consciously devote considerable time and effort to the primary functions of management—planning, organizing, motivating, and controlling."

As Tate sees it, managers do not move into this orbit by natural instinct. It is necessary to expose them to the concepts, discuss them so that the general principles are well understood, and to analyze systematically the appropriate applications of the principles of professional management in a given situation. For example, how many managers have open doors, encourage their subordinates to bring "all your problems to me," only to find themselves making most of the decisions for their subordinates? "The folly of this path," says Tate, "is not obvious to the manager unless he chances to think it all the way through—to ask who is responsible if the decision goes wrong."

The professional manager resolves this problem by applying the decision-level principle (decisions should be made at the lowest possible level consistent with judgment required and available facts). This principle makes it clear that the executive who makes decisions for his subordinates is working below his level and, viewed another way, his subordinates are "getting things done through him" or indeed, managing better than he. It is he who should be managing to get things done through *them*. Like other professional managers, Tate does not propose that the executive *not* be helpful to his team when indeed they may need assistance in thinking through a problem,

158

but rather approach the problem by asking questions designed to aid the subordinate in thinking through the problem and arriving at his or her own conclusions.

The timespan of decisions is a matter of interest to Tate. "The lower you go in the organization," he explained, "the shorter the timespan of the typical decisions. In my case, I make few decisions any more with a time span of less than a year. Formerly, I made them with a time span as short as a week, usually with customer-related problems. I now recognize that operating decisions should be left to your operating officers and the chief executive should refrain from invading that domain."

"The manager must have a philosophy of mistakes," says Tate. "The authoritarian leader does not allow mistakes; as a result he will find that his team will be willing to take fewer and fewer risks because of the hazard involved. It is essential to clear the air in this matter. There should be an area of freedom to err. Subordinates should be backed up when they make mistakes; they should be helped to understand them, and procedures should be discussed to make sure the mistake is not repeated. It should be a learning situation, not a fault-finding one. If the right to exercise delegated authority is withdrawn because of a mistake, there will be a credibility gap in management that will destroy the confidence and morale of the team."

The Organized Ones Versus the Mad-scramblers

Tate believes that every professional manager must be results-oriented. "Performance standards define the conditions that will exist when the key responsibilities are well executed. If results meet planned expectations, I am not concerned how they were achieved. I know they managed their time well. And usually, when results are not met, there is a serious problem in managing time. You can quickly separate your subordinates who are well organized from the mad-scramblers. The former meet deadlines easily. The latter always have difficulty. You must talk with them about their time, how they are using it, and what they are doing that should have been delegated. In the final result, most of the problems get back to ineffective delegation."

Secretary Acts as Carburetor

Tate agrees that a professional secretary is an invaluable member of the team. "She keeps my personal plans, calendar commitments, filters information in a way similar to the function performed by a carburetor in a finely tuned automobile engine. She has her fingers on the pulse of the office and is constantly screening incoming phone calls, drop-in visitors, and mail to determine those things which deserve my priority attention. During periods of my absence, a high degree of judgment is required in making decisions as to what matters require attention and by whom."

5. Paul de Marsano

Paul de Marsano, the chief executive of a multinational corporation, Lacoray, Inc., with headquarters in Switzerland, has lectured extensively, both in Europe and in America, on management principles and their application in his successful organization. He is a strong believer in the team approach to management problems. Since Lacoray has plants in a number of countries, it is important, according to de Marsano, that he be able to communicate effectively with his people in various places and to know in turn what they are thinking and doing. The key to this, in his opinion, is two basic rules which he and his people follow: first, they plan together, and second, they check results and take corrective action together.

When I asked him how he saw time management most directly affecting his operations, he immediately replied that it was in the area of delegation. He described his method of managing before he learned of delegation as spending most of his time chasing people and pushing and persuading them into doing things he thought they ought to be doing. He feared that the frantic pace and long hours would ultimately lead to his collapse. He invested some time at that point in talking with other successful managers about how they succeeded in getting their work done.

At this point he found out about delegation. He discovered at first that delegation filled him with anxiety about whether the responsibilities he had assigned to others would be carried out successfully. He not only worked hard during the day but worried at night about whether things would turn out all right. He found that you just have to take the plunge and assume that there will be some risk involved.

He also immediately discovered that it was important to have a philosophy of mistakes. You should not be afraid of them, for they are the best teacher. If you try to prevent a person from making a mistake, you will likely cause him to feel very insecure. It is likely that he will wind up doing nothing so that he will not run the risk of making any mistakes. As de Marsano put it, he would prefer to have a person make a mistake or two in trying, than make no mistakes because he was not trying. The two questions that he asks employees or managers who have made a mistake are: "What did we learn from this mistake?" and "How can we prevent it from happening again?"

De Marsano assumes equal responsibility along with the person who makes the mistake for any errors committed. He is the one who assigned the responsibility. He feels that it is likewise his obligation to see that the person succeeds in executing it.

The Prima Donna Itch

One of the most interesting concepts discussed by de Marsano is the "prima donna itch," which leads many managers into the trap of wanting to do things themselves rather than to delegate them to others. The need to achieve is a strong motivating force for most managers. If not controlled, this need can lead one to want to be a one-man band, to be the accomplisher of everything in the company. The solution to this problem is for the manager to recognize that the prima donna itch is natural. If he did not have the desire to accomplish, the manager would probably not have reached this position. He should control the itch and seek to become the stage manager rather than the star, thus seeing that each player takes his turn and plays his role to the best of his ability.

The Greatest Time Concern—Ineffective Communication

When asked to mention the greatest time concern in his experience as a manager, de Marsano, without hesitation, cited ineffective communication. "When people do not talk to each other in a way that they can understand, or when they do not listen to what is being said, then a great deal of time will be wasted." De Marsano continued: "Critical plans may be misunderstood, instructions may be confused, decisions may be miscommunicated, or vital feedback information may be misinterpreted."

If, as one sage put it, communication is the glue that holds the organization together, then it is important that it be accurate, adequate, timely, and reliable in every respect. De Marsano points out that it is human nature not to be good listeners. "Every person has his own preconceived ideas and is usually too intent on his own purposes and ideas to listen with care to what others are saying."

Don't Be the "Professional Problem-Solver"

De Marsano raised a very interesting point about the manager who becomes a professional problem-solver for his team. This encourages members of the team to bring their problems to him, and if he is too ready to give the answers, they will become overdependent upon him. The net effect of this is that they will stop trying to solve their own problems because it is easier to go to the boss and ask him for answers.

Rather than provide easy answers, de Marsano recommends asking skillful questions which will lead the person asking these questions to discover the answers himself. The person can then take pride in authorship and will feel that it is his own solution. He will very likely work harder to make it succeed than might have been the case if it were someone else's answer that he was implementing. "There is a real skill," said de Marsano, "in asking penetrating questions that will lead the questioner to his own solutions. For these reasons, even when you know the answer to the question being asked, it is often better *not* to provide it." De Marsano's stock response to a question is another question: "What's *your* recommendation?"

De Marsano's concern for his team includes concern for how they manage their time. He makes it a point to ask: "What's happening? Can I help in any way? What's taking your time? Can't your people help? Why don't you let them try and allow a mistake or two along the way? Don't expect it to come out perfect the first time around."

6. W. R. Harris

"I am a Timewaster"

Rusty Harris, vice-president and general manager, Pacific Western Airlines, Vancouvear, B.C., writes: "It seems to me that a serious attempt to improve the management of one's own time must come with an approach comparable to that used in many associations for self-improvement today—this being the public confession that 'I am a timewaster.' Having thus unburdened yourself, some concrete steps can then be taken to improve the situation.

"In my own case, the confession came two years ago during our first in-company time management seminar. The period since then has demonstrated conclusively the benefits of time management in improving managerial effectiveness. I see a distinct difference in every working day. The most effective changes I've instituted to bring about that improvement are: 1) A better, more effective secretarial relationship. 2) The institution of a quiet hour. 3) The adoption of a modified open-door principle. 4)A curtailment of the number of meetings and more effective use of meetings held."

Importance of the Secretarial Relationship

Harris continues: "Of these four, by far the most important is the relationship with my secretary. She, more than any other individual, including myself, is responsible for the organization of my working day, and consequently the periods of free time allotted for my required reading, required writing, and most importantly, required thinking.

As reported at the beginning of Section 7, "Were I to suggest to any other harried executive one single method of improving his work day, it would be to hire a competent, understanding, and compassionate secretary and then make her such an integral part of his working life that she becomes an extension to his right arm. Your secretary must know not only the operational details, your function in the operation and your responsibilities, but even your likes, dislikes, prejudices, biases, and the way you think, if she is to function most effectively.

"The item listed second in my timesavers was use of the quiet hour. This in itself won't function without the efficient secretary. Telephones continue to ring, department managers continue to have crises during the time set aside for quiet work and thought. But if your secretary is zealous in guarding this private period, it is surprising how seldom one is interrupted. The use of this quiet period for an hour each working day can eliminate or drastically reduce the bulging briefcase carried home each night.

"In common with the quiet hour, the modified open-door principle requires a good secretary to make it effective. The screening and scheduling of callers, the time allotment for appointments, and the interruption of and termination of appointments running much over time are in her hands. The minor interruptions and distractions for no other purpose than to pass the time of day or to set an appointment later cease almost magically, leaving more time for the tasks at hand.

"The number of meetings has been drastically curtailed and the length of the meetings shortened considerably. The use of minutes keeps nonattendees as well as those attending completely in the picture. Tasks are specifically assigned with due dates for completion and a follow-up system to check results. With the introduction of precirculated agenda, meetings may become still more effective. Following the seminar, our daily hour and one-half staff meetings with our top 12 executives were changed to a weekly meeting lasting approximately one hour. The savings in executive man-hours per week represented the difference between 90 hours and 12. Seventy-eight hours saved was of great benefit to the teams of these executives. Previously they had felt that their bosses were in meetings most of the time. They often resented this because of the relative inaccessibility of their bosses. Following the change, of course, their bosses were available much more. Also, the minutes of the staff meetings, which never before had been written, were circulated to all the top management team, who then felt much better informed than they had ever been before. As far as Pacific Western Airlines in general is concerned, I would have to believe that the change in the use of meetings has been the single most influential timesaver.

Measuring Effectiveness of Meeting Time

"Our president, Don Watson, was equally impressed with the improved utilization of meeting time. He agreed to an experiment with Alec Mackenzie in measuring his effectiveness in managing his time spent in meetings.

"The process, which I understand is described in detail elsewhere in this manual, was surprisingly simple and yet very effective. Two criteria were established: total time actually spent compared with time planned, and the extent to which the objectives of the meetings were accomplished.

"Before each meeting, Don estimated the optimum time he felt the meeting should take and identified the precise objectives of the meeting (for example: to inform, to plan, to coordinate, to generate possible solutions, to develop a consensus, or to motivate and persuade). After the meeting, his secretary, Eileen McKenzie, recorded the actual time and compared it to the planned or targeted time. If Don planned that the meeting should take 30 minutes and it actually took 60 minutes, the ratio of planned to actual time would be 30/60 or 50% effectiveness in time spent.

"At the conclusion of the meeting, Eileen also would ask Don to estimate the extent to which he had achieved his objectives. Assuming his objective was to inform his team and that he estimated 100 percent effectiveness, Eileen would double weight this factor, since Don had agreed with Alec that achieving his objectives was twice as important as adhering strictly to time limits. Thus Eileen would calculate Don's effectiveness by adding the figures:

>   50 percent
>   100 percent
> (2) <u>100</u> percent
>   250 percent

and dividing by 3: 83 percent effective.

"Don was understandably pleased to calculate his average effectiveness for three days of meetings at 79 percent. I understand that new criteria have now been suggested by Alec Mackenzie: the views of the meeting participants of the first two criteria (effectiveness of time spent and extent to which objectives were achieved). We believe these additional criteria are a sound addition to the calculation since the participants' views are important and could vary from those of the meeting leader.

"The other most effective timesaver arose from the recent acquisition of additional office space physically separated from the offices now occupied by the corporate officers. This physical move has made effective a long-standing policy which heretofore had never been completely observed—that of delegation of authority to the lowest practical levels. Day-to-day operating problems are now most often solved at supervisory and management levels rather than being carried to the officers, as so often happened when the officer was in close proximity.

"To reduce the time-wasting effect on fatigue, we are also experimenting with the 'gliding time' approach to office hours for accounting and staff. Although the measurement of its impact on fatigue reduction and on efficiency is difficult, a marked improvement in absenteeism and morale is adequate testimony of its worth."

7. Victor Milke

It was almost a year after Victor Milke had attended his first time management seminar in Mexico City. As the technical director of one of the world's largest and most modern bakeries, Central Impulsora, Mexico City, Victor's work was affected directly or indirectly by more than 3,000 of the 5,000 persons in the organization. He had attended the seminar because he needed more time. He was always busy, had great difficulty in finding time to take vacations, and never seemed to get caught up with his work. His acute sense of frustration doubled his determination to find workable solutions to his problems. When I asked him what was happening differently, he responded with obvious relish.

End of Overtime Work

"I don't work overtime any more. The 50–55 hours a week which I always worked before are gone, and I don't take work home. I get much more done in less time. Conservatively, I would say I save an hour a day while getting the same results.

"Perhaps the most important technique I use is the daily work plan. Now I arrange the things to do in order of importance, and I get number one done first. Then I work on number two. It used to be the opposite, you know. I would put off the important things until I could get time to devote to them. What I didn't realize was that getting the little things done was taking all the time I had. Now I leave the unimportant things to the last, and if they don't get done, I don't worry about it. I am much more satisfied, and I can leave my office on time without feeling guilty.

"I suppose one of the most important things that happened as a result of the seminar was my setting goals more clearly and specifically. Never before had I forced myself to write out what I intended to do and to prioritize it. I find that this makes it easy to discard a number of things, delegate a good part of the rest, and concentrate on doing myself those few things that only I can do.

"Another point that has helped me enormously is the 'do it now' concept. I have made a conscious effort to stop procrastinating. When I pick up a matter in the inbox, I attempt to dispose of it while handling it only once. This has made a great difference to my stacked desk, where such matters used to get lost in the pile. In fact, for the 50 managers from Central Impulsora who took the seminar, stacked desk and personal disorganization overall ranked as time concern number 2.

Time Concern Chart on Wall for Visibility

"I have found the concept of visibility extremely helpful. I have your time concern chart on the wall over my desk where it is always visible. I have checked off the 20 which are the most important to me, and a few of them I have double-checked for particular emphasis. As you can see, I have already stated that number one (shifting priorities and procrastinating) as well as the stacked desk has been much improved. My third time concern was crisis management because it seemed as if we lived from crisis to crisis. With our huge electronically controlled ovens, you can appreciate the kinds of problems encountered with mechanical or electronic breakdowns. We now try to anticipate the problems which will generate crises and are finding that we are able to manage them much better. While we agree with Winston Churchill that it is difficult to look into the future further than we can see, we are definitely finding that it is possible to anticipate the most probable crises and to develop contingency plans for minimizing their impact.

"You will be interested to know that the board of directors who attended your first seminar prior to having the remaining managers of the executive team attend it instituted a quiet hour from 8:30 to 9:30 a.m. This has set an excellent example for managers throughout the whole company to follow suit. The benefit in starting such a program at the top is obvious.

"I have closed my door; my secretary takes calls, makes appointments for drop-in visitors unless it is an emergency, and keeps my calendar at her desk.

"Since the entire top and middle management teams attended the seminars, we can see the benefit in having everyone on the same wavelength. We are taking the concepts now to lower levels of first-line supervision and are very convinced that effective time management from top to bottom is mandatory for the success of our company."

8. Gerry Achenbach

As president for more than 20 years of Piggly Wiggly Southern, Vidalia, Georgia, one of the most successful chains of supermarkets in the country, Gerry Achenbach has a number of credits worth citing. First, his track record for an unending series of sales records and profit records is one that would be the envy of almost any senior executive. Second, his commitment to professional management is reflected by his continuous and unrelenting application of the fundamentals of planning, organizing, delegating, motivating, evaluating, and controlling. Consequently, Achenbach has been in steady demand as a speaker before management groups in several countries, including the Presidents Association. Third, his unequivocal commitment to the principles of time management has led to his citation in a number of articles and to writing his own documents summarizing his position in support of these principles.

Sound management and good time management are inseparable in Gerry's opinion. Professional management is aimed at "getting more done in the same amount of time," he says. "We are all equal in the amount of time we have—we are unequal in the effectiveness with which we utilize it. We always have time for things that are important. Not having enough time is an excuse, not a reason."

Need for a Philosophy of Time

One of the highlights of his time management style is his recognizing the needs for a philosophy, of attitude toward time—as he puts it: "a sense of time urgency." Next, he believes the manager should determine his main objectives in life. He should prioritize them, analyze them, eliminate time concerns—those things preventing him from achieving his objectives. Having eliminated the unimportant, you delegate what others can do and reserve to yourself those things only you can do.

Another key element in Gerry's time management practices is his belief in the team. He incorporates the team in all his thinking. He takes a periodic time inventory himself to determine where his time is going and to prevent himself from falling back into his old bad habits. He recommends that his team do likewise. He believes that the team should participate in goal setting. While he does not feel that business is a democracy and that everyone is entitled to an equal vote, he is committed to participative management techniques. You can have a say, you can participate in the process of decision making without demanding an equal vote, as Gerry puts it.

Almost all routine details are delegated to his secretary. An effective secretary, in his opinion, takes an immense load off the executive. While delegation takes time in training and explanation, in coaching, counseling, and follow-up, it is worth every minute it takes. "After all," says Gerry, "you can't do it alone. We define management as getting things done through others." He is one of the few executives in my experience who equates effective delegation with sound training. He believes that managers grow by accepting tough assignments and learning how to do them. If he defers delegation of assignments until he has confidence that his people can do the tasks, he will deprive them of the experience they need to justify his confidence. Effective delegation, followed by support as needed, is the best on-the-job training there is. The do-it-yourself manager takes the easy way out of this dilemma, and he pays for it in the end. He will always be the only one who knows how to do the job, so he will have to do it again and again and again.

Achenbach prioritizes his "to do" list into three categories: "must do," "should do," and "could do." His best thinking time is early in the morning, so he is never without his portable dictating unit. By the time he arrives at work, his best thoughts are captured, his plan for the day is set on tape, and his secretary immediately gets it back to him on a typewritten list.

No Need for Crisis

There is no need for management by crisis, according to Achenbach. The careful setting of goals and objectives, the systematic prioritizing of them, and the development of plans for carrying them out should eliminate or significantly control nearly all crises which seem to afflict executives. Almost all effective executives, he observes, concentrate on anticipating the most serious problems and preventing them from arising. It takes three times the effort to correct a mistake than to do it right the first time. With just a little more thinking, we could get a lot more things done right the first time.

Like de Marsano, Achenbach refuses to make decisions for his subordinates. He will discuss their problems, ask them what alternatives they feel there may be for the solution, and will, when necessary, aid them in thinking through to the solution themselves. He is a strong believer, however, in requiring his managers to make the decisions that he is paying them to make. Otherwise, he could not hold them accountable for making the decisions work.

Given an opportunity, Achenbach will discuss with great insight, humor, and conviction a broad range of subjects within the field of professional management. Among the points of interest he touches are the art of listening, the ways of breaking bad habits (he is a William James supporter), and the three kinds of worry common to most executives. These are 1) worry about things which never happen, 2) worry about things which you can do nothing about, and 3) worry about things which you *can* do something about. One of the best energy conservers is to refuse to worry about the first two. "Energy," says Achenbach, "should be conserved along with time." Fatigue is another of the great time concerns. Finally, he is an advocate of results-oriented management. The key question is whether the objectives have been achieved.

9. Mark Dundon

Our first insight into time management in the medical profession came through discussions with Mark Dundon, administrator, St. Charles Hospital, Toledo, Ohio. Before he was practicing time management principles, Mark's day was pretty much represented by one interruption after another. His own staff, understandably, did the most interrupting. Mark's work was characterized by lack of overall direction and the lack of confidence which goes with not being certain of your objectives. Today, he says that he and his entire team have a definite sense of accomplishment and take real satisfaction in knowing where they are going through planning and measuring how well they are progressing according to plan by periodically evaluating results. They are finding more than enough time to accomplish both by controlling interruptions which had been stealing a great deal of their time.

When I asked Mark to tell me how he and his staff managed the turn-around, he put it this way:

The Key is Planning

"Planning, in my opinion, is the keystone to time management. Daily planning is important, but so are monthly and yearly planning. And tying all three together will bring the greatest degree of success and overall management effectiveness.

"I find that taking a period of time and setting it aside for nothing but planning is most effective. On an annual basis my management team and I go to a quiet location away from the hospital and spend two complete days planning for the year. This sets the overall direction and gives us specific objectives to shoot at for the entire year. By going to a remote location, we eliminate physical interruptions and the distraction of minds by concerns at home and office. We achieve a great deal more because of the greater concentration and improved communication over longer periods of time.

"From this point on we break up the objectives and prioritize them. Then we plan for periods—quarterly and monthly—in which the objectives will need to be accomplished. The planning and scheduling for a month is, of course, more detailed, and we fit tasks of lesser importance around the major objectives.

"We find that progress is achieved toward overall objectives much more systematically. Also smaller things such as file updating, revision of report systems, and reviewing and revising of policies also get done in a much better fashion. Then we ask what is going to get done today. The daily planning is the final step. It's where the action takes place. Having the yearly and monthly plans set, the daily planning is much simpler and fits into the big picture more smoothly. Finally I set priorities on the various items in my daily planner book and start to work.

"The principle that every hour spent in planning saves three to four in execution and gets better results is, if anything, on the conservative side. I would have to say that in our experience in St. Charles Hospital, effective planning has saved us considerably more than four times the amount of time we spend on it. In fact, one example alone will demonstrate that the results of effective planning can far transcend even

168

tremendous savings in time. As you know, we are in the middle of a $23,000,000 addition program. During our two-day planning session, the question arose whether there would be a parking problem. We anticipated that the planners might have overlooked a good solution to this problem, so we laid out a tentative plan. Our suspicion proved correct, and our plan was immediately implemented, less than two months before work on the parking lots was to proceed. We saved hundreds of hours of untold confusion, great frustration, and anger by solving it in advance rather than after the fact. By planning ahead and communicating with employees, physicians, and visitors, we found that there was ready acceptance of the change to a removed parking area. Employees even suggested that they could walk between the parking lot and the building rather than using buses as we had proposed.

"Another indication of the benefits of time management can be seen in the upcoming review by the Joint Commission on Accreditation of Hospitals. In the past 10 years I have gone through five such reviews, and they are typically a torment. By not planning ahead, but doing everything at the last minute, we were always in a panic situation. Right now this review is less than a month away, and our entire team is completely relaxed about it. Plans for preparation for the review were completed long ago, and the great bulk of required actions have already been completed. This is the first time in my life I have felt comfortable going into this review. At the present time I am not even involved. I'm spending no time at all in contrast to all five previous experiences. The principles of anticipation, advanced planning, and delegation have already proved themselves in this experience.

"At the end of a day I take time to review what was accomplished against my daily goals. This gives me an opportunity to assess how much progress was made and what the reasons were for failure to achieve any of them. It also gives me an opportunity to plan ahead as to when I will achieve them and to redouble my determination to do so. After all, one of the benefits of self-discipline in time management is to see in writing those things you intended to do which you did not accomplish. There is a self-correcting tendency not to want to continue putting off things that you have put down in writing you intended to do.

Importance of Controlling Interruptions

"You asked how I found time to do all this planning. The answer is simple — by controlling interruptions. After taking the first time management seminar, I took a one-month time log and discovered that I was wasting eight hours a week in interruptions. I set a goal to reduce this to four hours within three months. I took a check through a one-week time log at the end of 30 days and discovered that I had already reduced the eight hours to two hours. Thus, I had doubled my intended accomplishment in one-third the time. I believe, Alec, that as you would calculate effectiveness, if you can double your goal in one-third of the time, you have achieved a six times multiple of effectiveness in that particular measure of managerial effectiveness. I was very pleased, of course. Six months later, after the refresher course for our entire team on time management, I took another check and discovered that I had further reduced the time lost through interruptions in one week to only 40 minutes. I consider the savings of nearly one and one-half hours per day as a fantastic reward for the effort and money we have invested in the time management program. The principle of interruption control would have to place a close second in my mind behind the principle of planning as the key to effective time management.

"Of course, the team is a critical element in any such program. I determined after taking the time management seminar that my whole team would be involved. Therefore, all 50 of my managers were exposed to a two-day time management seminar and a one-day follow-up session approximately six months later. The benefits of involving the whole team have been incalculable. The whole concept of time management has been enthusiastically embraced by the team. Therefore, when one manager lapses into some old, bad habit, he is very apt to be reminded of it by a colleague. Supervisors and their subordinates have a joint goal for eliminating time concerns. With my team this has produced demonstrable results. There is a sense of enthusiasm and real enjoyment in achieving team goals in the time management area, and the effectiveness has been multiplied many times over what it would be if only I or a few of our managers had attended.

"We have offered a speed reading course for our managers; in all cases they at least doubled their reading speed, and in most cases are reading three and four times faster. With the amount of paper and information passed around in our industry, this has been an enormous timesaver for everyone.

"Of course, we should not overlook the role of the secretary as perhaps the most critical team member in terms of managing executive time. He or she controls three of the greatest interruptors—the telephone, drop-in visitors, and mail. I no longer see the great bulk of junk mail which used to clutter my desk. Our secretarial team which services our administrative suite of offices has developed great skill in handling visitors and telephone calls with diplomacy and tact. I do not know of any instances in which they have unnecessarily offended anyone. They also screen all incoming mail and reroute any matters which should be handled by other persons.

"The only things coming through to my desk today are those which warrant my attention. They are clearly prioritized, indicating which need to be handled first. While my savings in time on interruptions alone approximate one and one-half hours a day, it is the consensus of the team that the time originally lost through interruptions by the whole team has been cut more than in half. Any reasonable approximation of what this would amount to in manager-hours per day would indicate a tremendous savings in managerial time each day through interruption control.

Controlling Meeting Time

"Another aspect of team time management is control of time in meetings. In conferences of supervisors and managers with individual members of their teams, a discovery was made that preset meeting times had a great many advantages. First, they eliminated the necessity of interrupting each other whenever a new idea hit. Lists could be made of items to be discussed. Second, when the conference was held, many points could be discussed — in my case, as many as a dozen points may be discussed at one time with any one person on my team. This is a great timesaver in terms of interruption control. Third, we discovered that the parties to the meeting are much better prepared when they have written down the subject to be discussed. The time for reflection may have sharpened the focus, more facts may have come to mind, and in many cases the item is struck from the agenda as reflection proves that it is not as important as originally thought, or the solution becomes self-evident.

"Staff meetings are typically started late, conducted without an agenda, ramble from subject to subject because no one has come prepared, and usually last longer than planned without reaching satisfactory conclusions. Virtually all of these major problems have been eliminated in our meetings. We have had doctors at medical staff meetings preread all of their reports to themselves, rather than reading them aloud in one meeting. This has improved their grasp of what is going on, and it has saved a half-hour to an hour at each meeting. These staff meetings now are conducted in much less time, with agendas and with a savings in physicians' time which alone would have made the total investment of time and expense in our time management seminar worthwhile many times over.

"It is easy to compare the overall effectiveness of the team approach to time management with the individual approach. A number of hospitals in this area have attended your seminars represented by only a few of their managers. In sessions with their administrators we have often compared results, and it is clearly evident that the benefits of involving the entire team are far superior. A number of the hospitals, after comparing results with me, have made the decision to go ahead with seminars for their entire teams. There simply is no comparison in terms of total results.

"One of the most important results of time management has been the new awareness on everyone's part of the importance of time: his own and the other person's. Everyone is more conscious of interrupting the other person, and that has helped attitudes toward one another. Everything considered, time management has made our hospital and its management team a very effective organization and a better place to work."

10. Bruce Petersen

Bruce Petersen, The Taggart Group, Denver, Colorado, decided to apply many of the principles and techniques of time management to his very successful securities and investment business. In two years' time he doubled his net income while tripling his vacation time with his family from two to six weeks. Among his most valued techniques are: headphones to free both hands during the many hours of daily phone calls, delegation of all routine office activities and many nonroutine tasks to his secretarial staff, and the screening of telephone calls.

Bruce's overall objective was to maintain a balanced life in terms of equitable division of time between his family and his business.

For Further Reading

Mackenzie, Alec. *The Time Trap.* New York: McGraw-Hill Publishing Co., 1975.

Osborn, E. B. *Executive Development Manual.* New York: Economics Laboratory, Inc., September 1959.

Taylor, Harold. *Making Time Work For You: A Guidebook to Effective and Productive Time Management.* New York: Beaufort, 1982.

Webber, Ross A. *Time and Management.* New York: Van Nostrand Reinhold, 1972.

SECTION 9

Measuring Managerial Effectiveness

Measuring Managerial Effectiveness

Over the years managers have measured everything, it seems, but their own effectiveness. Bottom-line profit is usually suggested as the ultimate index of executive productivity. Yet even a casual observer of managerial performance realizes that many factors beyond the manager's control may exert a powerful impact on profit. The least effective manager, having the right product or service at the right time in the right place, may look very good indeed. Yet this may be because he or she is lucky. Profit performance will have resulted in spite of, not because of considerable efforts. A manager might reach or fail to reach goals largely due to uncontrollable circumstances.

Appraising Managers Against Goals

The best method devised to date for evaluating managers' performance is to appraise their performance against verifiable goals. However, goals that are reasonably attainable, yet require "stretch," are not easily set. There is a known tendency for managers to set goals unrealistically high in the initial phases of a program. Later, as goal achievement becomes a standard for appraisal and a determinant of compensation and promotion, a reverse tendency of understating goals to ensure achievement sets in.

Emphasis on short-term goals is common. In practice, goals rarely exceed one year and often are quarterly or less. Thus, long-range plans may be ignored or even undermined. Where job rotation is practiced this tendency toward short-range goal emphasis may be accentuated. The manager who knows he is not likely to be in the same position next year will understandably take greater interest in achieving short-range objectives.

Appraising Managers as Managers

The landmark work on appraising managers *as managers* was written by Koontz.* He grants that certain nonmangerial duties are undertaken at every level. However, the primary purpose for which a manager is usually hired and against which he should be measured is his performance as a manager and not his work as an engineer, accountant, or salesperson. He concludes that the effective appraisal program, therefore, must weigh both *performance in accomplishing managerial goals* and

---

* Koontz, Harold, *Appraising Managers as Managers*, New York: McGraw Hill Publishing Co., 1971.

performance as a manager in planning, organizing, staffing, directing, and controlling.

Koontz observes that a number of companies have attempted to appraise managers as managers, but found it difficult. The standards thus far have seemed too broad and too susceptible to general and subjective judgment. Koontz recommends using the basic principles of management as standards. Even though they are general benchmarks and will require a measure of subjective judgment by the evaluator, they are much more meaningful than the broad questions generally used relating to work habits, integrity, cooperation, judgment, intelligence, and loyalty.

Koontz proposes 73 questions for rating under the managerial functions of planning, organizing, staffing, directing, and controlling.

Typical of the questions posed by Koontz are the following:

Planning	**Rating**
1.m Does he set for his departmental unit both short-term and long-term goals in verifiable terms (either quantitative or qualitative) that are related in a positive way to those of his superior and his company?	(1-5) _____

Organizing

1. Does the organization structure under his control reflect major result areas? _____

The rating classification follows:

      5.0: *Superior*: a standard of performance which could not be improved under any circumstances or conditions known to the rater.

4.0 or 4.5: *Excellent*: a standard of performance which leaves little of any consequence to be desired.

3.0 or 3.5: *Good*: a standard of performance above the average and meeting all normal requirements of the position.

2.0 or 2.5: *Average*: a standard of performance regarded as average for the position involved and the people available.

1.0 or 1.5: *Fair*: a standard of performance below the normal requirements of the position but one that may be regarded as marginally or temporarily acceptable.

      0.0: *Inadequate*: a standard of performance regarded as unacceptable for the position involved.

        X: Not applicable to the position.

        N: Do not know accurately enough for rating.

A Managerial Audit

Mackenzie's Management Process Chart,* Exhibit 9.1 (see page 177), was first proposed as the basis of a "managerial effectiveness audit."† A systematic assessment of

---

* Mackenzie, R. Alec, and Emery, James H., "The Management Process," 1982.

† Mackenzie, R. Alec. M.E.M.0. 50, "Measuring Your Leadership Skills"—individual module for auditing managerial skills.

present levels of effectiveness on a 1-to-10 scale is completed for every function and activity of management deemed significant for the particular organization. These ratings are connected with a solid line showing a profile of present estimates of effectiveness. After "present" levels of effectiveness are completed, "desired" levels are plotted. Priorities are set for each area, and a development program geared to this assessment of executive effectiveness follows. The resulting "Management Audit" is shown in Exhibit 9.2 (see page 180).

Ray Watson, in an unpublished doctoral dissertation,* has proposed and sucessfully measured improvements in managerial effectiveness in 40 categories essentially combining those suggested by Koontz and Mackenzie.

Watson constructs a "Profile of Management Characteristics" which requires a determination of present level of effectiveness as well as a goal in each of the 40 categories. Each characteristic is rated on the basis of five categories: Limited, Moderate, A Great Deal, Exceptional, Extraordinary. (See Exhibit 9.3, page 181.)

A major finding of Watson's study was that communication effectiveness of a management education program may be measured in terms of changes in managerial performance in complex organizations. The data suggest that a significant improvement was made and was sustained after eight months in the on-the-job performance of the specific managerial functions defined for the study, as shown in the superiors' ratings. There was a 20.6 percent average increase in performance ratings of the experimental group compared to a 4.5 percent average increase by the control group according to the superiors' ratings. Referring to the Management Audit, Exhibit 9.2, it seems apparent that Watson's findings could be graphically represented by a "Beginning Level" and a "Level after Eight Months."

Koontz concludes his article on managerial appraisal by observing that it probably is the weakest link of the entire chain of the management process. He suggests that while his proposals may not completely solve the problem, they are believed to be important steps in the right direction. The thrust of this section is to propose one such additional step—the measurement and control of the factors identified by managers as their principal obstacles to managerial effectiveness, i.e., time concerns.

Need for More Effective Measurements

Executive time has long been recognized as one of the most critical resources of the manager. A survey of over 1,200 executives, nearly one-half of them presidents, concluded that executive productivity is a major concern and that a serious study of it is needed. In an analysis of overseas investment decisions, the most important difference between the experience of some 35 United States companies and the models of decision making is the failure of the models to recognize that executive time is the scarcest resource. A study of the failures of corporate mergers notes that the lack

---

* Watson, James Ray, "Communication Effectiveness in University Executive Management Programs: A Field Experiment," Doctoral Thesis, 1973.

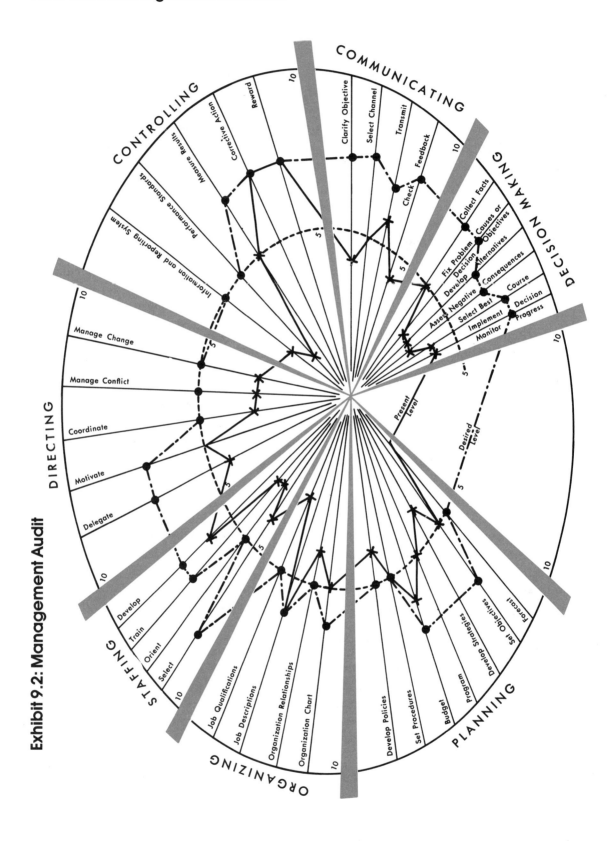

New Time Management Methods

Exhibit 9.2: Management Audit

COMMUNICATING

DECISION MAKING

CONTROLLING

Reward
Corrective Action
Measure Results
Performance Standards
Information and Reporting System

Clarity Objective
Select Channel
Transmit
Check
Feedback

Collect Facts
Fix Problem Causes or Decision Objectives
Develop Alternatives
Assess Negative Consequences
Select Best Course
Implement Decision
Monitor Progress

Present Level

Desired Level

DIRECTING

Manage Change
Manage Conflict
Coordinate
Motivate
Delegate

Develop
Train
Orient
Select
Job Qualifications
Job Descriptions
Organization Relationships
Organization Chart

Develop Policies
Set Procedures
Budget
Program
Develop Strategies
Set Objectives
Forecast

STAFFING

ORGANIZING

PLANNING

180

Measuring Managerial Effectiveness

Exhibit 9.3: Profile of Management Characteristics

Made by Immediate Superior for:

Title or Position _____

Name of Individual _____

Company Name _____

The purpose of this form is to get your opinion on the relative importance of various kinds of activities and functions that may or may not relate to the above position. Position requirements vary so greatly that different skills are needed in varying degrees. The only interest here is to understand the present requirements and the present performance for the above position as you know them at the present time.

Instructions:

1. On the line provided for each management variable (item), please place an "n" at the point which, in your experience, describes the degree of management skill which is now used in the performance of this job.

2. In addition, please place a "g" on each line at the point which, in your experience, describes the ideal goal for the degree of management skill which you feel is needed for a high-level performance of this job.

Example:

| | A Great | Excep- | Extra- |
| Delegate: Assign responsibility and exact accountability for results | Limited Moderate | Deal tional | ordinary |

James Ray Watson, "Communication Effectiveness in University Executive Management Programs: A Field Experiment," Doctoral Thesis, 1973.

of appreciation of the new demands on the time of executives in the acquiring company is one of the primary causes of these failures. Careful observers of the executive scene propose that minimization of demands on executive time deserves almost as much attention as businesspeople devote to profit maximization. In many decisions, return on time can be seen to provide a more useful criterion for action than return on capital invested. Time, not money, may be a company's most critical resource. Companies may very well be wise in making capital decisions on the basis of the return on the investment of executive time. It follows that organizations should make a practice of assigning staff the responsibility of helping executives make the best use of their time.

The critical need for more effective measures of managerial performance have nowhere been more evident than in a seminar on time management for 20 vice-presidents of one of the country's leading banks. The group was asked if they were satisfied with their criteria for measuring the effectiveness of the management teams of the various institutions and enterprises to which they had loaned funds. The group responded in the negative. They were then asked if they could think of any other factor which would have a greater impact on the future success of their own organization. Again their response was negative. Reflecting upon that brief exchange, one of the group later observed: "It's incredible that so little attention has been paid to developing measurements for so critical a factor in our future."

Criteria for Measuring Managerial Effectiveness

The time concerns most commonly cited by managers clearly qualify as key factors in the measurement of managerial effectiveness. For these are the factors that managers themselves say are preventing them from being as effective as they would like. It therefore seems logical to develop criteria with which to measure the degree to which these factors are operating in the daily lives of managers. In Exhibit 6.1 are listed some of the criteria by which the operative impact of the top seven of these time concerns can be measured. Some of the criteria may be identified simply by their existence (written objectives, priorities, and deadlines). Others will be identifiable by their incidence as recorded in a weekly time log (interruptions by telephone and drop-in visitors, doing a task which could have been delegated, agreeing to a request to which you should have said "No"). Either by simple conversion to weights or by arbitrary decision, percentage rates of effectiveness called "effectiveness quotients" can be determined, from which relative progress in improving managerial effectiveness can be measured.

A manager may choose to assign different weights to these criteria, depending upon which factors deemed most important at a given time. Arbitrary and subjective decisions may be used in assessing a weight. Assuming, however, that the same approach is used a second time around, one can measure relative (as opposed to absolute) improvement. Thus, even in the more difficult areas to measure, we are laying a baseline for measuring improved performance.

182

Measuring Managerial Effectiveness

Let's assume the manager has listed his/her top five time concerns or his/her group's top five time concerns as follows:

1. Interruptions
2. Crises
3. Lack of objectives, priorities, and deadlines
4. Ineffective delegation
5. Meetings

In the following Exhibits 9.4 to 9.8, a method is shown for calculating effectiveness quotients for each of these time concerns. For each time concern, several measurable elements or criteria are listed and each is assigned a varying number of points, depending on relative priority. A manager may adjust these priority weights as desired so long as the total remains 100.

For each criterion the manager rates himself or herself against the total. The total of these ratings equals the control or effectiveness quotient for that time concern. The resulting effectiveness quotients are entered according to the instructions at the bottom of each page, in the appropriate blanks of Exhibits 9.4 to 9.8 (see pages 184-188). Exhibit 9.9, page 189, yields the manager's overall effectiveness in controlling his/her top five time concerns at any given time. The quotients may be plotted on the graph shown in Exhibit 9.10, page 190. By connecting the points of the graph for each period plotted, a Management Effectiveness Profile is developed (see Figure 9.11, page 191). The profiles of several periods will indicate a manager's growth pattern in controlling his/her major time concerns, and thereby increasing managerial effectiveness.

Exhibit 9.4: Interruption Control Quotient

	Maximum Score	Your Rating
A. Strategy for controlling interruptions as evidenced by:		
1. List of principal interruptions in order of priority determined by frequency and seriousness. (Examples: telephone interruptions, drop-in visitors, unnecessary meetings, unscheduled meetings, mechanical breakdowns, human errors, noise, visual distractions, excessive paperwork, red tape, etc.)	10	_____
2. Written plan to anticipate, minimize, divert, or eliminate each.	10	_____
B. Effectiveness in resisting interruptions during measured period as evidenced by:		
1. Percent of potential interruptions anticipated, minimized, diverted, or eliminated.	30	_____
2. Total time spent distracted or diverted from intended tasks. (The shorter the time, the higher the score.)	10	_____
3. Beneficial, though unintended, results of interruption.	10	_____
C. Effectiveness of recovering from interruptions during measured period as evidenced by speed of recovery to original task and degree to which loss of continuity was minimized.	20	_____
D. Effectiveness of secretary or assistant in handling or screening as evidenced by percent of positive results achieved above without action by you.	10	_____
	100	( ) I.C.Q.

To compute your Interruption Control Quotient, take a one-week Time Log (Exhibit 3.1) taking particular care to record every interruption. Have your secretary or assistant do the same, noting in addition potential interruptions for you which were anticipated, minimized, diverted, or eliminated. Rate yourself on the seven criteria against the total points shown for each. Total the points for your Interruption Control Quotient.

Enter your Interruption Control Quotient on line 1a, Exhibit 9.9. Also enter your I.C.Q. on line 1, Exhibit 9.10.

Exhibit 9.5: Crisis Control Quotient

	Maximum Score	Your Rating
A. Strategy for crisis control evidenced by:		
1. List of types of crises in order of priority determined by frequency and seriousness. (Examples: mechanical failures, absenteeism, customer emergency, strike, loss of key manager, etc.)	10	_____
2. Written plan to anticipate, minimize, delay, or eliminate negative consequences of each. (Examples: contingency plan for rapid mobilization of resources; assessment of true importance and urgency of crisis; limitation of response to actual need; delegation)	10	_____
B. Percent of potential crises anticipated and avoided or effectively minimized.	60	_____
C. Number of cases of overreaction and relative waste of resources therein. (The lower the number and waste of resources, including time, the higher the score.)	10	_____
D. Effectiveness of secretary or assistant in anticipating, minimizing, delaying, or eliminating crises.	10	_____
Total:	100	( )C.C.Q.

To compute your Crisis Control Quotient, take a one-week Time Log (Exhibit 3.1) taking particular care to record every crisis and near-crisis. (A crisis may be defined as an unexpected interruption from the normal course of events of major impact necessitating immediate response.) Have your secretary/assistant do the same, noting in addition those near-crises which were averted. Rate yourself and your secretary/assistant against the maximum score for each criterion. Total the points for your Crisis Control Quotient.

Enter your Crisis Control Quotient on line 1b in Exhibit 9.9.

Record this rating by placing an "x" on the graph in Exhibit 9.10 on line 2 (Crises).

Exhibit 9.6: Achievement of Objectives Quotient

	Maximum Score	Your Rating
A. Long-range objectives as evidenced by:		
1. Written list of corporate or department objectives of one year or more for which manager assumes partial or full responsibility.	10	_____
2. Priorities and deadlines for each to indicate relative importance and date for completion.	10	_____
3. Written plans with interim goals and intermediate deadlines for each long-range objective.	10	_____
4. Percent of planned progress toward all objectives in measured period.	20	17

Example: Measuring Progress Toward Objectives

Objectives	Relative Weight	Extent Achieved	% Objectives Achieved
a. Project X	30%	1	30
b. Sales Report	30%	1	30
c. Salary Review	20%	0.8	16
d. Murray Case	10%	0.6	06
e. Job Description	10%	0.4	04
	100%		86%

Calculation: $\dfrac{86}{100} = \dfrac{X}{20}$ $X = \dfrac{86 \times 20}{100}$ $X = 17$

	Maximum Score	Your Rating
B. Short-range goals as evidenced by:		
1. Written daily, weekly, and monthly objectives, priorities, and deadlines.	20	_____
2. Percent of planned progress toward all daily, weekly, and monthly objectives during measured period.	30	_____
	100 ( ) A.O.Q.	

To compute your Achievement of Objectives Quotient, take a one-week Time Log (Exhibit 3.1) taking care to set daily and weekly goals. In setting relative weights, see that total equals 100%. In determining extent achieved, 1 equals total accomplishment. Rate yourself on all criteria against the maximum score for each. Total your points for your Achievement of Objectives Quotient.

Enter your Achievement of Objectives Quotient on line 1c in Exhibit 9.9.

Record this rating by placing an "x" on the graph in Exhibit 9.10 on line 3.

Exhibit 9.7: Delegation Effectiveness Quotient

	Maximum Score	Your Rating
A. Delegation framework evidenced by existence of:		
1. Up-to-date organization chart.	10	_____
2. Up-to-date job description including key responsibilities and degree of authority for each.	10	_____
B. Delegation effectiveness evidenced by:		
1. Ratio of actual to potential delegations during logged period. (How many tasks were actually delegated compared with the number which could have been delegated?)	40	_____
2. Ratio of refusals to get involved unnecessarily in detail to the number of opportunities to do so.	20	_____
3. Ratio of refusals of direct but inappropriate requests for information, opinion, suggestions, or decisions to the total number of such requests by subordinates (upward delegation).	20	_____
	100	( )D.E.Q.

To compute your Delegation Effectiveness Quotient:

1. Review "Maximum Score" column to determine your agreement. Revise, if desirable, ensuring that total remains 100.

2. Take a one-week Time Log (Exhibit 3.1) noting carefully all potential delegation situations. Have your secretary or assistant do the same, making similar observations to check your accuracy and detail of observation.

3. Rate yourself against the maximum on each of the five criteria.

4. Total the ratings for your Delegation Effectiveness Quotient.

Enter Your Delegation Effectiveness Quotient on line 1d in Exhibit 9.9.

Record this rating by placing an "x" on the graph in Exhibit 9.10 on line 4 (Delegation).

Exhibit 9.8: Meeting Effectiveness Quotient

	Maximum Score	Your Rating

A. Effectiveness in utilizing time.
   1. Estimate the optimum time you believe the meeting ought to take, assuming it is well planned and well run. (Optimum time-_____ minutes.)
   2. Record the actual time spent in the meeting. (Actual time-_____ minutes.)
   3. Divide optimum time (1) by actual time (2).

   $$\frac{\text{Optimum time (\ \ )}}{\text{Actual time (\ \ )}} = \underline{\hspace{1cm}} \% \text{ effectiveness.}$$

   4. Calculate your rating. _____% x 20. Insert to right.　　　　20　　_____

B. Effectiveness in achieving objectives of meeting.
   1. Identify intended objectives in meeting.
      a. to be seen ( )
      b. to contribute ( )
      c. to inform or explain ( )
      d. to generate or explore alternatives ( )
      e. to coordinate ( )
      f. to motivate or persuade ( )
      g. to review and agree, achieve consensus ( )
   2. To what extent did you achieve your objectives? (%)
   3. Calculate self-rating. _____% x 30. Insert to right.　　　　30　　_____

C. Participants' collective view of effectiveness of time utilization and extent of objectives achieved.
   1. Collect estimates from each participant of optimum time for meeting. Calculate from ratio of optimum to actual time spent the self-rating for each participant. Total these ratings and take their average by dividing by total number of participants. Multiply this average % by 20 and insert to the right.　　　　20　　_____
   2. Collect estimates from each participant of extent to which objectives for meeting were understood and achieved. Total these estimates and take average. Multiply average % by 30 and insert to right.　　　　30　　_____

　　　　　　　　　　　　　　　　　　　　　　　　　　　　　　100 ( ) M.E.Q.

To calculate Meeting Effectiveness Quotient: Add the Self-Ratings.

Enter your Meeting Effectiveness Quotient on line 1e in Exhibit 9.9.

Record this rating by placing an ''x'' on the graph in Exhibit 9.10 on line 5 (Meetings).

Exhibit 9.9: Calculation of Managerial Effectiveness

To calculate your overall effectiveness in managing the five time concerns shown, enter your self-rating for each as calculated on the correponding exhibits, total the points, and divide by 5 as shown.

1. Enter your 5 Effectiveness Quotients:
   a. Interruption Control Quotient   (Exhibit 9.4) _____
   b. Crisis Control Quotient   (Exhibit 9.5) _____
   c. Achievement of Objectives Quotient   (Exhibit 9.6) _____
   d. Delegation Effectiveness Quotient   (Exhibit 9.7) _____
   e. Meeting Effectiveness Quotient   (Exhibit 9.8) _____

2. Total sum of 5 quotients: Total   _____

3. Divide total quotient by 5 to obtain your average managerial effectiveness in controlling your top five time concerns.

$$\frac{(\quad) \text{ Total}}{5} = \underline{\quad}\%$$

Exhibit 9.10: Managerial Effectiveness Profile

Time Concerns	Relative Weight	10% 20% 30% 40% 50% 60% 70% 80% 90% 100%
1. Interruptions		
2. Crises		
3. Lack objectives, priorities, deadlines		
4. Delegation		
5. Meetings		

(1) To plot your growth in ability to control your chief time concerns, record your effectiveness quotients from Exhibit 9.9 by placing an "x" on the appropriate line above.

(2) When all five quotients are recorded, connect the points and designate that profile by a date as shown in the following exhibit.

(3) To calculate your average overall effectiveness, total the five quotients and divide by 5.

(4) Successive profiles are plotted in Exhibit 9.11 to demonstrate the manner in which continuous improvement can be plotted.

Exhibit 9.11: Example of Successive Managerial Effectiveness Profiles

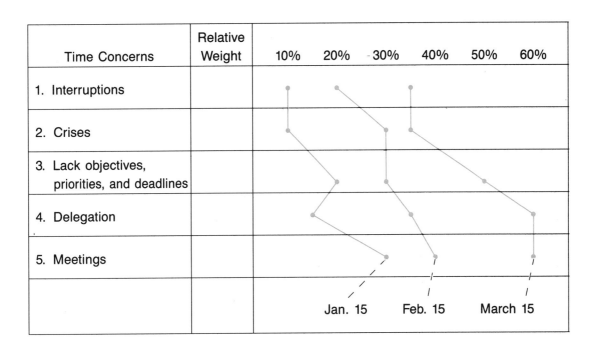

Time Concerns	Relative Weight	10%	20%	30%	40%	50%	60%
1. Interruptions							
2. Crises							
3. Lack objectives, priorities, and deadlines							
4. Delegation							
5. Meetings							
		Jan. 15		Feb. 15		March 15	

Calculation of monthly gains in overall managerial effectiveness

		Quotient	Quotient	Quotient
1. Interruption control	.30	x .10 = .03	x .20 = .06	x .35 = .105
2. Crisis control	.25	x .10 = .025	x .30 = .075	x .35 = .0875
3. Objectives control	.20	x .20 = .04	x .30 = .06	x .50 = .100
4. Delegation control	.15	x .15 = .0225	x .35 = .0515	x .60 = .090
5. Meetings control	.10	x .30 = .03	x .40 = .04	x .60 = .060
	Average effectiveness = 14.75%		28.65%	44.25%

Absolute gain in managerial effectiveness 44.25 - 14.75 = 29.5%
Relative gain in managerial effectiveness 29.5 ÷ 14.75 = 200%

For Further Reading

Albrecht, Karl. *Successful Management by Objectives*. Englewood Cliffs, NJ: Prentice Hall, 1978.

Koontz, Harold. *Appraising Managers as Managers*. New York: McGraw-Hill, 1971.

Odiorne, George S. *Management and the Activity Trap*. New York: Harper & Row, 1974.

SECTION 10

Time Management in Education

Time Management in Education

The interest of educational adminstrators in time management is evident across this country and in Canada. From management courses for college presidents to leadership skills workshops for elementary and secondary school administrators, the subject of time management arises again and again as one of paramount concern. A Connecticut public school superintendent was asked by a radio station interviewer during such a workshop why he was holding it for his administrative staff. He responded that education was, in a sense, really big business and that many of the basic principles of management which had been helpful in industry were equally applicable to the effective running of educational institutions. National and regional associations as well as state departments of education and city school systems are running seminars on the general subject of managerial effectiveness and including specifically the subject of management of time.

The "Educator Syndrome"

Despite the growing acceptance of management principles among educational adminstrators, many consider themselves educators first, and managers or administrators second.

The principal of a large New York high school observed that public school administrators do not usually view themselves as executives or managers and do not like to be viewed as generalists. It has been popular for principals to consider themselves as master teachers who have been promoted to positions where they can serve as curriculum specialists and instructional leaders. He pointed out: "In administrative circles it has been much more prestigious to describe oneself as a curriculum innovator than to admit to being an executive. Preparation for administation involves course work in such areas as curriculum, supervision, and building administration. Seldom is a principal exposed to the study of such vital managerial skills as office management, time management, delegation, planning one's work, and setting priorities for daily operation."

Always and Instantly Accessible

School principals frequently express the sentiment that education is different; that it is not amenable to the application of good management procedures. Of course, there are certain characteristics in education that commonly result in singular problems of management. For example, in a school the consumers are in the building and the feedback on administrative decisions is often direct and immediate. A carelessly formulated position can boomerang into a major confrontation before the words of the principal die out.

It is the expectation of many constitutents that the principal be always and instantly accessible. Particularly when a parent or student is irate, he or she expects to have immediate access to the principal by telephone or in person. In many districts it is commonplace for an aggrieved party to call the superintendent's office if he or she fails to gain the ear of the principal at once. Perhaps in overreaction to this demand, many principals proudly proclaim the open-door policy. A modified open-door policy recognizes the need from time to time for an educational administrator to have blocks of time set aside for uninterrupted concentration on major projects.

The expectation that the principal should see all, hear all, and know all is one of the unusual factors in the educational environment. To live up to this expectation in a school system of moderate to large size would be physically impossible. Yet the demands are such that the principal often has to discuss fast-breaking events before the public with little notice. If he pleads ignorance, he is viewed as not being sufficiently aware to manage properly. The more details he has at his instant command, the sharper he appears to his constituents. Any management analyst, however, would observe that such a requirement would make it virtually impossible for the principal ever to delegate any responsibility. The demands themselves make it essential for the principal to arm himself with the knowledge of managerial skills and the ability to carry them out effectively on a daily basis if systemwide objectives are to be accomplished.

The preference of many school administrators for the term "educator" rather than "manager" or "administrator" is not surprising when the boards of education and many of the administrators themselves have been slow to recognize the many ways in which the operation of school systems is, in fact, big business. Dr. John Perko, one-time assistant superintendent for business affairs of the San Bernadino Public Schools, was charged with all of the business and financial matters for a system with 60 schools. The salaries, supplies, buses, food for cafeterias, books, and materials—to say nothing of the planning necessary for future facilities—represented a level of responsibility many managers in industry would be ill-equipped to handle. Perko implemented a system for managing by objectives and was in demand as a speaker and counselor at management workshops for educational administrators. He was one example of many pointing toward the developing awareness of the importance of management principles in the field of education. Another is the emphasis on leadership skills, management practices in general, and time management in particular in the convention and workshop programs of the numerous national, regional, and state associations of educational administrators.

New and Unrelenting Pressures

Concern of taxpayers over budgets and the difficulty of measuring results have sharpened the focus of attention on management practices. Public pressure on boards of education has had a similar effect. The demands of teachers and of students for a voice in determining decisions has had a direct effect on the time management of many school and college administrators. A share in the governance of colleges and universities and participation in the decisions of school boards and school administrations have been demanded by educators through newspapers of the institutions, local press, teachers' unions; and by students appearing individually at local school board sessions without invitation in some cases, and in others sitting as participating members of the board.

Today's chief school administrators must respond to intense and unrelenting pressure on a broad front. The average tenure of school superintendents is now less than four years. No wonder. What folly for society to make so critical a position so untenable!

A Unique Time Concern

Time concerns appearing in the lists compiled by educational administrators generally are the same as those of all other managers. One time concern that we do not find on the lists of other groups is "Enhancing the democratic process." Faculty, students, and even staff members interpret "democratic" to mean "equal vote" and demand it as a right. Unprepared for this new demand, many chief school administrators and college presidents seem to have failed to distinguish between the right to share in the decision-making process and in the deciding itself. The former implies representation, the latter equal voting rights. The former can lead to orderly process involving real participation and a voice in the affairs of the institution. The latter, as many administrators have discovered, can lead to virtual anarchy; or at least, interminable delays and much wasted time in the decision-making process.

Accountability for decisions must rest with those making them. Boards hold the chief school administrator accountable, and it is he who should make the critical decisions. Once the responsibility for decision is settled, many avenues should be explored for an orderly process of communicating the views and the recommendations of those who will be affected by the decisions.

Time Profile of Six College Presidents and Their Teams

A consortium of six college presidents and their administrative staffs combined their estimates on time utilization in a composite time profile of a college president and his staff as shown in Exhibit 10.1. This profile, shown first in *The Time Trap*, is repeated here because of its implications for advanced study of time management patterns. Electronic equipment for collecting and collating large amounts of data now make this model extremely useful for patterning and assessing time utilization behavior not accessible heretofore.

Beginning at the center with the inner band of the president's profile, presidents apportioned their time to "managerial" functions as follows:

Planning—25 percent
Organizing—10 percent
Staffing—15 percent
Directing—20 percent
Controlling—30 percent

For the activities involved in each of these managerial functions, see Exhibit 9.1: The Management Process. The presidents felt that their relative allocation of time to these functions would depend on several factors including: 1) the given situation (or emergency) at the particular time; 2) the years of experience of the president and his years in the present job; 3) the time of year such as the planning and budgeting period, annual fund drive, opening of school, closing of school, etc. The figures derived were derived from estimates based on the six presidents' time logs.

The outer band of the presidents' profile indicates the amount of time they estimate was allocated to each of the "operational" functions as follows:

Development and external affairs—70 percent
Student affairs—8 percent
Academic affairs—14 percent
Business affairs—8 percent

The 70 percent of their time allocated to development and external affairs reflected the extreme financial pressures on small, private colleges which demand inordinate amounts of the chief executive's time.

The outer circles represent profiles of the administrative officers of the college president's team. Although there was a variance of titles, the four operational areas seemed fairly uniform: development, academic affairs, business affairs, and student affairs. The time allocations represented in these profiles were derived by combining two composite profiles—that of the group of administrative officers of the six colleges charged with that particular responsibility with respect to how they thought their time should be allocated ideally, and the composite views of their presidents as to how they thought the time of these officers ought to be spent. There were a few interesting variances between the views of the two groups. For example, the development directors felt they should be spending more time in planning for institutional advancement and less time in fund raising than did their presidents. In general, however, there was a great similarity between the two profiles. (The reader may wish to refer to the Time Profile of a President's Team, Exhibit 2.4, for comparison of an industrial model with this model for educators.)

Time Concerns of College Presidents

A group of presidents of small colleges attending a Management Institute for College Presidents individually logged their time for one week and listed their top time concerns in order of priority. Their time concerns were weighted by priority and compiled as follows:

	Time Concern	Weight
1.	Scheduled meetings	36
2.	Unscheduled meetings	34½
3.	Enhancing the democratic process	34
4.	Lack of priorities	31
5.	Failure to delegate successfully	30
6.	Unavailability of people	28
7.	Interruptions	28
8.	Junk mail	24
9.	Lack of planning	19
10.	Outside (civic) demands	17
11.	Poor filing system (information retrieval)	16
12.	Fatigue	15½
13.	Procrastination	15
14.	Phone calls	13
15.	Lack of procedures for routine matters	12
16	Questionnaires	12

Note: The method of compiling weights was to have each president list his top five time concerns. Each time concern was weighted, five points for number 1, four points for number 2, etc. Then the ranking assigned to each time concern was determined by total weight.

The list of time concerns reveals the strong views held by college presidents about the time they spend in meetings, both unscheduled as well as scheduled. A connection between meetings and the No. 3 time concern (Enhancing the democratic process) is evident. Time wasted in scheduled meetings should be subject to the control of skilled conference leadership. Time wasted in unscheduled meetings may be a partial reflection of management by crisis. The tendency to respond to the "urgent" while neglecting the "important" may also be a factor. Calm reflection after a crisis leads many administrators to admit that an immediate response might better have been withheld. In retrospect it often appears that what seemed urgent at the time was not really important in the long run. Nevertheless the diversion of attention and energy to assumed crises is a daily occurrence for most. Consequently, we are often postponing action on more important matters.

New Time Management Methods

Exhibit 10.1: A Time Profile of Six College Presidents and Their Teams

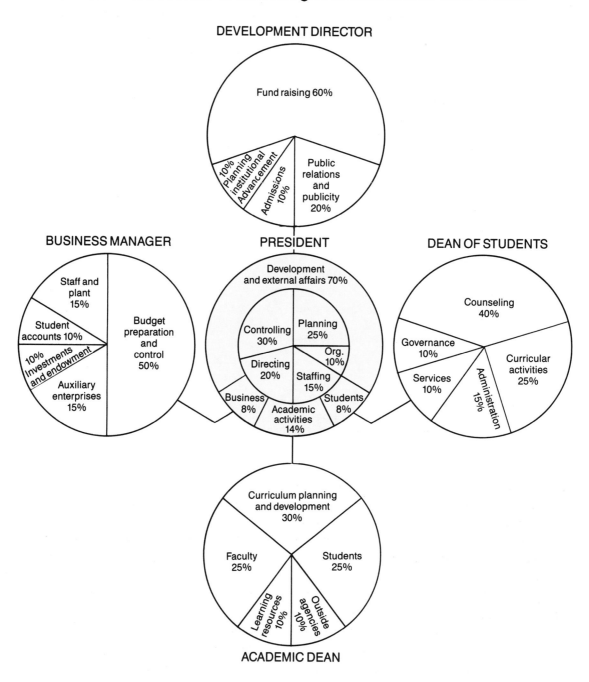

200

Time Concerns of Public School Administrators

For comparison purposes a list of the top time concerns of 375 public school administrators follows. The group consists of approximately one-half superintendents and principals and one-half assistants and central office administrators who attended seven different seminars on time management.

Time Concern	Weight
1. Telephone interruptions	516
2. Ineffective delegation	505
3. Drop-in visitors	416
4. Meetings	300
5. Crisis management/shifting priorities	300
6. Lack objectives, priorities, daily plan	223
7. Stacked desk/personal disorganization	189
8. Indecision/procrastination	128
9. Attempting too much at once/unrealistic time estimates	74
10. Inability to say "No"	72
11. Confused responsibility & authority	70
12. Over/unclear/undercommunication	56
13. Leaving tasks unfinished	29
14. Mail, paperwork, reports	24

The only difference between their list and that of any other group of managers is that delegation ranks higher than usual. However, this is common among educational administrators who typically will not have thought a great deal about professional management in general or the complexities of delegation in particular.

"Time Banks" for Uninterrupted Concentration

Dr. Kenneth Dunn, former superintendent and nationally known author and lecturer, took a deep interest in time management. Not only did he expose his administrative staff to the concepts of time management and leadership skills, but he also personally lectured on the subject of time management for students and parents.

Dunn observed that involvement in the political realities of the community poses special time management problems for the school administrator and that the power of interruptions to destroy one's effectiveness is unequalled. Recognizing that interruptions increase in frequency and intensity as involvement in community affairs increases, Dunn predicted that the effective school administrator would be forced to analyze his situation carefully. He begins with a log of his activities to determine where his time is actually going. He then develops a game plan to set aside "time banks" for periods of uninterrupted concentration, while remaining sensitive to the insistent demands on his time. He must stay flexible so that he can accommodate to the changing scene.

Dunn found that setting aside time blocks where he could work without interruption, such as arriving in the office at 7:00 a.m. and working without interruption until 9:00 — or working from 5:00 p.m. to 6:30 p.m. — enabled him to accomplish most of his tasks requiring uninterrupted concentration. This left him free to remain much more flexible to the varying demands upon his time during the day. In this fashion, a school administrator should be able to remain responsive and yet achieve his own objectives.

Flexible Response to Outside Demands on Your Time

A major difference cited by Dunn between administrators in education and other enterprises is the extreme people emphasis in the school profession. Almost all of the work of the educator is carried out with people. While this is true in certain segments of industry, there are very few instances in which managers' decisions and actions are so visible, so subject to immediate scrutiny by so many client groups. The multiplicity of demands upon the time of the educator and the speed with which priorities can shift with new emergencies stagger the imagination. It is virtually impossible for school administrators to set clear priorities at the beginning of the day and to follow them systematically throughout the day. Flexibility is an absolute requirement.

"It takes judicious reaction," said Dunn, "to avoid being pulled unnecessarily in many directions at once. Nonetheless a certain responsiveness to immediate demands is mandatory." In most businesses, many of the problems which arise along the research, engineering, or production lines are far enough removed from the end customer not to come to his attention at all. By contrast, an oversight by a school administrator with a parent, a problem with a student, a crisis on a bus or in a classroom is immediately evident to one or more of the many publics being served by the school administrator.

Those Evening Meetings

An example of the unique demands upon the school administrator is the number of evenings per month that the average chief school administrator—particularly principals—spends attending school-related activities. It is not uncommon for them to average between 10 and 15 evenings a month when you include PTA meetings, athletic events, cultural activities, and committee meetings of all kinds. When this time is added to the normal workday, it extends the time which appears to be expected of school administrators enormously. Many school administrators attend these functions from start to finish.

It is my conviction that they ought to limit their attendance when possible by attempting to attend a part of a school-related activity so that they are seen and have some familiarity with how things are going. But to expect school administrators to attend all of these sessions in their entirety is far too much. I am constantly encouraging educators to reconsider their priorities in this regard and to attempt to limit the time they allow themselves to be involved in all of these activities. Dr. Dunn discusses this problem with his administrators; they chart out all of the meetings where the administration needs to be represented; they consider the skills and expertise that will be required in the meetings; and they attempt to distribute the responsibilities in an equitable fashion.

Consolidating Meetings, Arriving Late, Leaving Early

Another useful technique is to combine meetings on the same evening, arranging them successively so that those who need to may attend all of them. This has the benefit of grouping meetings, getting them over in less time because of the discipline that is imposed automatically, and saving travel time for those attending more than one.

A principal of an open elementary school in New York State told me of an excellent solution that she had worked out for the problem. When her purpose in attending a meeting was simply to be seen, she would ask the chairman if it was all right if she just appeared for a few minutes. If the chairman had any particular part of the program that was especially important and had a desire for the principal to attend during that time, this was quickly agreed upon. In general, she has found that, with proper notice, she is able to attend most evening meetings for a short agreed-upon portion of the meeting. Usually she arrives late and leaves early. For the seven years that she has practiced this policy, she feels she has never gotten into any serious difficulty with it. She highly recommends it as a form of time conservation. Her visibility is increased while time spent is reduced. Ken Dunn views this as a very sound approach in which openness and candor between the concerned parties will almost always work out an equitable solution that will be respected by all.

Clock to Monitor and Timed Agendas

Evening meetings are not the only ones of major concern to educators. One of the most persistent time concerns for school administrators is meetings during regular working hours. With his team, Dunn approached this problem in a number of ways. Placing a clock in clear view of all participants and agreeing that interruptions would not be tolerated except in emergencies made a considerable difference.

A timed agenda ensured that time would be devoted to topics in proportion to their importance. An ending time was determined prior to the meeting, and the group exercised considerable discipline in sticking to the agenda and ending on time. They found that all benefitted by knowing the meeting would start and end at the appointed time. Without time wasted in waiting for the meeting to begin, they could plan for the time immediately following the meeting with assurance that the meeting would not be extended.

Take an Inventory of Your Committees

One public school staff surveyed the number, purpose, and accomplishments of committees. They discovered some 53 committees in existence, 40 percent of which had already achieved their intended purposes. As a result, 20 of the 53 committees were abolished, and a great saving of time was immediately realized.

Stacking Meetings Back to Back

One progressive principal believed in predetermining the starting and ending times of meetings, "stacking" them back to back, and occasionally accomplishing a committee's purpose without a meeting. He sent me the following agenda of meetings conducted one afternoon:

1:45-2:15 Physical education staffing
2:15-2:35 Foreign language
2:35-3:15 Department chairpersons (weekly meeting)
3:15-3:45 Budget cuts

Each succeeding meeting was scheduled to begin at the minute the preceding meeting ended. When I asked him how that could possibly work, he responded that it was simple. A minute or two before the new meeting began, all of the participants entered the room and asked the other group if they would mind adjourning because they were ready to start their meeting. Meetings were announced ahead of time by means of a notification sheet. In order to carry out such a program effectively, participants must be briefed in advance as to the schedule, purpose, and who will attend the meeting. A typical meeting notice follows:

Meeting at 2:15–2:35 on Tuesday
Topic: Staffing for next year
Purpose: To correctly identify possible staffing problems in French
Participants: Principal, assistant principal, and department chairperson

This method of stacking meetings back to back and providing advance agendas resulted in meetings being completed in one-half the normal time.

A Committee Without a Meeting

When the superintendent established a three-member committee to review a policy on participation in interscholastic sports, the principal asked the other two members of the committee if they really wanted to have a meeting on the subject. Their response indicated that they would favor any way that could be devised to accomplish the purposes of the committee without having to meet. With a few minutes of concentrated effort, they came up with some potential revisions. By agreement the principal had the revisions typed and forwarded to the other two members for reactions. Two telephone conversations resulted in a final proposal, and the objectives of the committee were completed without a formal meeting. Not only were the committee members pleased with the new policy, but they all felt an added pleasure at having accomplished very satisfactory results without the series of two-hour meetings and extensive travel time which such a process usually required. A little creativity, it seems, plus a little initiative, can go a long way.

Dr. Hugh Partlow, former superintendent for Professional Development and Educational Services of the Borough of North York in Toronto, devoted considerable attention to the problems of time management with school administrators. One of the two largest school districts in Canada, North York had at that time over 5,000 professionals on its staff. Dr. Partlow attended a time management seminar and carried back the basic concepts, determined to make them available to his people.

Time Management for Teachers, Too

Over the years Dr. Partlow sponsored a number of management seminars on basic leadership skills and on time management. He considers the effective utilization of time as one of the most needed skills of the educator. As he put it:

> It is my belief that time management is just as important to the school administrator as to the manager in business and industry. Unfortunately, it has not been studied as intensively in the field of education, but it should be. Educational leaders may not have recognized its importance and therefore have not provided sufficient in-service opportunities for staff members to develop competencies in this area. Teacher-preparation courses prior to certification have concentrated on such things as educational philosophy, curriculum development, and teaching methods. They have omitted or neglected the study of time management. These skills are valuable not only to educators in leadership positions such as the superintendent, the principal, and the consultant, but to every teacher in the school.

The Famous Five—a Unique Team

Some six months after the first time management seminar in the North York (Toronto) school system, a short refresher session was offered to those participants who wished to review their progress, problems, and plans for improved time utilization. Although this session lasted only one hour, it was evident that it had a significant impact on those attending as each recounted what steps had been taken and with what results. As one person would state what action he had taken, other heads would nod with apparent agreement that they also had done that or eyebrows would lift evidencing real interest. There seemed a general conclusion on many points that "If they can do that, why can't I?"

Five of the participants attending this refresher session decided that to achieve the full potential of the seminar they should continue to meet occasionally on an informal basis. Their names and positions held at the time are: Lynne Brenner, Consultant in education research services; Carl Hogg, coordinator of history; Henry Johnson, administrative assistant; John Mergler, coordinator of art; Beverly Wood, assistant coordinator of information and utilization services. Although they held different positions in the system, they knew each other and had varying degrees of contact. This presented opportunities for reinforcement outside of the meetings themselves.

In a year of meetings spaced approximately one month apart, the group came to some definite conclusions collectively and as individuals. A measure of the group's elan, good humor, and espirit de corps may be seen in the name they chose for their group: the Famous Five. Their conclusions, selected from the tapes of three different sessions of the group, are as follows:

1. The meetings have provided each one with a keen awareness of where his/her time is going, ideas of how to better control its utilization, and strong reinforcement to follow through on plans to implement these ideas.

2. A new candor has been developed in treating problems with time and priorities honestly. Instead of saying, "I don't have time," a term they rarely if ever use any more, they respond with, "It's not important enough to change my present plans," or perhaps, "I'm sorry, but my priorities won't permit the time that would require."

3. Sound time management techniques have been internalized. At first a conscious thought process was involved when an identified time concern was encountered. For example, one might say to oneself, "Time to start the in-box. Oh, yes, I want to try handling as many items as possible on first picking them up—to make the decision or take indicated action without putting them down." As Carl Hogg put it, the process has become automatic. The habit has been established so firmly that he is barely aware of the process. He goes through his in-box once and disposes of almost everything, or takes whatever action can be taken on nearly all of the items.

4. Priorities are now clear. It has also become habitual to think about what is most important each day and to focus energy on getting these things done first.

5. Much more work is getting done than was previously thought possible. Bev Wood estimates she is getting from two to three times as much work done today with one-third the staff she previously had. This is a direct result of concentrating on priorities. Saying "No" to less important interruptions becomes much easier when you know your priorities.

6. Indecision and procrastination have been minimized. Clear priorities make it much easier to make decisions and to take initiative in executing them. As Carl put it, in the time I used to take speculating about whether or not to do something, I now have made the decision and taken the first action. My habitual response used to be to think it over. Now it is to decide and act, almost simultaneously. If it's worth doing, why not get it out of the way while you're still thinking about it. Then you won't have to worry about remembering to do it later. The time span required for decision making has been markedly reduced.

7. Secretaries are included as members of the team. Some of the secretaries attended the time management seminar. All were considered proficient previously. Afterward, they assumed a more effective role as members of the team and became even more effective, partly due to their boss's new awareness of time, and partly due to being allowed to do many things their bosses previously had insisted on doing themselves.

8. Opportunities are maximized. Congruency and dovetailing are utilized to take advantage of timing. Carl recounted an incident where planning the output at the time of the input gave him an excellent time advantage. On a Tuesday he was to present a summary to 30 principals concerning the priorities in Canadian Studies in Program Development for the next year. On the preceding Sunday he was attending the final session of the conference on Canadian Studies. Instead of leaving the session without considering the pending report, as nearly all of the other attendees did, he decided to outline his report and decide the important elements before leaving the session. With the session fresh in his mind, the report outline was simple and

completed with little effort. If he had waited until he was in a different environment, and the details of the session had faded from his mind, the task of preparing the presentation would have been many times more difficult and undoubtedly have taken much longer. Timing was the key to maximizing the opportunity by getting better results in less time.

9. Planned unavailability has become a reality. Some of the group don't have doors but are in an open environment. Their secretaries screen their calls and their drop-in visitors as well. Bev Wood was surprised how quickly she was able to switch to a modified open-door policy—that is, closed from time to time to permit concentration when needed. Carl has no door but has his back to the opening. His secretary has an excellent reputation for screening visitors without appointments and handling them in a professional manner without offending. By working as a team, he and his secretary have enjoyed combining time management techniques such as protecting the boss from interruptions and enabling him to complete 15 telephone contacts with principals within a two-hour period.

   Taking callbacks during a period of uninterrupted concentration gains two direct advantages, they discovered. First the freedom from distraction permits much more to be accomplished. Second, on returning a number of calls they can be arranged in priority and necessary facts already gathered by the secretary to expedite the discussion. In many cases, the secretary herself will return the call with the answer. So the time spent on calls themselves will be radically reduced.

10. Tuning out of meetings when nothing worth listening to is going on has helped optimize the utilization of time previously wasted. When priorities are clear in your mind, instead of becoming hopelessly bored you can be thinking through a problem, organizing your day, and planning next steps while apparently listening.

11. Efficiency and effectiveness have been distinguished by the group. Again priorities turn out to be the key. Being efficient on a low priority matter will result in low effectiveness. Being efficient on a high priority matter, however, will result in high effectiveness.

12. Conflicts of priorities have been discussed by the group. There is the problem of finding that your top priority is at the bottom of someone else's list. When such a conflict of priorities occurs, it may take skill and diplomacy to work out the problem. Congruence of your own priorities with those of your boss is seen to be of paramount importance. Conflicting priorities are best resolved by discussion.

13. The paradox of needing time without interruption to accomplish your own objectives and yet to be available to others whose requirements it is your responsibility to serve was discussed by John and Henry. Neither had found it easy to resolve this difficult situation. Others in the group questioned them, suggesting first that serving others had to be viewed as a key objective for those in service departments. Second, they questioned the right of those being served to demand instant action without notice. Clearly it is impossible to serve all of the people all of the time. It seemed reasonable that priorities be set. Except for emergencies it would be reasonable to serve first those who requested your services first. In many cases, asking people to phone ahead for an appointment would be reasonable, particularly in the case of salespeople seeking to sell their own products.

14. Whether doing routine tasks is a time concern, when you have no one to whom to delegate, was discussed. It was agreed that certain things simply must be done. Hence if you are the only one who is around it will likely fall to you to handle routine tasks. However, as Lynne pointed out, it is quite possible to take an hour to do a five-minute routine task. That would be wasting time. The same holds true of many other matters such as making decisions and handling the in-basket. Decisiveness in these routine matters will save a lot of time. So the key to handling routine details is not whether you have someone to whom you can delegate, but rather it is in how effectively you handle them.

15. Time to laugh a little was a benefit identified by at least two of the group. Both said they were working a lot harder last year and getting a lot less done. Now they have learned that it isn't how hard one works but rather how well that determines how much is really accomplished. Effectiveness permits you to run relaxed, while achieving much more. You can be more flexible to take advantage of opportunities. You can laugh a little and enjoy your work and your life much more.

16. It all applies to life, said most of the group. The same principles which were helping them at work were helping them in their homes to get more done in less time. This was giving them more time with their families.

17. The final conclusion of the group. . . . They would never have experienced comparable success alone. The greatest value of time management was experienced after they began reinforcing and supporting each other. These values were deemed so great that they were determined to continue meeting as an informal group so that they could continue to improve the management of their time and therefore their lives.

We recognize these were educational administrators, but the importance of this unique experience must not be lost on other managers. The same discoveries could be made by any group of administrators at any time.

For Further Reading

Drawbaugh, Charles A. *Time & Its Use: A Self Management Guide for Teachers.* New York: Teachers College, 1984.

Neal, Richard G. *Managing Time: An Administrator's Guide.* Manassas, VA: Neal Associates, 1982.

Shipman, Neil J. and Martin, Jack B. *Effective Time Management Techniques for School Administrators.* Englewood Cliffs, NJ: Prentice Hall, no date.

Wisehunt, Donald W. *Administrative Time Management: Tips for Administrators and Aspiring Administrators.* Lanham, MD: University Press of America, 1987.

SECTION 11

Managing Time in the Home

Managing Time in the Home

Dual Career Families

In my seminars it has been interesting to note the change in the make-up of the participants. Once it was not at all unusual to make a presentation to an all-male group. Increasingly, however, we see a rapid rise in the number of women managers. News accounts of awards in the millions of dollars for back pay for women who have been discriminated against in salaries indicate that the position today has changed.

From time to time people ask about the relative competence of women managers as compared with men. While there are people better qualified than I to make a definitive analysis of the issue, it seems clear that because of discrimination in wages women have had to demonstrate far more competence than men to reach the same level. This suggests that women with the title of vice-president are apt to be more able and more intelligent than their male counterparts. Equal pay for comparable work, while proving difficult to implement, offers hope for correcting the situation.

Unequal Work Distribution in the Home

This discrimination in salary has its parallel in the home. When a woman goes to work, there often is tacit assumption that she will also still manage the home. She can delegate tasks to the rest of the family, but the burden of seeing to it that the household functions efficiently is usually left to her. However, most husbands, who delegate to others at the office, willingly accept being delegated to at home. They are happy to pick up the loaf of bread on the way home but do not readily assume responsibility for checking the refrigerator to see what items are needed. One possible reason for this is that, in most cases, the wife's salary is lower than her husband's so that they both feel her second job (outside the home) is less important than his. To compensate for bringing home less money, she has continued to assume the role of home manager, protecting her husband from onerous household details. When a homemaker goes to work, she needs to increase her effectiveness markedly. She is now managing two jobs; she must plan better and carry out those plans more effectively. She stops doing unnecessary tasks because there isn't time. She must do as well in the office as her competition, often a man who is handling only one job. A Harris Poll showed that working women end up with about 10 hours less free time per week than either full-time homemakers or employed men. There is some evidence that as more husbands realize the burden on their working wives, they are beginning to assume more of the home chores.

Doubling Your Effectiveness

A frequent example of the dual role of working women is found among elementary school principals. In a typical group of 25 principals, more than half will be women who are married and have families. These women, almost without exception, will be managing most of the family affairs in addition to managing the elementary school. How *do* they manage? They tell me that, of course, management of the home is a full-time job and management of a school is a full-time job; but they have to cut back on their rigid housekeeping requirements. Instead of dusting their homes every day, they do it once a week, realizing that this is adequate. They recognize that none of their friends come to visit for the purpose of inspecting their home, but rather to enjoy their company and friendship. Many hire cleaning services.

These principals, of necessity, plan wisely. They double their output often by cooking not for one meal but for many, utilizing their freezer as a timesaver. Assignments to members of the household are given on a much more systematic basis, and schedules are often posted. A list of meals prepared ahead for an entire week ensures that any teenager can get a meal ready with a minimum of effort. Likewise, in their jobs, professional women must manage to perform within the levels expected and without the freedom to work overtime and to take work home—so extensively relied upon by their husbands and male counterparts at work.

When I was flying back from a week of seminars in Germany, my flight companion was the wife of an engineer in the midwest who had raised three children and for 13 years had been a successful elementary school principal. In addition, she had developed a slide presentation called "Mission Impossible—the Role of the Elementary Principal." From time to time, she would visit state associations of teachers and school administrators to give her talks. With extensive use of delegation, planning, and minimizing such things as overhousecleaning and overdecorating, she was able to manage her home as efficiently as she managed the school.

The principal had left her school without notice a few days earlier after receiving a call from Germany that her daughter was undergoing emergency surgery. I asked her what kind of chaotic situation she would be returning to after four days of unplanned absence. Her response: "None at all—everyone knows whom to go to for decisions necessary to keep the school functioning." I concluded she was a better principal than most I encounter and it was because of sheer necessity. She had decided she wanted to be both a successful homemaker and a successful principal and realized that this required planning and anticipating unexpected absenses. Required authority was delegated in advance as part of her contingency plan.

Managing the home is a tough business. Food prices tend to rise, yet there is a budget to balance. Family disputes must be resolved, children chauffeured, pets fed, etc. We know that all the management principles employed in the office have to be employed in the home at one time or another. The principles of planning, for example, are so obvious as scarcely to need mentioning. The amount of planning necessary for budgeting makes most managers glad it isn't their task. The purpose of our

212

discussion here will be to compare the impact of time on the manager's activities in the home and in the office. We will seek to determine whether there are any significant differences and whether there are principles which come to play in one situation and not the other.

Time Concerns of 18 Wives and Their Young President Husbands

Much depends, of course, upon the particular situation of the homemaker. If the homemaker is a woman whose sole concern is the management of the home and she does so without outside assistance, the time management implications will be different from those of the single person who has a full-time job on the outside and has some assistance in handling usual housekeeping chores. In a meeting in Mexico City with members of the Young Presidents Organization and their wives, it became immediately evident that nearly all of the homemakers in the group had maids and/or housekeepers full time. A time log for one of these women showing all activities on a given day would vary markedly from a similarly placed woman who had no help in the home. In a similar meeting of wives and husbands, also senior executives and members of the same organization in Pittsburgh, lists of time concerns for each group were compiled. See Exhibits 11.1 (page 214) and 11.2 (pages 216-217).

At first glance the lists look surprisingly similar. However, the universality of the time concerns themselves perhaps explains the similarity. For example, telephone interruptions, drop-in visitors, and crises are certainly common to both the office and the home. One time concern on the homemakers' list which did not appear on any of the executives' lists was chauffeuring children. The startling similarity between these lists is recognized by noting that ineffective delegation and telephone interruptions rank first or second on both lists. Attempting too much ranks third for the homemakers and sixth for the executives. No daily planning ranks fifth for the wives, and failure to set goals and deadlines ranks fifth for their husbands. Crisis management and shifting priorities rank sixth for the homemakers and fourth for their husbands. Leaving tasks unfinished ranks seventh for the women and fifteenth for the men. Drop-in visitors ranks ninth for the wives and third for their husbands. Inability to say "No" ranks tenth on both lists. Personal disorganization and stacked desk ranks twelfth for the women and seventh for the men.

Several of the wives noted that they held part-time jobs in addition to managing their homes. Candor and a lively sense of humor characterized the contributions from the wives to the meeting. For example, one of them listed in her time concerns "Irregular Meal Hours, Sloppiness, and No Place to Hide." One suggested, "Don't like to start jobs after 2 or 3 p.m." A few other interesting time concerns included boredom with household jobs, reading too much, jumping from one job to the next without finishing any of them, TV, too large a house, too many steps, not well planned, lack of self-discipline, husband talking, and fatigue. One can hardly restrain the conjecture as to whether there might be any relationship between the last two—husband talking and fatigue.

Exhibit 11.1: Time Concern Profile

18 Wives of Presidents (4 were part-time or volunteer workers)

		Number Reporting	Weight
1.	Doing it myself 9/63 Involved in routine 6/26 Ineffective delegation (with help) 3/14 Too much attention to detail 1/10 Doing too much that children could do 1/5 Family jobs children could do as well 1/2	21	120
2.	Telephone interruptions	17	99
3.	Attempting too much/unrealistic time estimates 11/77 Too many interests 1/8 Starting too many projects 1/6	13	91
4.	Chauffeuring children 9/63 Beauty parlor 2/13 Doctor & dental appts. 1/7 Family schedules 1/5	13	88
5.	No daily plan 3/22 Poor planning of errands and shopping 3/18 No self-imposed deadlines 3/17 Comparison shopping 2/15 Not planning meals ahead 1/8 Not setting goals 1/2	13	82
6.	Crisis management (plumbing, appliances) 6/32 Shifting priorities 6/38 Coping with the unexpected 2/11	14	81
7.	Leaving tasks unfinished	10	64
8.	Indecision/procrastination	10	47
9.	Visitors 4/22; children's interruptions 3/15	7	37
10.	Not saying "No" to children, volunteer requests, etc.	8	35

Note: Weights were determined by having each participant express her time concerns. A weight of 10 is assigned to number 1 concern, 9 to number 2, etc., to 1 for number 10. The weights for all participants are combined. The first number following each time concern indicates the number reporting that particular concern. The second number represents the weight. Numbers in the columns represent the sum of the numbers of related time concerns grouped under those concerns.

As evidenced from the time concern profiles of the senior executives and their wives, the telephone may be our best friend or worst enemy, either in the office or at home. Husbands typically accuse their wives in an only semijesting fashion about being long-winded on the telephone. Yet secretaries in my seminars list as one of their most common complaints of the boss that he or she never gets off the telephone. Shirley Belz of the National Home Study Council is a strong advocate of staying *off* the telephone when possible. According to Belz, friends who hang on the phone with you for half an hour or longer often are using you as a substitute therapist. Introducing some of your own problems into the conversation is a good way to cut short the call.

The tendency to make unrealistic time estimates afflicts everyone, and the value of a daily written plan is quickly acknowledged by homemakers and office managers alike. Most homemakers, as we know, make lists of "things to do" including shopping requirements. Getting things onto lists frees the mind for more important matters and also ensures against forgetting.

But a "to do" list, as Phil Perkins pointed out in Section 8, does not solve the problem of planning the day and mapping out the hours so that one doesn't get side-tracked and procrastinate.

Victor Hugo's observation makes it clear that the principle of planning applies equally in the home or the office:

> He who every morning plans the transactions of the day and follows out that plan, carries a thread that will guide him through the maze of the most busy life. But where no plan is laid, where the disposal of time is surrendered merely to chance, chaos will soon reign.

New Gadgets Don't Save Time

A study on *The Use of Time*, written under the general editorship of a Hungarian socialist, Alexander Szalai, showed that the array of modern conveniences and technological timesavers made no difference in the amount of time spent on housework. The average woman in West Germany who has conveniences that might only be dreamed of in a small town in Yugoslavia got her work done in only one minute less per day than the Yugoslavian housewife.

Deadlines Usually Must Be Met at Home

Surely the pressures in the home may be just as unrelenting and deadlines as imperious as those faced in the office. When company is due for dinner at 7:00 p.m., who would dream of waiting until the guests arrive to announce you hadn't made the deadline? Would they mind coming back tomorrow night? You could be ready by then. The manager who misses a deadline in the office may shrug his shoulders and say: "Well, you can't win them all." A missed deadline in the home, whether for a social event, a school requirement, or a medical appointment, may have as serious and immediate consequences as most of those in the office.

When I asked Dr. Doris Williams of Bowling Green State University how a home

Exhibit 11.2: Time Concern Profile

24 Members, Young Presidents Organization

		Number Reporting	Weight
1.	Telephone	20	151
2.	Ineffective delegation 7/52 Doing it myself 11/63 Routine, detail 5/15 Upward delegation 2/14 Switchboard operators 1/6 Doing others' work 1/1	27	151
3.	Drop-in visitors	22	142
4.	Shifting priorities 11/52 Crisis management 7/46 Firefighting 7/37	25	135
5.	Lack objectives, priorities, daily plan 9/51 No self-imposed deadlines 2/8 Lack planning 3/7 Preoccupation with problems (No planning) 1/8 Outside deadlines 1/10	16	84
6.	Attempting too much at once	14	79
7.	Cluttered desk 7/37 Personal disorganization 3/19 Mail 1/10; junk mail 1/5 Paperwork 1/4	13	75
8.	Meetings	13	73
9.	Procrastination 6/35, indecision 3/18	9	53
10.	Inability to say ''No''	10	51
11.	Inadequate staff 2/14 Inadequate secretary 2/7 Untrained staff 1/16	5	37
12.	Ineffective communication	8	30
13.	Personnel with problems 3/12 Problem personnel 2/11 Unions 1/2 Listening to grievances 1/1	7	26
14.	Incomplete information	5	26
15.	Leaving tasks unfinished	5	21
16.	Socializing, long lunches	4	20

Exhibit 11.2: Time Concern Profile (Continued)

17.	Overlooking poor performance	3	17
18.	Mistakes/ineffective performance	2	16
19.	Wanting all the facts	3	16
20.	Duplication of effort 1/6 Solving same problem twice or more 1/6	2	12
21.	Lack self-discipline	2	12

Note: Weights were determined by having each participant express her time concerns. A weight of 10 is assigned to number 1 concern, 9 to number 2, etc., to 1 for number 10. The weights for all participants are combined. (See explanation in footnote to Exhibit 11.1.)

economist views the impact of time in the home, she summarized her thoughts as follows:

1. Learning to write schedules for different processes that must go on in the home, i.e., meal management and timing of various stages of preparation.

2. Learning to use time in relation to energy levels.

3. Learning how to use 'dovetailing' to save time.

4. Understanding my own motivation and value systems relative to the use of time.

5. Understanding the balance of work and leisure in relation to priorities for obtaining personal goals.

6. Learning that time is a valuable resource and at times warrants the extravagant use of other resources, i.e., money.

Management Principles in the Home

Larry Appley, when he headed the American Management Association, was a strong advocate of the application of the principles of professional management to every area of organized human endeavor. In a memo to his key staff members, he once wrote:

This pattern (of professional management) says that if one will: set objectives, organize required human and physical resources, establish standards, review performances, provide growth and corrective measures, and reward for work well done, much more can be accomplished in any form of human activity than by any other means. This applies to one's own individual life, to the family, to any community activity, to a business, a government, a labor union and on the farm. It is tried and true. It is a way of life that will provide greater assurance of success in any activity than will leaving things to chance.

For Further Reading

Mackenzie, Alec and Waldo, Kay. *About Time! A Woman's Guide to Time Management*. New York: McGraw-Hill, 1981.

Miller, Elizabeth L. *I Just Need More Time*. Wichita Falls, TX: Woman Time Management, 1984.

Pepitone-Rockwell, Fran (ed.). *Dual-Career Couples*. Beverly Hills, CA: Sage, 1980.

Silcox, Diana with Moore, Mary Ellen. *Woman Time*. Ridgefield, CT: Wyden, 1980.

Szalai, Alexander. *Use of Time: Daily Activities of Urban and Suburban Populations in Twelve Countries*. Hawthorne, NY: Mouton, 1972.

SECTION 12

Time and Territorial Management for Salespeople

Rising Cost of Calls

Priorities Questioned

Conclusions of Vizza and Chambers Study

Improving Sales Performance

Planning

Implementation

Control

Key Recommendations

Influencing Support People

Salespeople as Managers

Travel Time

Managing Their Absence

Waiting Time

Will Somebody Catch That Phone?

How Time Tactics Controls Ten Top Time Concerns

Time and Territorial Management For Salespeople

In none of the operational functions of management have concepts been changing more rapidly than in marketing. The function of marketing poses direct problems in the area of time utilization. The editors of *The Sales Executive* have been quoted as saying: "The most important link in the marketing chain is the salesperson; how best he utilizes the hours available to him often determines the success or failure of the overall marketing program."

Under the sponsorship of the Sales Executives Club of New York, Robert Vizza and Thomas Chambers conducted a study on "Improving Salesmen's Use of Time," which concluded that:

> The field of Sales Management is taking on a more scientific posture. In this transitional state, guesswork and intuition are being replaced by principles and scientific methods. This study has found that principles and methods for planning the efficient use of salespeople's time exist: they are being practiced by some companies researched. But the area is still regarded as the number one problem of sales management. A major conclusion to be drawn from this apparent paradox is that what is needed is not so much the development of new principles, but a more wide-spread adoption of the existing ones.[*]

Ten years after this report a second study was sponsored by the same organization to determine the impact of the intervening decade on this vital area of sales management. At least two factors were isolated as contributors to the importance of efficient time utilization by salespeople: 1) the nature of time itself and 2) the rapidly rising cost of salespeople's time. Unlike all other resources of the salesperson which can be accumulated and committed at will, the salesperson's time must be spent as it becomes available, increment by increment, evenly—constantly. Most resources are planned for and put to use according to a plan. Expenditure of these resources can be withheld pending completion of a plan. Not so with time. It keeps coming at a fixed rate. If there is no plan for its use, it is wasted. Hence the vital importance of an on-going practice of planning one's time on a daily, weekly, and monthly basis.

Rising Cost of Calls

As nearly everyone in business recognizes, the cost of a salesperson's call has risen steadily over the years. According to the Dartnell *25th Sales Force Compensation Survey*, the average cost of a face-to-face sales call is $64.80, with averages by

---

[*] Vizza, Robert F., "Improving Salesmen's Use of Time," Sales Executives Club of New York, Inc., 1961.

industry ranging from $25.00 to nearly $250.00 per call. This figure represents only compensation, benefits, and related expenses. In brief, regardless of what industry you are in, it costs a lot of money to make a sales call.

In addition, the amount of time a salesperson spends in face-to-face selling is diminishing. One study indicates that in spite of working a nine-hour day, the average industrial salesperson is able to spend only three hours and 52 minutes in face-to-face selling. Traveling and waiting for interviews along with paperwork take up slightly over half the day. A more recent survey indicated that industrial salespeople spend approximately a third of their time in face-to-face selling. My own surveys of life insurance agents and securities reps indicate the average time spent in face-to-face selling is only one hour per day.

Priorities Questioned

The diminishing of selling time increases the cost per call, and raises the serious question as to the effectiveness of the priorities being placed on the activities of salespeople. It must be recognized that success in selling is a result of *what* a salesperson does, in addition to *how* it is done. Much attention has been paid to the "how" of selling skills, i.e., handling a sales call. Too little attention has been given to "what" a salesperson spends his/her time doing.

Conclusions of Vizza and Chambers Study

As a result of a three-year study of questionnaires and selected interviews in 257 companies, Vizza and Chambers drew the following conclusions:

1. Although most respondents felt that time utilization represents an area for improvement, less than half (46 percent) have formally investigated how their salespeople actually spend their time in order to effect improvement.

2. One-fourth of the respondents do not have a system of classifying accounts according to potential. In these cases it would appear doubtful that calls were made in relation to potential, and therefore that time was being used effectively. The 75 percent of the companies which have adopted the approach of account classification by potential indicates an encouraging trend in this direction.

3. 30 percent of the companies surveyed do not use call schedules for the salespeople. Much time is wasted deciding "where to go" and "whom to call on" by the salespeople, without the discipline provided by a formal approach to setting call schedules.

4. Over half the respondents do not determine the number of calls it is economical to make on an account. Their salespeople thus lack guidelines as to the amount of effort they should and can devote to accounts in relation to potential. The danger of too many or too few sales calls is very real.

5. 83 percent of the firms surveyed do not determine an approximate duration for each call. As a result salespeople have no formalized approach to determine how much time they can spend on each call in relation to the potential.

6. Over half (51 percent) of the firms surveyed do not use a planned sales presentation. In many instances time management focuses *around* the sales call, whereas other companies have discovered that sales call time can be more effectively used through a planned approach.

7. 24 percent of the respondents do not set sales objectives for accounts. A lack of objectives makes control of salespeople's activities difficult. Also, the amount of sales effort required by an account is elusive in the absence of objectives. The development of selling strategies, so essential to the proper coverage of an account, is almost impossible if not done within the framework of sales objectives.

8. 72 percent of the companies surveyed do not set profit objectives for accounts. It appears that the major obstacle to setting profit objectives is still the difficulty involved in measuring profitability. At a time when profits are shrinking, it is even more imperative to come to grips with the measurement problem.

9. 81 percent of the firms surveyed use a call report system, and of these, 69 percent require the salespeople to report on every call made. Many companies have not yet recognized the advantages of applying the principle of management by exception to sales reporting systems.

10. 63 percent of the companies surveyed do not use prescribed routing patterns in covering their territories. The possibility of wasted travel time appears great.

11. 77 percent of the respondents do not use the computer to assist in salespeople's time and territorial management. When companies indicated that the computer is being used, further investigation revealed that the predominant application is sales analysis, that is, print-outs of sales by product, by customer, by salesperson, by territory, and a combination of these, are being produced. In very few instances are salespeople's call activities and time utilization programmed into the system. Nor could systems be found in everyday use that include the variables of account potential, call frequencies, call scheduling, routing plans, and balanced sales and prospecting activities.

Improving Sales Performance

The underlying concept of the report is that sound territorial planning is the key to effective time utilization. Shown following is a Model for Time and Territorial Management designed by Vizza and Chambers to describe the process of territorial planning, implementation, and control (Exhibit 12.1, page 224).

The Vizza and Chambers study is a call to action for improved time management for salespeople based on more effective territorial management. The model identifies the elements of the management process: planning, implementation, and control.

Planning

It is through planning that goals are established, resources to implement these goals are identified, and the strategies necessary to accomplish the goals are decided. A well-designed plan begins with the analysis of accounts in a territory to determine which have the greatest potential. The authors use the concept of "expected value"

Exhibit 12.4: A Model of Time and Territorial Management for Salespeople

TERRITORIAL PLANNING

- Account Analysis
  - Identification
  - Analysis of Needs
  - Classification
  - Expected Value
- Goals and Objectives
  - Share of Market
  - New Business
  - Company Image
  - Account Objectives
  - Product Objectives
- WORKLOAD ANALYSIS
  - Number of Accounts
  - Number of Calls
  - Duration of Calls
  - Travel Time
  - Non-Selling Time
- TIME ALLOCATION
  - Value of Time
  - Return on Time Invested
  - Opportunity Costs
- SELLING STRATEGIES
  - Product Mix
  - Territorial Coverage
  - Call Frequency Patterns
  - Selling Appeals

IMPLEMENTATION

- Territorial Coverage
- Call Schedules
- Routing and Traveling Plans
- Planned Sales Calls
  - Identifying Decision Makers

CONTROL

- Standards of Performance
- Collection of Data
  - Call Reporting Systems
  - Time and Duty Studies
- Analysis
- Corrective Action

From *Time and Territorial Management for Salesmen*, Vizza and Chambers (The Sales Executives Club of New York, Inc., 1971).

as a measure of potential. They describe "expected value" as the product of market potential, estimated share of market, and probability of getting that share. Once the expected value of each account in a territory has been revealed, a salesperson is ready to set measurable time and effort goals based upon number of calls, travel time required, and return on time invested (ROTI). By comparing the ROTI of various accounts, the salesperson can decide which accounts are most profitable. The calculation for ROTI is as follows:

If total sales are $750,000
and nonselling costs are $600,000
then gross profits are $150,000
If salesperson's direct selling costs are . . . .$ 30,000
then,

$$\text{ROTI} = \frac{\text{GROSS PROFITS}}{\text{COST OF TIME INVESTED}} = \frac{\$150,000}{\$ 30,000} = 5$$

See Exhibit 12.2, page 226, for calculating ROTI for a particular account.

Implementation

In order to cover territory effectively, the salesperson creates a call frequency pattern — the number and duration of calls on each account. Vizza and Chamber point out that as calls increase, so do sales — up to a point. After that, the sales level off and additional calls produce little in the way of additional sales. Opportunity costs are high when a salesperson continues to call on accounts that produce little more in sales compared to those accounts in early development.

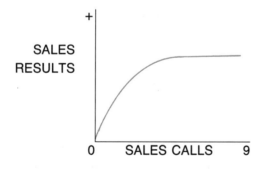

The same relationship holds if "time per call" were substituted for "number of sales calls."

One approach in establishing call frequencies is to classify accounts so that those with the highest profit potential are classified "A." They will be called upon most frequently. "B" companies will be called on half as often as "A," and "C" companies will be called on one-fourth as often as "A" companies. Of the accounts selected, 15 percent are designated "A," 25 percent "B," and 60 percent "C." Accounts that would least affect profits if they weren't called upon would be scheduled last.

225

Exhibit 12.2: Account Investment Analysis Form

Account Name: _____

I. Potential
    1. Past sales   _____
    2. Additional potential sales   _____
    3. Total potential   _____
    4. Probability of realizing potential   _____
    5. Expected value (3x4)   _____

II. Time Required to Realize E.V.
    6. Number of calls required   _____
    7. Approximate duration per call   _____
    8. Call hours required (6x7)   _____
    9. Travel time per call   _____
    10. Total travel time (6x9)   _____
    11. Total time required (8 + 10)   _____

III. ROTI
    12. Gross margin on Expected Value   _____
    13. Cost of time invested (Item 11 x cost per hour)   _____
    14. ROTI (12 ÷ 13)   _____

From *Time and Territorial Management for Salesmen,* Vizza and Chambers (The Sales Executives Club of New York, Inc., 1971).

An effective routing pattern drawn on a map of the territory might include all "A" accounts, one-half the "B" accounts, and one-fourth of the "C" accounts each time the cycle is repeated.

While it is important to get a salesperson to the right customer or prospect in the shortest time, there is considerable time wasted on the call itself. Time utilization is enhanced when a salesperson knows who the decision makers are and has information about the company called upon. Effectiveness is further increased when the salesperson allocates some of his/her time to writing a selling strategy that includes opening remarks, an approach to presenting the benefits of the product or service, anticipation of objectives, and the closing techniques to be used. See Exhibit 12.3, page 227, for an example of a sales call planner suggested by the authors (Vizza and Chambers).

Exhibit 12.3: Sales Call Planner

1. Person/persons to be called on:

Name   Title

_____

_____

2. Background Experiences:

_____

_____

3. Objectives of this call:

_____

_____

4. Strategies
   a. Opening remarks:

   _____

   _____

   b. Appeals to be stressed

   _____

   _____

   c. Method of demonstrating

   _____

   _____

   d. How to relate features to customer's needs

   _____

   _____

e. Benefits to be presented	Corresponding Product Features
f. Objections to Anticipate	Logical Answers
g. Closing techniques to be used	

From *Time and Territorial Management for Salesmen*, Vizza and Chambers (The Sales Executives Club of New York, Inc., 1971).

Control

Any effective control system assures that performance proceeds according to plan. Once standards of performance have been established, actual performance can then be compared to them and corrective action taken if required. The standards of performance are an outgrowth of the territorial objectives set in the planning stage. They might include:

Number of calls on existing accounts
Number of calls on potential accounts
Average time per call
Total call time
Average travel time per call
Total number of hours spent traveling
Hours spent waiting
Number hours spent on nonselling activities
Number of presentations made
Number of demonstrations made
Number of meetings attended
Number of customers called on
Number of prospects called on

Working together, the sales manager and salespeople quantify the standards. An excellent tool for collecting data on actual performance is the salesperson's Time and Duty Analysis shown in Exhibit 12.4, page 229. The vertical columns represent sales activities and might vary according to the company and actual job. A two-week period will give a representative sample for analysis.

The salesperson checks the appropriate column to indicate time spent on the activity and at the end of each day totals the check marks in each column, converts them to hours, and then calculates the percentage of the day spent on that activity. Analysis of performance reveals strengths and weaknesses and suggests corrective action required for below-standard performance and poor time allocation.

Sound principles of time and territorial management do exist, say the authors, and more companies must adopt them while developing additional principles in other areas.

Key Recommendations

Summarizing the key recommendations:

1. Use of a Time and Duty Analysis to know how time is presently being utilized or wasted in order to increase its productivity.

2. Call frequency patterns, including number, duration, and interval between calls, should be developed based on account potential. These patterns should be established and adopted as standard operating procedure for the salesperson.

Exhibit 12.4: Salesperson's Time and Duty Analysis

DAY _____

DATE _____

TIME	SALES CALLS										SERVICE						TRAVEL	WAITING	ENTER-TAINMENT AND LUNCH	ORDER EXPE-DITING	REPORT WRITING	TELE-PHONE CONTACTS	MISCEL-LANEOUS
	CUSTOMERS					PROSPECTS					CUSTOMERS												
	A	B	C	D	E	A	B	C	D	E	A	B	C	D	E							
8:00-8:30																							
8:30-9:00																							
9:00-9:30																							
9:30-10:00																							
10:00-10:30																							
10:30-11:00																							
11:00-11:30																							
11:30-12:00																							
12:00-12:30																							
12:30-1:00																							
1:00-1:30																							
1:30-2:00																							
2:00-2:30																							
2:30-3:00																							
3:00-3:30																							
3:30-4:00																							
4:00-4:30																							
4:30-5:00																							
5:00-5:30																							
5:30-6:00																							
TOTAL TIME																							
PERCENT OF DAY																							

From *Time and Territorial Management for Salesmen*, Vizza and Chambers (The Sales Executives Club of New York, Inc., 1971).

3. More attention must be given to assisting salespeople in sales calls. This includes gathering marketing intelligence, identifying decision makers, and planning sales presentations. These enable the salespeople to save time on calls and to do a more effective job, geared to the *identified needs of the buyers rather than the obvious needs of the seller.*

4. Computer capability must be developed beyond present control applications to optimize time utilization. Call frequency patterns, analysis of customers' potential and needs, routing and travel patterns, and establishment of sales objectives all lend themselves to systems analysis and computer application. Additional research will be required to develop computer-based time and territorial management systems for salespeople.

5. Finally, the focus of sales volume must be shifted to sales profitability. Measurement techniques must be developed to overcome this major obstacle. Companies are applying the concept of profit contribution to the sales force, despite lack of absolute measurement. Comparisons of results are being made customer to customer, salesperson to salesperson, product to product, time period to time period, in various combinations. This is a start into the most important measure of effectiveness—profit.

Influencing Support People

Virtually all of the typical time concerns encountered by managers are encountered by salespeople. Even those time concerns specifically related to the problems dealing with a team of subordinates have comparable factors for salespeople. While the salesperson is not in a position of direct authority, there are always people with whom he/she must deal, who must be influenced to prepare research data, to aid in assessing customer requirements, to provide needed information and all of the backup support which salespeople must have to close their sales. Whether a special request for a modification can be included within a set delivery time and within the quoted price requires cooperation from production and often from engineering as well as accouting personnel.

Salespeople as Managers

Salespeople are managers. They must be skillful in their management of corporate personnel whose assistance they need to make the bid, to close the sale, to ensure timely delivery, and to keep the customer well-serviced and satisfied. There are other resources to be managed—financial, material and, most critical of all, the time of others and oneself. So practically all of the basic principles of management, with the exception of delegation, apply to a salesperson's work. Even delegation, in the special sense described above, must be utilized judiciously with nonsubordinates including clients and customers. For the thousands of salespeople with secretaries or support staff, delegation often becomes a serious problem.

230

It comes, therefore, as no surprise that the time concerns cited by salespeople are very similar to those of other managers. Interruptions, the telephone, confused orders, poor communication (always with headquarters—not the customer it seems!), waiting for information (needed to complete a quotation), and ineffective delegation are but a few of those most often identified. But singular to the salesperson's list of time concerns is the absence of "drop-in visitors" and in its place the time spent in travel and in waiting for appointments. (The salesperson is one of the drop-in visitors listed by many managers among their top time concerns!) So important are these two impediments of travel and waiting to selling time that it is surprising to discover so little conscious planning to master them.

Travel Time

Travel time is most subject to the control of the salesperson. Optimizing the utilization of travel time calls for skillful blending of the factors cited in the Vizza and Chambers study. This would include, but not be limited to, the potential of the account in question, the distance to be traveled, the availability of the decision maker, the probable state of his/her need and estimated readiness to decide, other calls which can or cannot be made in conjunction with the one considered, timing of the proposed trip, and barriers such as weather and traffic to be anticipated according to the time of day, day of the week, and local conditions.

Managing Their Absence

Those who travel often fail to manage their absence from the office. What anticipated event will occur during your absence which ought to be provided for? What action can be readied by a simple request which will prevent an unnecessary delay in accomplishing desired results? What actions should others be requested to take during your absence which will create an optimum situation for achieving objectives? Some managers call their team together for a few moments to designate the person in charge, to ask what problems are anticipated, and to discuss what objectives will be achieved by the time they return. Using this opportunity to suggest a few goals of your own, which you would like to have completed in your absence, provides a hedge against Parkinson's Law being forced into action by team members catching up on their work and not having additional goals ready and waiting to be attacked. Underutilization can destroy morale of secretaries and support staff as quickly as overwork.

Waiting Time

Far less control is possible over the waiting time for appointments. Suggestions range from the last-minute call to confirm the appointment prior to departure, to the "foreshadowing" of an early departure by discreet mention to a receptionist or secretary of a later appointment which obviously will preclude an extensive time delay. The feel for the situation and one's own ingenuity will determine the salesperson's willingness to use such techniques to attempt to limit time wasted waiting for thoughtless or otherwise involved persons.

Effective managers of time anticipate the unexpected moments when they must wait. Reading material and routine but necessary reports make excellent standby material for such times. Minutes spent in this manner are not lost. They are utilized in another, though secondary manner, and they represent a saving of time which would be required to accomplish the same task later. A salesperson told me he always scans the Visitor Log when he signs in. If he spots the name of a competitor he often mentions it during his sales call as a means of finding out if the competition has "anything new."

Will Somebody Catch That Phone?

A sales manager in one of the major insurance companies recounted an experience of a senior salesman who was leaving the office shortly after opening hours to make a round of calls. The phone rang. The salesman stopped in the door and turned around to return to his desk to take the call. Suddenly he stopped, recalling the numerous time concerns he and the other salespeople had identified the day before in a seminar. He called out, "Will somebody catch that phone?" as he turned out the door and disappeared to make his calls.

The odds were very great that this was a call for service, explanation, or information not directly related to new sales. Others in the office could at least take the message allowing him to return the call at a time convenient to him. Very possibly they could provide the requested information so he would have saved time for the more important matter of selling. This example demonstrates a fundamental principle of priorities in action.

Many forces are focusing attention on the salesperson's time. Spiraling costs, the profit squeeze, new methods of purchasing, and intensified competition are but a few of the forces crystallizing the concept of the salesperson as territory manager. Managing a territory requires that one plan, implement, and control. By mastering these skills in managing his/her territory and available corporate resources, the successful salesperson will maximize his/her time utilization, productivity, and profits.

How Time Tactics Controls Ten Top Concerns

The new time management systems introduced over the past five years have been the greatest single advance in the history of time management. They have, for example, outmoded the perennial favorite, Daytimer's pocket calendar. The new systems which are recommended provide for:

- Functional use—a place to record everything you have to do or remember.

- Retrievability—permitting retrieval of any information within seconds.

- Priorities—Both long-range and short-range priorities are recorded, deadlined, and tracked at regular intervals to ensure timely accomplishment.

232

- Deadlines—are kept visible where they cannot be overlooked.

- Progress reports—as scheduled on Project and Objectives Sheets to ensure that progress conforms to plans.

- Contact logs—to record key conversations by individuals to permit instant retrieval when needed.

Time Tactics controls ten of the top time concerns in the following ways:

1. Crisis management/shifting priorities. Priorities are deadlined so potential problems can be anticipated and prevented. Overresponse on less important matters is avoided because top priorities are kept visible to maintain concentration. Temptation to move to lower priority tasks is deflected by having written prioritized daily goals and time to accomplish them blocked out on the daily schedule.

2. Telephone interruptions. Contact Logs tell you exactly what was discussed in your last conversation and what you want to discuss the next time. Decide instantly whether or not to take the call based on the information on the Contact Log. All prior discussions and decisions are instantly retrievable to avoid misunderstandings. With your priorities in front of you on your daily plan, you can easily deflect phone calls that are a lower priority than your current task or that should be handled by someone else.

3. Lack objectives/priorities planning. Written and quantified annual/monthly/weekly goals are scheduled. Progress is monitored. Corrective action can be taken in time to ensure meeting your goals.

4. Drop-in visitors. Your written daily plan showing your goals for the day provides an excellent tool for dealing with drop-in visitors effectively and without offending. You can see yourself falling behind schedule, and you can tell instantly if the task being interrupted has a higher priority than the concern of the interruptor. When appropriate, ask if the problem can wait, if someone else can help, or if the person can handle it on his/her own.

5. Meetings. For the repetitive meetings, create a section with a Time Tactics special tab (e.g., Staff Meetings). Use Contact Logs to develop the agenda and to record actions taken at the meeting for quick retrieval when needed. Specify dates for progress reports and completion on important decisions, noting these in your Weekly and Monthly Plans.

6. Inability to say "No." Because you now have a daily, written, prioritized plan to follow, no more being at the mercy of the priorities of others—unless they supersede yours. Use your schedule to show why you should not interrupt your plan. This makes it easy to say "No" without offending.

7. Attempting too much. Your daily plan shows your number-one priority and the time set apart to complete it. You can see at a glance what your plans for the week are. You have monthly calendars to indicate when you are planning too much in the future. When you focus on top priorities first, tasks not done are the least important. Project Sheets and Contact Logs give you the control needed to plan and delegate effectively. Delegating more and tracking progress frees you to do what is really important. Use calendars to record paperwork to be done before it's due. Use Contact Logs to record actions taken and information still required for red tape tasks.

8. Procrastination/indecision. No more "To Do" lists that simply list everything you have to do but never say when or in what priority. You develop a prioritized, written plan to achieve your objectives on a daily/weekly/monthly basis, with checkpoints for measuring progress periodically. Interim deadlines prevent procrastination. Use a Time Tactics project sheet for each of your projects. Tracking progress is automatic as deadlines keep you from forgetting. Use Project Sheets and Contact Logs to keep track of every task delegated to you. This kind of record keeping will feed tasks to your daily plan on a timely basis and force you to do what you should do, when you should do it.

9. Ineffective delegation. Delegated tasks and important discussions are recorded on that person's Contact Log. Checkpoint and due dates are entered on your calendar. Follow-up is automatic. Project Sheets make it possible to develop the action plan for a whole project and then key that plan to the Contact Logs of those to whom you delegated tasks. You know at a glance what you delegated, to whom, and when it is due.

10. Personal disorganization/cluttered desk. With only one place to record what to do, when to do it, what has been delegated, and checkpoints for deadlines, nothing falls through the cracks. Because Time Tactics provides the places to record information exactly where you will need to retrieve it, you'll never again have to answer the question, "What did I note so that I wouldn't forget it, and where did I put it? Time Tactics contains the information you need to handle phone calls, track projects, and be ready for meetings. No more notes on scraps of paper, backs of envelopes, and separate "To-Do" lists that keep getting lost.

For Further Reading

Adelman, Conrad. *How to Manage Your Sales Time.* Westwood, NJ: IBMS, no date.

Mackenzie, Alec. *Time to Sell* (audio). Chicago: Dartnell, 1988.

Quebein, Nido R. *Get the Best from Yourself.* New York: Berkley Books, 1983.

SECTION 13

Time and Technology

Answering Machines and Voice Mail

Electronic Calculators and Schedulers

Computers

Copy Machines and Fax Machines

Cellular Phones

Word Processors and Memory Typewriters

Pagers and Beepers

Teleconferencing and Videoconferencing

SECTION 13

Time and Technology

Perhaps the best thing to happen to business in the past few years, in terms of time management, is the emergence of electronic devices and new business services which speed the transfer of information and data and save time every business day.

These devices and services were designed to organize information, process data, arrange files, create documents, or convert old information into new, allowing each of us to communicate in new and exciting ways.

We can illustrate the many time saving uses of these electronic devices by using a page from a modern business person's daily planner as an example.

Answering Machines and Voice Mail

7:30 a.m.—Check answering machine at office for new orders. Check voice mail for overseas messages from salespeople.

What was once nothing more than a tape recorder attached to a telephone is now a sophisticated telephone-answering system complete with computer circuitry.

Today's answering machines, for example, allow users to monitor and screen incoming calls without answering the phone and to pick up messages using any phone anywhere in the world.

If an office is too small to have a full-time receptionist, or if it's important to answer the telephone when no one is in, today's answering machines can accomplish about everything a receptionist can, and the cost of the machine is a one-time expense.

One of many practical uses of an answering machine might be to accept overnight orders and retrieve them in the morning, saving time by compressing all the evening's requests into one recording which could be played back, and stopped and started at will, freeing up time for other important activities. Some machines make the caller's voice audible, so you can pick up the receiver, override the machine, and take the call personally if you choose. This avoids the danger of missing a vital call.

But as efficient as today's answering machines are, what they can't do is directly answer a caller's questions or direct private messages to a specific person. Where even the most sophisticated answering machines leave off, voice mail picks up.

One of the newest services to reach the marketplace is voice mail. Unlike the Postal Service's method of delivering the mail, voice mail utilizes computer systems, software, and the telephone to save time and energy and increase productivity, all the while ensuring you never miss a phone call or message.

Essentially, voice mail is a very sophisticated answering system whereby a caller can communicate with another person using a recorded message. Coupled with the organizational power of a computer, the system is 100 percent private, just like a telephone is, and gains its appeal to business people from its many unique features.

For example, let's say you are the sales manager of a large corporation and need to deliver a message to your entire staff of 30 salespeople. By utilizing a voice mail system it's possible to leave the same recorded message for each salesperson and later verify that it was received by each of them.

Obviously, the time savings are enormous. Rather than recording 30 different messages, and perhaps mistakenly recording some of the facts in a few of them, the message is recorded only once but played back in its entirety only to the individuals you choose.

Or if necessary you could record a different, private message to each salesperson and retrieve a private reply. Just like the note in the business person's daily planner, checking a voice mail box is as easy as using the telephone.

If, for example, a private reply from overseas salespeople was directed to your voice mail box, using the telephone, you could easily retrieve each one, replay it if necessary, and even record a reply to be retrieved later. And all this is accomplished using a touch tone telephone.

Voice mail saves the time and expense of telephoning and missing the person you need to reach, eliminates the possibility of adding unnecessary long-distance charges to the business telephone bill, and yet offers features not found in other telephone systems and equipment.

All of these voice mail features and many more are managed by a computer at a central location and billed to subscribers of the system. And even though the service is relatively new, there are voice mail systems which offer their subscribers features too numerous to mention here.

Regarding the cost, there is an initial training and set-up fee applied to each new account and then a per minute usage fee assessed. Your monthly charges then depend upon how often you access and use the system.

Whether you choose the one-time expense of an answering machine or the continuing convenience of voice mail depends upon your needs. You may answer the following questions and determine which system is best for you.

Comparing the Need for an Answering Machine versus Voice Mail

1. Are you away from your office for long periods of time? Yes _____ No _____

2. Do you need to communicate with clients or members of your staff while away from the office? Yes _____ No _____

3. When communicating with clients or staff, do you feel the need to personalize a message to each of them? Yes _____ No _____

4. Can you afford the continuing cost of a voice mail
   system?   Yes _____   No _____

5. Are your staff or clients willing to use a voice mail
   system?   Yes _____   No _____

If you answered yes to many of the questions above, chances are an answering machine will not help you as much as voice mail.

Electronic Calculators and Schedulers

8:30 a.m.—Compare today's schedule in daily planner with electronic scheduler. Bring calculator to staff meeting.

The daily planner may be an excellent way to permanently record the day's events; however, if schedules change, memos need to be recorded, and telephone numbers need to be on hand, and all these items must fit in a business suit or purse, an electronic scheduler may be a helpful time management device.

The size of an electronic calculator, a scheduler can, among other things, find the number of days between two dates, find the day of the week for any date, keep track of appointments by storing them in memory, compute the time for any location in the world, and ring an alarm when a preset time is reached.

The daily planner, like a diary, is perfect for the office and for permanently recording a daily schedule. But having all the features above and more in a small package, and the information available instantly, it could be said that schedulers are really electronic time managers.

For managing time and information, schedulers are unparalleled in their abilities; but for so-called "number crunching," electronic calculators have also come into their own.

It wasn't very long ago that cumbersome adding machines dominated offices everywhere. In the office of the past, the bulky adding machine was a mechanical device which served just one purpose: it added numbers.

In today's offices and briefcases are electronic calculators which will find a monthly payment on a real estate mortgage, find the internal rate of return for an investment, compute the break-even point or return on investment for a business venture, or statistically analyze a set of important data.

Unlike computers, which are only limited by available software, electronic calculators are typically capable of performing only one set of tasks. For this reason, they tend to fall into categories. For example, there are calculators for business, science, and engineering or for just doing simple arithmetic.

The simplest calculators only do arithmetic. Calculators which only add, subtract, multiply, divide, and do a few other things like percentage calculations would fit this category nicely.

Scientific and engineering calculators, on the other hand, have many preprogrammed functions built in. Scientific calculators are used by computer programmers as well as astronomers, mathematicians, statisticians, and physicists. Engineering calculators perform tasks unique to that discipline.

Business calculators would include those which solve problems common to business. For example, it's possible to calculate the time value of money or find a return on investment. Mathematical problems like these, which in the past delayed important decisions and took a significant amount of time to solve, can now be answered in seconds with machines that are conveniently hand held.

The modern business person wouldn't want to forget an electronic calculator when attending an important meeting—especially if mathematical problems might be discussed during that meeting. Even the most accomplished math user knows that checking the results of a calculation is as important as attempting to arrive at an answer. And for "crunching" numbers, today's calculators let business people make decisions rather than waste time solving math problems.

In addition, as a calculator's calculating power has increased, the price per unit has, over time, continued to fall. For example, even though it may have double the calculating power, a calculator which five years ago cost about $150 today is priced at half that amount.

It's easy to see why the bulky adding machine is gone. But as electronic machines of the future continue to diminish in size, we can expect them to increase their powerful contributions to business.

Computers

10:00 a.m.—Run spreadsheet on computer, confirm new entries.

The workplace tool which has become as common as the telephone is, of course, the computer. And just like the electronic calculator, computers are relatively new to business.

The computer entered the scene only a few years ago but since has taken over many of the office responsibilities of accountants, secretaries, typists, clerks, messengers, and trainers. What were once dreary, menial tasks performed by the lowest paid staff member have been taken over by a machine which will very often perform those same tasks with more accuracy.

Without having to call in an accountant, and without having to wait days for the results, today's business person can key data into a personal computer and within minutes have a complete and accurate spreadsheet detailing, for example, the complete financial health of the business.

In terms of time management, the computer may be an all-time champ. The computer accomplishes tasks which shave years off jobs which might never have been attempted simply because they weren't cost or time effective.

The typical office computer is composed of two major parts: hardware and software. The hardware part of a computer is analogous to a record player. A record player

240

has a tone arm, a platter, and a needle, things which can be touched and seen.

A computer has a keyboard, a display screen, and a central processing unit called a CPU which processes all the information and manages the parts of the system. These pieces of the device, when connected, make up the hardware part of the computer: that is, the parts of a computer you can see and touch.

But before the computer can perform even the simplest task, it must have software.

If a record player with its physical parts is analogous to the hardware part of a computer, then the record played on the record player is analogous to computer software.

Software is what a computer needs to tell it what, when, and how to perform a task. Like a record player without a record, there is no output from a computer without software. And most recently the number of software products made available for business has increased dramatically. There are programs which will process your every word, balance the books, keep track of every client, and perhaps most importantly, keep track of your daily schedule.

Generally speaking the price of a computer is dependent upon two things: the size of the computer's memory, meaning how much information it can store, and the speed with which it processes data. It you plan to buy the most recently introduced computer, one which does everything at three times the speed with double the memory of the last introduction, you can plan on spending top dollar for your purchase.

You will also have to decide whether or not you want your computer to stay in the office or go on the road with you. The size of today's computers, the laptop versions, for example, allow business people to carry them aboard planes, work in hotel rooms or even taxis, and once that work is completed, using a telephone and a device called a modem, send it to a computer permanently stationed back at the office. All this obviously makes the traveling business person a great deal more productive.

We have grown dependent upon computers to the point that it's a rare business which does not own at least one. And with the introduction of more and more software products, the time spent performing routine tasks can't help but continue to diminish.

Copy Machines and Fax Machines

11:00 a.m. — Copy spreadsheets from computer printout, fax to regional offices.

Technology has added another device to the office which, rather than decreasing the amount of paper we all must handle, at the very least doubles it.

The first copy machines forever removed the carbon paper from between two sheets of paper. At first, time savings came from the ability to "make a copy" of just about anything on a standard sheet of paper almost instantly. Today those copies can be bound together, copied in color, reduced or enlarged in size, or collated and sorted — and everything is done by the modern copier.

Copy machines virtually recreate any document and sometimes even enhance it. And in the course of disseminating all this information, they also tend to bury us under a growing mountain of paper.

Like much of high technology, the copier, once it was perfected, offered engineers and vendors the challenge of creating something new to keep up with a very competitive marketplace. Hence the emergence of the color copier. Where once only black and white copies were possible, the color copier, at a much higher price, is beginning to make its mark. Today's color copier will reproduce lifelike copies in brilliant colorful detail.

When the highest quality presentation is a must, for proposals or for full-color presentations, the color copier eliminates the inherent delays trips to the printer can cause.

And if adding color to your copies wasn't enough, now there is a machine resembling the familiar copier, attached to a phone line, which is capable of speeding a copy of a document virtually anywhere in the world.

Fax, or facsimile, machines have rapidly become part of the modern office. It's common to hear business people jokingly wonder if a business is "in" business based solely upon whether or not they have a fax.

A fax machine combines a telephone, a copy machine, and a computer modem for sending and receiving documents. The combination of the three devices in a fax work as follows:

When a person dials the telephone number of another fax machine, the computer modem (a device which converts digital information to audio information) inside the distant machine automatically answers the telephone. It then sends a tone seeking another fax machine. If that tone is answered by the sending fax, the transmission process begins. The sending fax begins to scan the document, converting it into sounds, which are sent down the telephone line, and which the other fax "understands." As it receives these digital audio signals the distant fax machine converts them into a document again by printing them on a roll of special paper.

The daily planner above reminds the business person to update and print a spreadsheet using a personal computer. Then, using the printed results, that same spreadsheet can be delivered at the speed of light via the telephone to any or all affiliated offices. There's no need to wait for overnight mail, a courier, or even a telegram if a facsimile of the original document can be on the addressee's desk within minutes. Any office anywhere in the world with a telephone line and a fax machine can accept fax transmissions.

The basic features of fax machines remain the same on different models. The differential in cost between the most economical and most expensive is the number of so-called "bells and whistles" a person wishes to have on the machine.

If you wish to send your documents to a distant location, taking advantage of economical overnight telephone rates, then timed document transmission is a must. If you wish to have an automatic document feeder, a printed record of every fax sent

242

and received, or a telephone attached to your fax, then you can expect to pay a little more for yours then you would for the basic machine.

By sending price quotes, contracts, orders, or confirmations when a personal visit isn't required, the fax machine is unparalleled for managing time more efficiently.

Cellular Phones

12 Noon — Lunch with Henry. Bring portable cellular phone.

If high technology is trendy, then the cellular telephone wins the award for being the trendiest. Until a few years ago only a lucky few were able to communicate by telephone from his/her vehicles. Since the transmission of voice signals was handled exclusively by radio, and there were only a small number of frequencies available, the maximum number of car phones which could be used in any one area was limited.

This limitation persisted until cellular technology came into wide use. Today almost everyone can enjoy cellular telephone service either from his/her car or from a portable unit. The only restriction is whether a geographic area is currently served by cellular technology. And some areas of the country are not.

Basically, cellular phones work because of the availability of electronic cells within a given area. Without these cells there is no cellular service.

As a cellular telephone user passes through a cell, a computer automatically processes the two-way conversation while it is within range, and when it is not, the call is passed along to the next cell. Since there are several cells within a service area, there can be many more cellular telephone users than ever before.

And in association with the fax machine and special equipment, a cellular telephone makes document transmission from just about anywhere within a cellular area a possibility.

Cellular telephones come in two distinct styles and price ranges. The most popular style is the phone installed in a vehicle. The phone, along with a power unit and antenna, is permanently installed and its use is restricted to inside of the vehicle. This style of phone is the more inexpensive of the two versions.

Another style of cellular phone is the portable version. The phone's power source, antenna, and telephone system are completely self-contained and, because of its portability, can be used anywhere within the cellular service area — either within a vehicle, a restaurant, a client's office, or any other location. Of the two styles of cellular phone, this is the more expensive.

And whether you buy an installed or portable version of a cellular phone, you may be required to pay a programming fee, a one-time hookup fee to a cellular telephone company, a monthly service fee, and per minute charges for every phone call. In some cases charges start whenever you dial a number and continue regardless of whether or not anyone answers the phone.

At a business lunch, like the one mentioned in the daily planner, it may be important to have a cellular phone handy in case an order must be immediately placed. Also, information which isn't on hand, but is necessary for the meeting, can be supplied by only a simple phone call. Obviously, if you can obtain information or transact business by telephone, thus saving a personal visit, time is being managed more efficiently.

Choosing whether you need an installed or portable cellular phone can present some interesting challenges. Use the following questions as a guide to your cellular purchase.

Should You Choose an Installed or Portable Cellular Phone?

1. Is cost a factor in your cellular phone purchase?   Yes ____ No ____

2. Is portability important to you?   Yes ____ No ____

3. Is your work dependent upon being away from the office a great deal?   Yes ____ No ____

4. Must you be in contact with your office or clients continuously?   Yes ____ No ____

5. When working away from the office are you also often away from your vehicle?   Yes ____ No ____

Cellular telephones weren't designed for everyone, so thoughtful consideration of the preceding questions could make the cellular phone decision-making process somewhat easier.

There are some metropolitan areas which do not yet have cellular technology. But with the popularity of this telephone system, it would seem just a short time before they are in use throughout the world.

Word Processors and Memory Typewriters

1:00 p.m.—Pickup new word processor at supplier. Drop off at office for new typist.

Limited only by the kinds of software available, a computer can take on a variety of office jobs. But if all an office needs is a good word processor—that is, a means of creating professional quality documents which can be stored and later retrieved—a complete computer system may be a waste of money and time.

There are many companies today which sell machines designed to do only one thing: process words into quality documents using the most desirable word processing features. Perhaps the most desirable feature of stand-alone word processors is that they are completely self-contained. There is no reason, therefore, to separately buy a computer monitor, keyboard, printer, word processing software, or CPU. The word processors of today have all these features built in. They come complete with word

244

processing software and a CPU to control all of the hardware and software, a keyboard, and a monitor, and sometimes a printer. Some word processors also come complete with computer modems so they can communicate with other computers.

A typist, by job description, isn't going to have the responsibilities which warrant a complete personal computer system. So for a more reasonable price, it's possible to purchase a word processor which will do all the things similar computer software will do and save the time it would take to do each job on a conventional typewriter, with much better results.

For the price, if all that's needed is assistance with word processing, these packages are a very good alternative to buying a complete computer system.

Another alternative, and the least expensive way the modern office can take advantage of the electronic revolution in word processing, is the memory typewriter. Although it looks like a standard typewriter, it doesn't act much like one.

Memory typewriters can store limited amounts of text in their memories, can memorize document styles, can correct a word or sentence before committing it to paper, use different typefaces and spacing to print a document, and even check a document for correct spelling using built-in dictionaries.

Although no substitute for the power of a word processor or computer, memory typewriters can fill a need which a standard typewriter cannot by making communication between people easier and faster.

Use the following table to compare the features offered by computers, word processors, or memory typewriters.

Comparing the Features of Computers, Word Processors (WP), and Memory Typewriters (MT)

	Computers	WP	MT
1. Large memory?	Yes	Yes	No
2. Several fonts?	Maybe	Maybe	Maybe
3. Easy to learn?	No	No	Yes
4. Portable?	No	No	Yes
5. Expensive?	Yes	Yes	No

Computers, word processors, and memory typewriters serve different needs. Consequently, consider how the device will fit your workplace now and in the future before committing to any one.

Pagers and Beepers

2:30 p.m.—Contact Charlene's beeper in Calcutta. Remind her of p.m. meeting with G.M.

Perhaps the most unobtrusive way to keep in touch with the office or clients is through pagers and beepers. They've each been around for a while in one form or another, and dollar for dollar allow a person to efficiently keep in contact with the office or clients.

There are a variety of services and kinds of pagers and beepers available. The choice is really dependent upon the budget of the person intending to use one.

For example there are voice pagers, numeric pagers, beepers, and voice and vibrating pagers. There are some which are used in conjunction with telephones allowing an associate or client voice contact with you or, using a telephone keypad, the option of keying in only a telephone number.

When the variety of pagers and beepers is coupled with the geographic area to be served by the devices (using satellite technology it's even possible to receive pager messages anywhere in the world), you can roughly estimate the relative cost involved in carrying one with you. It's possible to lease one for as little as a few dollars a month or spend larger sums keeping in contact. And, as you might have guessed, the final cost for leasing a pager or a beeper is dependent upon two things: the size of the geographic area in which you intend to receive pages and the kind of device which will be providing the service.

Thus, it's entirely possible to "contact Charlene's beeper in Calcutta" and remind her of the important meeting with the G.M. even if you are in Minnesota. And if, for example, reminding Charlene of the meeting is fundamentally important to continued business success, the time saved by dialing her beeper and sending the message could be directly translated into profits.

Use the table below to compare the features separating the most common pagers and beepers.

Comparing the Features of Pagers and Beepers

		Pager	Beeper
1.	Voice communication	Yes	No
2.	Numeric display	No	Yes
3.	Vibration	No	Yes
4.	Distance from office	Variable	Variable
5.	Cost	Variable	Variable
6.	Use with telephone	Yes	Yes

Since there are so many variables associated with the choice of pagers and beepers, it's wise to check with a reputable vendor before making a commitment.

Teleconferencing and Videoconferencing

3:00 p.m.—Videoconference at the Conference Center.

Imagine a sales staff of 100 people, with each person in a different location around the globe, listening to you, the manager, speak to them on the telephone about the next new product introduction—and it's all taking place simultaneously!

What you are imagining is teleconferencing. And for about the cost of a person-to-person phone call, with a minimum of two other people, you have a teleconference.

There are several companies in the United States whose business is setting up conference calls which may serve as many as 100 people at a time.

In light of the alternative of having to travel to 100 locations around the globe, or assembling 100 people from around the globe in one location, or making 100 phone calls to different individuals in different locations, teleconferencing makes a great deal of sense. And since some companies offer rates equal to person-to-person phone calls, communicating with groups in this way is exceptionally practical in terms of time and dollar savings.

Setting up a teleconference means contacting one of several businesses who do this full time and giving them the name or names of the people you wish to call, their phone numbers, and the time you intend to speak to them. At the appointed time the company arranges for each person to be on the line, and the discussion commences. You are billed as if you had individually made a person-to-person call to each person. It's that simple to arrange a teleconference and avoid the wasted time and money associated with travel.

But if seeing the party you wish to speak to is important, another way to confer without the hassle of travel is through video conferences. When traveling to several different locations to present the same message to several groups is too costly or impractical, this form of communication makes sense.

Using video cameras, microphones, large screens, and the latest in satellite technology, a person or firm can carry on a two-way conversation and view a televised image of individuals or groups anywhere in the world.

Not only does this service involve leasing or renting equipment, namely satellites, video, and audio equipment, but it also entails the added expense of meeting rooms in the locations receiving the closed circuit broadcast, particularly in instances where a company might not have suitable space.

Since meeting rooms are commonly used to accomodate the attenders of the video conference, larger hotel chains, through arrangement with video conferencing companies, are happy to arrange all the details of the video conference.

Consequently, it wouldn't be unusual for our business person to have a video conference written in the daily planner. And instead of traveling a great distance, spending a night in a hotel, buying meals, and traveling back again, there is perhaps a short drive to a conference center where a large screen is set up alongside a video camera and some microphones. And from distant points groups can experience everything about a meeting without having to physically attend.

The following questions may highlight your need for either a video or telephone conference.

Choosing Teleconferencing or Videoconferencing For Your Next Electronic Meeting

1. Is it important to you that you see the people you are communicating with in an electronic meeting?   Yes ____No ____

2. Is cost an important factor?   Yes ____No ____

3. Does the substance or content of your electronic meeting justify the rental of meeting space and the lease of cameras, microphones, and satellites?   Yes ____No ____

4. Are the attenders of the meeting sufficiently dispersed geographically to warrant an electronic meeting?   Yes ____No ____

If you answered yes to the majority of the questions, you can assume you have a need for at least a teleconference and maybe even a video conference.

For Further Reading

Parikh, Girish. *The One Minute Organizing Secret: Finding Electronic Files, Papers, Books, and Almost Everything Fast!* Chicago: Shetal, 1985.

Epilogue

Time

Time, the elusive fourth dimension
Time, the shapeless evanescence
Time, personally condensable, awesomely expandable
Time, the backward infinity, the limitless forward
Time, hopelessly nonmeasured by clock, star, water, crystal
Time, cosmic-slowed, Einstein speeded

    The precious commodity, time
    The irretrievable moment, time
    The dragging minute, time
    The fleeting year, time

    Measured by birthdays, time
    Canceled on calendars, time
    Ruefully reviewed, time
    Prospectively hoped, time

Time, the healer of wounds
Time, the luxury of dalliance
Time, the allotment of span
Time, the grim finality

    Entrances and exits, time
    Beginnings and endings, time

Mortimer Abramowitz, Former Superintendent
Great Neck, New York, Public Schools

Index